THE
WORLD
WALK

THE WORLD WALK

7 YEARS. 28,000 MILES. 6 CONTINENTS.

A GRAND MEDITATION,
ONE STEP AT A TIME.

TOM TURCICH

Skyhorse Publishing

Skyhorse Publishing books may be purchased in bulk at special discounts for sales promotion, corporate gifts, fund-raising, or educational purposes. Special editions can also be created to specifications. For details, contact the Special Sales Department, Skyhorse Publishing, 307 West 36th Street, 11th Floor, New York, NY 10018 or info@skyhorsepublishing.com.

Skyhorse® and Skyhorse Publishing® are registered trademarks of Skyhorse Publishing, Inc.®, a Delaware corporation.

Visit our website at www.skyhorsepublishing.com.

Please follow our publisher Tony Lyons on Instagram @tonylyonsisuncertain

10 9 8 7 6 5 4 3 2 1

Library of Congress Cataloging-in-Publication Data on file.

Edited by Jesse McHugh
Interior design by Joshua Barnaby
Cover design by Kai Texel
Cover and interior photographs by Tom Turcich
Maps by Veronica Dall'Antonia

Print ISBN: 978-1-5107-7901-3
Ebook ISBN: 978-1-5107-8127-6

Printed in the United States of America

To Savannah, my only constant.

CONTENTS

PREFACE

If you're considering traveling, I would advise against it. If you're reading this while already skimming a foreign land—especially if by train, bike, or foot—say bon voyage to your future happiness. Traveling, you see, is a perpetual revealing. By simply existing in new places, being exposed to new sights, flavors, and misunderstandings, the world unfolds before you and you unfold before the world, unraveling yourself until you become unrecognizable. In the moment, there are few things more rewarding, but the longer this goes on, the more ruined you become.

For the sake of your happiness, it's best you stay in your hometown with your cousins and the friends you knew as a child. By staying, your connections will be deep, your intentions understood, and your heart protected by an umbrella of familiarity. There's nothing ignoble in this. Across the world, having generations of history to a place is the norm. Some of the most wonderful people I've met have been sixth or seventh generation to a place. They've hosted me with warmth and assuredness and revealed to me hidden wonders of everyday places that I would have otherwise overlooked. A piazza to someone who's known it all their life isn't just something beautiful, it's a collage of memories: the adrenaline of holding hands for the first time, the scent of the farmers market on Tuesday, the breeze rushing over the café in the evening. People who stay hold the history and details to their home—no small thing.

But if you travel too far, your hometown will be lost to you. There's no avoiding it. In fact, your hometown is one of the first things to go. Rather than experiencing it through that collage of memory, you'll begin to compare it. Of course, there are better views in Tuscany, better infrastructure in Copenhagen, and warmer people in Turkey, but that has little to do with the matter. Your hometown is fine. The thousands of people living in it like their restaurants, their parking, and the gossip that drifts in the air like a mist. The problem isn't your hometown, it's you and how you've returned.

My hometown, a suburb in South Jersey, a few miles from the Ben Franklin Bridge, was in many ways a utopia. I grew up on a back street with no through traffic, two blocks from a river. My friends and I played build-up-the-army—climbing fences and garage roofs to avoid being tagged. I never worried for my safety. I walked to elementary school and high school, and after college, I returned to live with my parents. Before walking around the world, I didn't have a bad thing to say about my hometown. I was motivated to leave, but in no way jaded.

Traveling can't be undone, though.

At the outset of your travels, the unfolding is noticeable. Everything is new and exciting and as you bumble your way across new cultures, the big lessons hit you first—you're dumb, naïve, and everything you've read amounts to nothing. In a certain way, these lessons are easy to live with because they come with a hunger for greater understanding. And for that hunger, there's food: more travel.

So, you press into ever more remote regions of the world and the unfolding becomes more subtle. Lessons don't hammer you over the head like they used to. They come in small gestures—a hand to the heart to signify contrition, a pause where before you would have spoken, an invitation accepted rather than feared. With enough time and enough cultures, you become so removed from your past self that you lose the thread of how you've grown. The change quits being noticeable and an unnerving quiet sweeps over you because that sense of progress that traveling provided no longer exists.

Nonetheless, your progress continues, whether you know it or not. Once you lose that sense of growth, you become capable of feeling places in a way that was before impossible. You stop seeing the world in terms of individual interactions. You understand that men are small; that geography, history, and government dictate life more than anything aside fortune. This understanding—that man is separate from his failure and success—offers relief but brings frustration. It means the stakes for good systems are unimaginably high and that the great populations oppressed by self-serving government, harsh landscape, or strict culture cannot be helped with the stroke of a pen or the proffering of kind words.

Travel—by that, I mean experiencing places for what they are and allowing those places to change you—is probably more than we were meant to take. It expands your perception, but not your influence. Over time, this incongruence leads to an uncomfortable balance—you see the systems divining people's fates, but know you'll never possess the power to change them.

You are, and always will be, human.

Perhaps an underwhelming revelation, but the road to this knowledge is peppered with joys small and profound. Many are born of serendipity, that fantastic and forgotten virtue which veils itself in the unknown and only graces those willing to bump against it. Serendipity leads to bruises and scrapes, but it also marks the path to wisdom. To know the world, you must exist in it. And to exist in the world, you must accept that you will be wrong, that you will be hurt, and that you will be made a fool a thousand times over.

I traveled in a strange manner, by walking with a companion at my side—my dog, Savannah. For seven years we walked the world, covering thirty-eight countries and twenty-five thousand miles. There were stretches of long solitude, particularly in the deserts of Peru and Chile, but Savannah provided me with a baseline of companionship that filled the gaps of isolation. No matter how poorly a day went, each difficulty was forgiven the moment we sat at our campsite and took in how far we'd come.

My desire is to give you our adventure and the memories that glimmer in my mind, but unfortunately there's no substitute for being there. There are too many details—mangoes hitting the ground, the taste of the air in the Páramo, and knowing what satisfaction comes from walking twenty-four miles a day for years on end. The World Walk is for myself and Savannah only. Still, I've done my best to give it to you here.

LEARNING TO LIVE

As snow drifted over the mountain edge, the vision of sliding to a gruesome death was clear in my mind's eye. I moved a step at a time—tamping out a place to put my foot, finding my balance, then pressing out a place for the next foot. After each step, without realizing it, I crouched a little lower until I was halfway across, clutching the snow with my hands.

"Don't do that!" called Husnidin. "Stand straight. You have to stand straight."

Over six years, I had crossed every terrain imaginable, yet taking a single step farther was suddenly impossible. I was slipping; millimeter by millimeter the snow was giving way. So near to the end of my dream, I was going to die in the mountains of Kyrgyzstan.

For most of my life thoughts of death followed me to bed. When I was young, I would place a pillow over my eyes so I couldn't see, press my thumbs to my ears so I couldn't hear, then lie perfectly still so I'd lose the sensation of having a body. From there, I would search for a stillness that resembled the nothingness of death, but always as I searched, thoughts crept in. And in death, there are no thoughts.

Whenever that idea resurfaced, my meditation turned to panic and I would open my eyes in terror. Too many nights with that fear forced me to give up trying to imagine death. I wrote it off as something impossible to resolve and I went about my life. I was young, comfortable, and prepared to live the quiet suburban existence laid out for me. Time slipped by in a steady stream, and it might have gone on forever that way, but at seventeen, my delicate peace was shattered.

Lowering the music in his father's convertible, my friend Kevin answered his phone, then turned to the back seat to tell us our friend Ann Marie had died.

"In a jet ski accident."

A little while later we sat cross-legged in the front yard of Ann Marie's best friend's house. Shannon was Kevin's girlfriend, my neighbor, and she would die three years later in a car accident. Lines of mascara streaked her freckled cheeks, Britny's blue eyes were etched red, and tears hung from Kevin's long eyelashes.

I didn't cry.

After an hour, I walked across the street to my house to lie in bed and stare at the ceiling.

A few days later, there was a service for Ann Marie. The procession went around the block. People fanned themselves in the sun. The service was closed casket, so I never saw Ann Marie again. Her father, Jack, was broken. Even at seventeen I could see that. I knew him from growing up. He'd been soft-spoken and gentle, but now he leaned forward and had a fretful stare as though perpetually realizing he would never again take a full breath.

From then on, I thought of death obsessively. I carried a pain in my chest that I identified as a bit of Ann Marie—her life caught in me like shrapnel.

Ann Marie and I grew up a block apart, my house on Morgan Avenue and Ann Marie's on Fern. We walked to elementary school together.

Through high school we existed in the same circle of friends. Early on I recognized that Ann Marie was better than me. She was a better student, which wasn't difficult, but more importantly, she was kinder. She was kind to the point that it annoyed me. When we would spend time together, I spent most of it trying to get her to say anything less than immensely generous, but I never succeeded. She never spoke a bad word about anyone and yet, at sixteen, she was dead.

My senior year began in a fog. I felt death looming over my shoulder, his hand turning the air cold on the back of my neck. I barely slept. Every night, I tried to imagine death like I had when I was younger: pillow over my eyes, thumbs against my ears. But now my thoughts turned too quickly and there was never silence. My grades slipped. The fog thickened.

It wasn't until someone played *Dead Poets Society* in class that I found a way out.

"Carpe diem! Seize the day. Make your lives extraordinary."

My classmate only played a few clips of the film, but I knew in an instant I had found the counterpoint to death that I had been searching for all my life. I would soon be dissolved, but while I lived, I would reach as far and deep into life as I could. Where before death's inevitability terrified me, it now provided my liberation. With the ending decided, what was left to fear? Only cowardice, only laziness, only a self unexplored—a life not lived.

Carpe diem became my guiding light.

I kept the phrase on the background of my phone. I wrote it idly in my notebook during class. For weeks, I watched *Dead Poets Society* every night, attempting to absorb the lessons of Thoreau, Whitman, and Frost. I read *Walden* twice, *Leaves of Grass* once, and "The Road Not Taken" a hundred times. On empty afternoons I rode my bike to Harleigh Cemetery to sit at the grave of Walt Whitman. What were the essential facts of life? What verse would I contribute? What path less traveled would make all the difference?

Those questions, illuminated by the phrase *carpe diem*, became the principal sounds troubling my soul. In order to answer them, I had to know myself, and in order to know myself, I had to take action. But for

3

months, despite knowing what I had to do, nothing changed. I read new books, thought new thoughts, and knew at the heart of *carpe diem* lay action, but I was unable to break from my nature of deference, timidness, and introversion.

My frustration came to a head when I stood on the sidewalk, kicking myself for not kissing Britny yet again.

We'd been on three dates, and I had the chance to kiss her during each of them, but instead, once more, I slunk down the street, sat on the curb, and opened my phone to gaze at the phrase I claimed to be embracing but that seemed to be mocking me. I intoned the words a million times and believed what they promised, but I had yet to act on them. Moments of opportunity abounded, yet I hadn't grabbed one.

I knew that if I didn't take action soon, my window of clarity would shut and I would go through the remainder of my life embittered by all the things I should have done.

So I texted her, asking if she would come outside again.

It was cold enough that I could see my breath, but the adrenaline was what made me shiver. I waited for a shadow to pass across the light of her door. I thought of taking my gloves off to hold her cheek with my bare hand, but then she was outside and walking over to me.

I put a hand to her cheek and kissed her.

When we broke apart, she stepped back and smiled. I didn't know what to say.

"Well, goodnight," she said, before hurrying back inside.

"Goodnight," I said belatedly.

Inside me, the universe was expanding, possibilities unfurling like ribbons let loose in a hurricane. I stretched out my arms and leaned my head to the sky. There were only a few stars visible, but I felt a billion passing through me. I felt each of them, the same as I felt every word from Frost, Whitman, and Thoreau. The opportunities I'd been seeing weren't mirages, they existed just as the poets promised and they held all the potential I imagined and more.

I took off in a sprint, jumping to slap every street sign I passed on the way home.

From that night on, I understood one fundamental truth: an extra-ordinary life exists in the realm of action.

After the kiss, I had no fear of taking action. I saw opportunities as I did before, but I now possessed a decisiveness that was previously dormant. If a single kiss could set me alight, what would happen if I packed my days with the new?

"You should join the swim team," my best friend Fitz suggested.

I hadn't been on a swim team since thirteen and I hated every chilly morning, but now waking at 5:00 a.m. to dive in a cold pool seemed like an adventure.

"You should join the one-act," said my choir teacher.

I had nothing else planned after school in winter, so why not? I joined the production of *Once Upon an Island* and was cast as a tree, but what better time to socialize than when you're a tree without lines?

I felt myself growing, changing, learning. Each choice I made, each action I took, revealed new aspects of myself in a way that the passive drifting through life never had. When I took action, I set a course. And through my actions I was able to evaluate what it meant to me to live a full life.

I was already on the course for higher education—I received early acceptance to Moravian College—but what did I want beyond that? Who did I want to be?

I knew I wanted to travel.

Two years prior, I had taken part in an exchange program where I lived with families in Ireland and England for a month. That whetted my appetite, but my desire to travel came more from my father than anywhere else.

In our living room, propped loosely in front of a framed photo, was an image of my dad in the brambles of South Point, Hawaii: hair below his shoulders, arms skinny as the branches around him, and wearing a bright orange shirt that read: SEX, DRUGS, AND ROCK AND ROLL. Throughout our upbringing, our father regaled my sister and me with his many lessons from living under a tarp in Hawaii for four years. He spearfished for food and harvested sugar cane for money. At the time, we made fun of him for telling the same stories over and over, but naturally his priorities grew into us without us noticing.

My mother would never find herself living under a tarp. She was an artist, just not the "living-under-a-tarp" type of artist. It was from her that I knew I wanted a greater understanding of the world. She was a toy designer for most of my childhood, then a freelance artist, a master gardener, and finally a landscape designer. Attached to our garage was her studio. During the day, the sunlight came through a skylight and the paintings that hung to the ceiling ricocheted with color. More often than not, she worked into the night when the skylight revealed the stars. She was a perfectionist, often depressed, and thus either motivated with a fire to see her through fourteen-hour days or caught in some unknowable abyss.

"Be sure to pay attention," she told me at museums, botanical gardens, or in passing as I sat reading.

For much of my life, I didn't take her advice. I didn't understand it. It wasn't until Ann Marie passed that I understood what my mom meant: Life is here now.

While my dad danced through life, my mom was forced to wrestle it. I fell somewhere between—light enough in disposition to seek adventure but weighted enough in spirit to struggle for understanding.

Toward the end of my senior year, I began looking for cheap ways to travel—cheap because I only had a thousand dollars to my name. What I found first were people taking the rail across Europe. I offered the idea to my cousin, Aileen, who was the same age as me, in a stage of rebellion against her parents, and looking for any way to escape the quiet rectitude of her Quaker high school. She loved the idea, so we set backpacking Europe as our plan for the summer.

With a plan set, I grew even more excited about a life filled with travel. Late most winter nights, I ignored any assigned reading in order to lose myself in a blue light of travel blogs. I read everything I could about backpacking, attempting to divine the perfect order of European capitals until being waylaid by a story about Steve Newman, an Ohioan who had walked around the world in the seventies. After discovering Steve Newman, I found Karl Bushby, an ex-British paratrooper who was in Russia after walking from Patagonia, through the Darien Gap, and swimming across the Bering Strait. Between the two men, they had walked every continent except Antarctica.

Amid that wild unfurling of possibilities that occurred after kissing Britny, one ribbon suddenly illuminated itself above the others—I would walk around the world.

I knew as quickly as that.

Walking around the world was as big an adventure as I could imagine, and it would be deeper and slower than traveling in any other form. Even cycling meant zipping by villages when it suited me, but on foot, I would be forced to spend time in every place—the interesting, the dull, the beautiful, and the ugly. I would see it all.

By seeing the world without bias in my route—other than visa-friendliness—I would see the details of real life. Of course, I wanted to see the beautiful, but I didn't *only* want to see the beautiful. If I sought to understand anything, I first had to acknowledge that the world is too complex to seek palatable histories and photogenic places. There isn't anything made less wonderful for its multitudes and idiosyncrasies. The same goes for attempting to live a full life. A life guided by the essential facts and in search of the essential facts means striving to know the self in all its depths and facets.

Walking around the world would test me at every level. It would bring me to the boundaries of myself.

A few months later, in the same Speech and Communications class that introduced me to *Dead Poets Society*, I gave a speech outlining how I planned to walk around the world. No doubt I was written off by most everyone; teenagers have wild, unfulfilled ideas all the time. But I meant what I said, and by some quirk in personality, once I made my goal of walking around the world public, I felt there was no turning back. I could imagine few things worse than becoming someone who talks about the great things he's going to do then does none of them.

I wanted to leave immediately and as the school year neared its end, I broached the idea with my mom.

"You're going to college," she stated flatly. "If you have a degree, you have a backstop. You have a minimum. I hope walking around the world works, but you can't put all your eggs in it. Get a degree then go. You'll be better for it, and you'll get more out of it."

What she knew at the time, but didn't say, was that I was about as naïve as a person could be and if I started a walk around the world at eighteen, there was a high chance that I would never make it home. I was the soft, untested product of an idyllic North American bubble and being young and inexperienced made me blindly confident. Thankfully, my mom had the foresight to insist I grow up before setting out.

Aileen and I never backpacked Europe. Instead, I installed solar panels to save money and the following autumn, I started at Moravian College. The year after that, I met Layla.

"What is this?" I said, tapping her flip phone at a party. "It's the twenty-first century. We have smartphones now."

"I like my phone."

"That's because you don't have a smartphone to look up how out of date your phone is."

She laughed a singular, sarcastic laugh.

"The first thing I'd look up on a smartphone is where you can get a new shirt."

Layla flicked a button on my green oxford, then tilted her head and smiled widely and full of braces.

When my dad met her, he said, "She's full of life."

In another world we would have married, but after three years together, when she was a few months from graduation, I realized if I continued a life with Layla, The World Walk would grow out of reach. My responsibilities would become increasingly difficult to throw off. We would move in together, buy furniture, build careers, fall deeper in love, and eventually start a family. Part of me wanted those things. All of me wanted them with Layla, but nothing stands alone and each step down one path is a step away from another. I had money to save. I had student loans to pay. By moving out, I'd be spending thousands on rent and food. My loans that might be paid in a few years by living at home would instead take ten years to rid. And who would I be in ten years? What responsibilities would I carry?

So, with an unsteady and unwilling hand, I broke things off. I wanted to be with Layla, but I knew in order to walk around the world, I couldn't be.

After college, while my friends pursued masters and PhDs, moved in with their partners, and built careers, I lived with my parents. The job I worked every summer through college, installing solar panels, paid as well as it ever had, so in a little over a year, I paid off half of my student loans and began to envision the start of the walk. With a couple more years of work, I would be in good shape. My loans would be paid and I would have enough saved to see me through two years of walking, which I figured was time enough to prove myself and corral a sponsor. But, unbeknownst to me, my parents were losing their house.

My mom lost her job during the recession and the massive solar arrays my dad had lined up to develop were put on ice. My parents, my father especially, had a strong instinct to shield me and my sister from money concerns, so despite my parents being underwater on their house for years, I had no sense of it until my mom approached me in the kitchen one afternoon.

"I hate to ask this," she said. "But we're going to need some money to keep the house."

The severity in my mom's voice was surprising. Usually, she tended to myself and my sister, Lexi, with the same light touch she used to tend to her plants and paintings. She listened, considered, and offered advice, guiding us this way or that, but rarely, if ever, did she prune us, erase us, or approach us with the directness she did that afternoon.

"How much do you need?"

"Five thousand for now, and we'll probably need more after that."

Over the next few months, I wrote my parents more checks. My plan to begin the walk was delayed, but for my family I would have delayed the walk indefinitely if that's what was needed.

I continued working, living at home, and saving as best I could. But eventually, it became clear that we didn't have the funds to keep the bank from foreclosing, so my parents stopped asking for money. At twenty-five, three years removed from college, I decided I needed my life to break one way or the other. My parents were easy to live with but I had to begin a life of my own. I didn't have enough saved to pay off my loans and walk two years. After another year of work I still wouldn't, but there was no way I was moving out of my parents' home to pay rent without giving the walk my best shot. Ending my relationship with Layla was meant to change my path, not keep me on the same one without her.

On my twenty-fifth birthday, I resolved to begin the walk before my twenty-sixth.

With a date set, my focus narrowed.

THE UNEXPECTED SUPPORT

I had known for years the route I wanted to take. I drew it with two things in mind—how to walk every continent, and how to do that with as little visa trouble as possible. Under those criteria, estimating I would average fourteen miles a day including rest days, I believed my walk would take five years. My first year would be from New Jersey to Panama City. My second, from Bogotá to Montevideo. At the end of the South American summer, I'd catch a boat to Antarctica. Year three was Ireland, the UK, down Western Europe, and across North Africa. I wanted to walk sub-Saharan Africa, but Africa was enormous, a Gordian knot of visas, and would likely add three years to an already long walk. So, after Morocco, Algeria, and Tunisia, I would head up Italy, make my way to, then across, Turkey, Central Asia, and all the way to Ulaanbaatar, Mongolia. After that it was a few months down the coast of Australia and a six-month homecoming across the US, from the west coast to my front door in New Jersey.

There were only two season-sensitive sections of the walk. To catch a boat to Antarctica, I had to finish the South American section by the end of their summer. That meant if I began the walk on April 2nd, the day before my twenty-sixth birthday, I had a little under two years to make it to Uruguay. During those two years, I would be walking through a perpetual summer—the North American summer for six months, the temperate zone for a year, then the South American summer.

The only other season-sensitive section was the walk to Ulaanbaatar, the capital of Mongolia. That part of the world was so far north that I would only have a brief window to walk it before an impassable winter set in. But that section was years away, and what was currently on my mind were the details of how to begin.

The first thing I did once I knew I was leaving was order a baby carriage that could be attached to the back of a bike. What I learned from the two weeks of total backpacking I had done in my life was that I hated backpacking. I had no desire to attach a seventy-pound tumor to my back for five years. I wanted my things in a cart.

I took the bike carriage to a business off Haddon Avenue, thinking I could have the arm modified to attach to my waist. The Factory Workers was an early twentieth-century theater repurposed into a maker space. I had never been inside, knew no one there, but I figured if I stood around long enough in a place where people built things, I could find someone to build something for me.

I was outside the entrance for only a few minutes when someone approached—a bearded man with the flicker of warmth in his eyes.

"You need some help, bud?"

"I have this baby carriage for a bike." I pointed to the carriage inside my one-hundred-dollar Jetta. "I need the arm modified so I can attach it to my belt or around my waist."

"Can you get it out of there so I can see it?"

I withdrew the cart and sat it on the ground between us. He tilted the carriage back by its arm.

"This is aluminum. I don't have an aluminum welder. But anyway, you'd be better off getting a new arm than welding this one."

"Could you do that? Build an arm for it?"

"You're planning on pulling this? With a kid inside? Are you running? They have strollers for that, you know? There are people running Cooper River with jogging strollers all day."

"I don't have a kid. I'm planning on walking to South America. I was thinking this would carry my gear."

The man studied me. It was the first time in years that I told anyone outside my immediate circle that I was planning the walk and I remembered why. It felt ludicrous. Who was I to make such a claim?

"Where are you from?" he asked.

"Haddon Township."

His crow's feet pinched. "What street?"

"I grew up in the Bluebird Section, but we moved to Hampton a few years ago."

"You know the Maros?"

"Fitz is my best friend."

"I grew up with Sandy. What's your name?"

"Tom Turcich. You?"

"Tom Marchetty."

We shook hands.

"Do you rent space here?" I asked. "I've heard it's amazing."

"I own the place. I could use fifty grand to refurbish the murals, but it's coming along. How'd you get the idea of walking to South America in your head?"

"Actually, the plan is to walk around the world. All seven continents over five years."

"You're best friends with Fitz?"

"Since fourteen or so."

"And when are you leaving?"

"In six months."

"You have a sponsor?"

"No, but I've been saving for years."

"You get any press?"

"I've haven't told anyone. I only told you because I need to figure out what to do with this cart."

"Well, I have friends at the *Inquirer* and Matt from NJPen.com works at the coffee shop inside. I'll make some calls and we'll set up a press conference to get your story out. Are you free now? I can introduce you to the businesses renting space. One of them will sponsor you. Hell, they should all sponsor a kid walking around the world. We need to scrap this bike carriage, though. It won't hold as much as you need, and you'll want to push it sometimes. I can build you something tougher and bigger. Something you can lock, too."

"How do you have so much confidence I'll actually walk around the world?"

"You don't look like someone who says something without meaning it. And anyway, the Maros are a great judge of character." He gestured to himself.

I met Tom a few more times over the next couple months. He was gregarious and willing to talk about my plans in exactly the way I needed. Where I found it painful to promote myself, Tom did it energetically. He introduced me to the businesses renting space from him and helped me find my first sponsor, Wildfire Radio, who promised to host and run my website. When I told Tom how tight I thought I would be on money, he decided to throw a send-off fundraiser at The Factory.

The send-off was scheduled two weeks before my birthday. A month before, Tom called a press conference with the largest newspapers in the Philadelphia area. Soon, journalists were interviewing us and scribbling notes on Ann Marie, my planned route, and what I hoped to gain out of such an enormous undertaking.

Displayed at the center of The Factory, surrounded by lathes, saws, planers, drills, and presses, was the cart Tom had constructed—a metal box with run-flat tires that looked like a white ice cream cart with THE WORLD WALK decals pasted on the side. The cart would hold everything I would need and then some. The newspaper photographers asked me to push it around.

The next day, unbeknownst to me, the owner of another local business was at lunch with his son, reading my story.

While I stood behind the host counter of Indeblue, the Indian restaurant I had been waiting tables at the previous six months, I received a text from a friend I went to high school with, Brian Mehmet. He said his father owned Philadelphia Sign, a local sign-producer, and he wanted to meet me and talk about funding my entire trip. I read the text twenty times to be sure I wasn't missing something.

A few days later I was meeting with Brian and his father, Bob.

"Are you crazy?" Bob said as he entered his office.

I stood from the sofa to shake his hand.

"No sir."

"Had to ask." He took the chair across from me. Brian sat beside him, smiling. Behind them, a wall-sized window revealed a rock garden.

"You're really going to do this?"

"There's nothing I've been more certain about in my life. And now that it's in the newspapers there's no turning back."

Brian laughed. Bob didn't seem to notice I had made a joke.

"How much do you think it will cost?"

This was a question I had considered a thousand times over the years and researched endlessly by way of travel blogs, but now I could tell Bob anything. Fifty thousand dollars! Sixty thousand! A hotel every night. Gourmet meals in every city. But there was no need for that. If someone was willing to pay for my dream, that was more than enough.

"I think I could do it on fourteen a year."

"That's less than minimum wage."

"I don't need much, just food and the occasional hotel."

"Maybe we'll put you down as an employee. I'll ask payroll to figure something out. I want to do something for Ann Marie, too. Maybe we could donate a dollar a mile to her scholarship fund."

"That sounds great, but just so my intentions are clear: I have to tell you I'm not doing this for Ann Marie. I'm doing it because of her. I don't want to misrepresent myself. I never thought of this as a charity walk. I just want to see the world."

"Okay, but it's important we donate in her name. How many miles will you walk a year?"

"My guess is forty-five hundred."

"Perfect. We'll donate a dollar a mile."

"We should do Shannon's, too," said Brian. "They were best friends. You all were."

The night before I was set to leave, I looked over my things spread across the dinner table with my sister, parents, and my girlfriend, Catherine. After our first date, I told Catherine I was leaving in a year, but that we could enjoy the time we had before I left. She agreed, and she was wonderful, but I never permitted myself to open up to her. After ending things with Layla, I wouldn't allow myself to get tied to anyone until the walk was finished.

Catherine held up a pack of Spanish flash cards and the Spanish version of *The Sorcerer's Stone*.

"What about these?" she asked. "Won't they be too heavy?"

"I have to learn Spanish before I get to Mexico."

"You're going to trash that chair before the week is through," said my dad.

"It barely weighs a thing."

"A tarp on the ground weighs less."

I found space for the chair anyway. It folded to the size of a water bottle. I tucked it beside my camp table.

"Why can't you just walk across America?" asked my mom, wiping tears from her eyes.

"Because I don't want a six-month adventure. I want to see the world. I want to see what I can become."

I took the paper maps of the bike route I planned to follow to Florida and slipped them into my backpack.

"But it's just so far and you'll be gone for so long."

"It wouldn't be a big dream if he wasn't," Lexi put in.

"Call if you need anything," my dad said. "You won't be far for a while, but even when you're in Maryland or Virginia. We know people there. Mitch lives in South Carolina and Michael will be in Virginia next month."

"Okay."

"Will you ask for help if you need it?" asked my mom.

"Of course. When I rode my bike to the shore and cut my hand on the spokes, I knocked on doors until finding someone who could help."

"But you have to be smart, too. Not everyone is nice, Tom. You can be naïve, you know?"

"I know."

"But most people are nice," my dad said.

"But not everyone," my mom interjected.

"But most," he reiterated.

"*Tom.* Not now. He has to be careful."

"He'll be fine," said my sister with a wave of the hand.

"I'll be fine."

"Just pay attention," said my mom. "And don't be an idiot."

"And meet people," said my dad. "That's why we're here. That's how you learn places. That's how you really learn places."

"I know. I will."

"He'll meet loads of people," said Lexi.

"Are you sure you need to bring so much food? There will be grocery stores all along the east coast."

I looked at the two plastic crates packed with pasta, bread, peanut butter, jam, granola, trail mix, protein bars, protein powder, dried mango, canned tuna, sardines, and chocolate. My mom had a point. It was more food than I could eat in a week, but I had already bought it, so I figured I might as well bring it.

"It'll get eaten eventually."

"I'll go to L&M for donuts tomorrow," said my dad. "There will be a lot of people here."

The next morning, I woke at six. At seven, neighbors and friends trickled in. The first person to show was our neighbor, Bob, a World War Two vet and the person I spent the most time with while living at home. On my free afternoons we sat beside his record player and listened to Tommy Dorsey and Frank Sinatra. Bob gave me his 1933 track medal for good luck. I put it on a chain and hung it around my neck. At seven thirty, I clipped my backpack around my waist and pushed my cart out the front door. All told, there were about twenty people to see me off.

The crowd cheered in our driveway. A camera was slung over my shoulder and a small solar panel dangled from my backpack. Outside my neighbor's house, I turned and took a photo of everyone. My mom had a napkin to her nose, my sister was smiling, and my dad was waving.

"See you in five years!" I hollered.

Down the block, I turned at my elementary school then onto Haddon Avenue. A few people who had seen me off honked as they passed in their cars. The sky was an unbroken blue. The sun was gold. I thanked Tom outside The Factory, then followed Haddon Avenue through Collingswood until reaching the bent iron fence of Harleigh Cemetery. At the stone gates, I looked in on Uncle Walt. "Oh me! Oh life!"

I was beginning.

A BLISTERED BEGINNING

I woke to the burr of cyclists and the smell of shit, but I might as well have woken to Chopin and roses. It was my twenty-sixth birthday, and I was on an adventure. I was camped on a patch of grass between the Schuylkill River Trail and a sewer treatment plant, but after eight years of saving and maneuvering, I was living the dream I had carried since seventeen.

The Schuylkill River Trail took me to Valley Forge. On the highest hill, I bent over my cart to rest and catch my breath. In front of me was the National Memorial Arch. Through the arch was an American flag and three wooden bunkhouses. In the valleys to either side, a fog rested like a militia of wintering ghosts. When it began to drizzle, I unlocked my cart to find my rain jacket and saw with fresh eyes the sheer quantity of unnecessary things I had brought. My dad was right: the table and chair were absurd, as were the Spanish flashcards and the Spanish *Harry Potter*. Still, I couldn't bring myself to toss them just thirty miles from home.

Around midday, the rain stopped. At five, I found a clearing in a forest to set camp. Down the hill, I could make out a house and the smoke leaving its chimney. The house was far enough away that I doubted they'd be able to see light from my camp.

I staked out my bright orange tent, then unfolded my chair and table beside it. At my feet, I boiled water for a dehydrated meal. The rain made the air cold and creeping. I zipped my down jacket to my chin and pulled my beanie over my ears. When a breeze rolled over, raindrops fell from the maples. I ate dinner, lit a cigar, then opened my box of Spanish flashcards to study. For a while, I thought of Layla and the life we might have lived.

After my birthday, nothing went right.

Rain began and didn't stop. In my great wisdom, I had brought a table and a chair, but no waterproof gloves. My hands were so cold from clutching the cart's metal handle that when I reached a bus stop or a church awning to escape the rain, it took five minutes of rubbing my hands together before they could make any shape other than a talon.

Even though Pennsylvania wasn't densely populated outside of Philadelphia, the houses were close enough together that finding somewhere to hide away for the night was nearly impossible. The night before Easter, I slept in a patch of woods tightly encircled by eight houses. The night after that, I camped in a forest opposite a high school where kids walking home spotted me, then shouted and waved. Another time, I didn't reach a woodland until after dark. When I clambered out of my tent in the morning, I was greeted by a woman shouting and a cop asking if I knew I was on private property.

The bike route I intended to follow to Florida didn't work as planned either. After the Schuylkill River Trail and the path through Valley Forge, I nearly died a dozen times walking the narrow, sinuous roads that the maps recommended. I had to sprint around one blind bend after another. Twice, I barely made it to the top before a car spotted me and slammed on their brakes. After a few harrowing roads, I flung the maps into the trash.

My custom-made cart was failing in remarkable ways, too. Three days in, when I moved off a road to make space for a car to pass, my cart sank into the earth and its run-flat tire snapped clean in half. Luckily, I was only fifty miles from home, so Bob and the warehouse manager, Pat, were able to drive out two inflatable tires. But after that incident, I winced each time I rolled the cart down a curb and fixated on the things I knew I should toss to cut weight.

I thought because I had been an athlete my entire life that walking every day would be an easy adjustment, but my body wasn't accustomed to the new demands I was making of it. I was in pain—my knees ached, my ankles were swollen, my feet were blooming with blisters, and my hamstrings cramped constantly. There were times each day that a cramp caught me with such ferocity that I fell to the ground and quickly slung a shirt around my foot to stretch my hamstring and keep it from charley-horsing. During one of those episodes, my grandparents video-called me.

"I thought you were supposed to be walking?" shouted my grandmother upon seeing the grass I was laid on.

"I thought I'd be able to walk more than fifteen miles a day."

"Oh God. I don't like this, Tom," said Pop-Pop while putting his hands to his head. "What'll happen when you need to stretch in Mexico?"

"My body just needs time to adjust."

"How are your feet?"

"I've got a blister or two. There's a big one on my heel that I'm waiting to pop."

"Oh God."

"It's fine."

"Where are you?" asked my grandmother.

"Almost to Maryland."

"Maryland! Well, hitch a ride home for a pedicure and you'll be back before nightfall." She cackled gleefully at her own joke.

By the end of my first week, I had made it to the small town of Parkesburg. I was exhausted, but instead of falling into bed after a long day, I was once again searching for a place to camp. Just outside of town, I came to a patch of woods lining the road. Yellow PRIVATE PROPERTY signs were stapled on every large tree, but from looking at Google Maps,

I knew there wouldn't be another patch of forest for miles, so I left my cart on the road and tramped into the woods. Just a few feet in, my pants were caught with thorns. I loosened each prickle, then navigated a maze of bushes until reaching the top of the hill for a better view. The woods beyond were thornier and more uneven than the area beside the road. There was nowhere to camp.

I returned to my cart and gazed down the road. I could have fallen asleep standing there, but the day was dwindling so I returned to the main road and kept walking. When I cleared the edge of the woods, a pickup pulled over on the opposite side of the street and a man called to me.

"I know you!" he said.

I didn't recognize the man, but I was eager for any excuse to take a break, so I dropped my cart to a stop.

"I saw you on the news!" The man glanced up and down the road, flung open his door, then jogged over to me. He stretched out his hand and shook mine vigorously.

"Mr. Ed, pleasure to meet you."

"Tom. It's a pleasure."

Mr. Ed stepped back, put his hands on his hips, and looked over my cart.

"The World Walk in my neighborhood. I can't believe this." He turned back to his car. "Kara! I told you it was him!"

Kara smiled and waved from the passenger seat.

"I recognized you from *Good Day Philadelphia*. Kara didn't believe it was you even though she had a better look at your cart than I did. She thought you were homeless. I said you were walking around the world and a man that's walking around the world is never homeless."

"That's a nice way of putting it."

"In my neighborhood." Mr. Ed clapped. "You're going to see the whole world. No one sees the whole world. Everyone lives in the same town they've lived in their entire lives. There are people in this town that ain't never been to Maryland. Ain't that so? They live their life in a box, but not you. That's why I remembered you. I told Kara when we were watching you on the news, 'Now there's a man who knows how to live.' Which way are you going?"

"Heading uphill if my hamstrings don't snap."

"You mind if I try?" He gestured to the cart.

I stepped back to allow Mr. Ed free rein, then I walked beside him as he pushed the cart uphill with an ease that suggested the cart wasn't actually packed to the brim.

"You're saving me," I said.

"It's a smooth ride. Bigger than I thought, though. Heavier too. It's a whole life in here, isn't it?" Mr. Ed tilted the cart to a rest then snapped his head back.

"Kara!" His body jerked when he called her. "Kara! Get out the damn car! Come take a picture of us."

Kara ran across the street and took a picture of me and Mr. Ed with our arms around one another. Then Mr. Ed took a picture of me and Kara.

"Is there anything you need? Anything at all I can get you?" he asked.

"I have everything I need right in here. Thank you, though. I appreciate it."

"Anything at all. I want to get you something."

As I considered if there were any luxuries I might want, I felt the sting of the cool air against my parched throat.

"Some Gatorade would be nice, I suppose."

"Consider it done. I'll be back in fifteen minutes."

"Oh," I said as they were turning to go. "Do you know if there's anywhere I could camp for the night?"

"Hmm . . . camping here is tough. Nothing but guns and private property. Ain't that so?"

"What about the church?" Kara pointed up the hill to a white steeple pinned to the sky.

Despite my desperation to find places to sleep over the past week, I had never considered a church. They made sense, though. They were safe havens, like home base in a game of build-up-the-army. They'd have water, manicured lawns, and if someone asked what I was doing I could tell them I thought no one would mind me taking shelter beside a house of God.

"Now that's a bit of bright thinking." Mr. Ed pulled Kara in to kiss her cheek. "We'll meet you at the church in fifteen!"

Kara and Mr. Ed drove off. I pushed my cart with renewed energy.

Once I reached the church, I found a flat spot of grass that made an ideal place to camp, then I sat at the front entrance, undid my sneakers, and slid them off. I had six blisters, a few on the tips of my toes and a pair of larger ones on my heels. I leaned forward and grabbed my toes to stretch. Then I lay on the concrete and shut my eyes.

It had been only a week, and I was overjoyed to be living my dream, but the rain and cold were draining, and I couldn't help but fantasize about being home, sitting around the dinner table with my family, while a hot shower and a warm bed awaited me upstairs. I missed Layla, too. Three years had passed since we separated, but visions of her still played in my thoughts—how she leapt when she made a point, and how she tilted her head and smiled when she teased.

I turned to my chest and pressed my forehead against the concrete. I stayed like that until the pebbles were painful against my skin, then I turned over and sat up to meditate. Placing my hands on my knees and counting my breath, I leaned into my mind the same way I did when I was young and in search of what it meant to die. Gradually, I lost the sensation of having a body, but that only made my sadness more pronounced—I had left everyone I loved. I set myself on a path of loneliness. If I couldn't make it to Maryland without crumbling, how was I supposed to make it to South America? I was doomed. Mr. Ed wasn't going to return. Fifteen minutes went by, then twenty, then twenty-five. The next five years would have no love, no companionship, no Sunday dinners.

A car door slammed.

"Mr. Tom!"

Mr. Ed and Kara were walking over.

"We have Gatorade, some yogurt parfaits, and granola. I hope it'll do for you."

Mr. Ed set the bag between us.

"Listen here," said Mr. Ed, taking my hands in his. "I want you to hear this. We're family, you and I. Not friends, *family*."

He kissed my hand.

"I can't tell you how much I needed this," I said. "I didn't even know how much I needed it until now."

"Family," he said.

I nodded.

"Now, is there anything else we can do for you? You want dinner? I didn't bring no dinner. I know you have food in your cart, but I thought he can't keep no yogurt, so that's what I'll bring him."

"The yogurt is perfect, thank you."

I glanced back to my cart to consider if there was anything I needed but didn't have.

"Do you have a tire pump?" I asked.

"A tire pump?"

"One I can bring with me. I know it's a strange request, but I had run-flat tires when I started. When they snapped, I replaced them with regular tires and I didn't bring a tire pump with me."

Mr. Ed held up a hand then jogged to his truck and searched the back seat before returning with a brand-new portable tire pump.

"You had this in your back seat?"

"I bought it yesterday for the little one's new bike."

"You need it then." I tried to hand it back, but Mr. Ed raised his hands to show he wouldn't accept it.

"Let me pay you at least."

"Mr. Tom, what did I tell you? We're family, you and I. You're going to meet a lot more family along the way. Pay it back when someone needs it."

"I will."

"All right then."

We shook hands. Mr. Ed and Kara drove off. I set my tent beside the church and sat on the grass to watch the day fade. The forest I walked out of an hour before was below me. Its leaves were dark and unsettled.

After sunset, I crawled into my shelter thinking of the choices I'd made and why I made them. Layla and South America felt equally close—the place I left, and the place I was going.

THE DARKER PATH

By the time I reached Savannah, Georgia, and turned off the coast to make my way to Texas, I had a decent handle on the basics of living out of a cart and traveling by foot.

Back in North Carolina, I swapped the cart Tom Marchetty built me for a Thule jogging stroller. The stroller wasn't as large as my old one, but it had shocks, a foam handle, and a back basket for things I wanted quick access to like my water and camera. Compared to the first cart, the Thule felt as though I were pushing a quarter of the weight, but that was helped by the fact that I dumped half of my things as I went. I left my camp chair and camp table at a church and put my Spanish copy of *Harry Potter* and my Spanish notecards in a tiny library.

The only luxuries I kept were a camp pillow and my heavier inflatable sleeping pad. I prioritized the pillow and sleeping pad because I knew how critical sleep was to feeling strong the next day. Each night, I needed as much sleep as I had since I was a teenager, about ten hours. Thankfully, I had honed my ability to use Google Maps to find an adequate church, clearing, or patch of woods to hide away in each night. I also realized that as long as I was comfortable with a bit of car noise, I could get away with camping just out of sight from a road. That meant I didn't need large swaths of forest to feel hidden; a small, well-positioned strip would do fine.

I also worked out exactly how much water and food I needed. I was burning close to five thousand calories a day, so I forced myself to eat more than I enjoyed. Usually, that meant drinking a liter of milk on top of my meals. Other times, it meant loading up on fast food until developing a sodium headache.

But as I moved further west, subtler forms of my naïvete revealed themselves.

One afternoon, as I sat on an embankment on a dusty back road, the driver of a red sedan waved as he passed, then doubled back a few minutes later to pull alongside me. He leaned over the center console, gazed at me with glassy eyes and spoke with a thick, almost unintelligible accent.

"Whatcha doing pushing that thing?"

"Walking from Jersey."

"You pushed that thing from New Jersey?"

"Yes, sir."

"Why the three wheels?"

"Good for walking and jogging, I suppose."

"You headed to town?"

"That's the plan."

"Once you hit the light, I'm the first house on the left. You should come by, I have some people you should meet. It's not every day a man from New Jersey walks into town. You should come by, meet the youngins."

It was a kind offer, but I had already walked twenty-four miles that day and I knew in another hour I'd be too tired for pleasantries. The man must have noticed my hesitation.

"You should," he pressed. "I'm good people and you seem like good people."

"Maybe. I have to get back to it, though."

"Think about it."

The man drove off and silence returned.

As the road lifted and fell, I could feel the day in my legs. I hadn't eaten since noon. It was hot and humid but there were oaks on either side for shade. I listened to *This American Life* and fantasized about the hose shower I would take at The House of the Lord—the church three miles up the road where I planned to sleep. In my backpack, I had a bar of soap that would wash away the grime that had built up on my arms and legs. I could almost feel the cold water on my back, chilling me to goosebumps.

The red sedan reappeared over a hill. The man stuck his head out of the window and said something incomprehensible as he passed. A minute later, with his arm draped over the driver-side door, he came to a stop beside me.

"I just wanted to let you know that you really should come by. Meet my youngins and my sister. I'll cook you something. It's good to have a hot meal."

"I don't know. I have to find a place to sleep, and I've walked eight hours already. I probably don't have time."

"Where do you sleep?"

"Churches or the woods usually."

"I'm sure we can figure something out. I want you to come by. I'm good people, won't hurt you none. Never hurt anything."

I looked into the man's car. It was new and clean. He had a lighter in his hand, and on his forearm was a streak of blood. I wondered if he killed something, maybe a small animal, but then I noticed his arm was marked with bumps and that one of the bumps was open.

"I'm sure we could throw that thing in here and take you to town," he said.

"No, no. Thank you. I'm walking. Have to walk. One continuous path."

"You really are walking, aren't you?"

"I've come this far."

"To the middle of nowhere, Georgia."

I peered down the road. It had been an hour since I'd seen another car. "Name's Rob."

"Tom."

When I looked Rob in the eye, it was as though a thin film separated us. I was unable to immediately connect with him the way I did with most people.

"Ya know, I had a pit that I used to run on this road, had him until he was two. We used to run this road damn near every day. Then one afternoon, I'm standing outside my house and a car runs him over. The car runs him over and doesn't even touch his brakes. Right in front of my youngin' too. Doesn't even stop. So I'm raging. I'm pissed. This dog really had me, you know? We connected. I had other dogs, but once I got this pit, it was something different. So I get into my truck and I follow this guy all the way to his house and I go right up to this n–"

The veins on Rob's neck bulged as he yelled at the man in his story, but I stopped hearing him. I wondered why he would tell me about his dog getting killed just minutes after meeting me.

"Anyway." The rage dropped from his face as quickly as it appeared. "You should come by. You really should. I don't mean anything about that talk about Black men, you grow up down here and that's how it is. I'm good people and you seem like good people. You seem real interesting. Really you should come by. Left at the light and I'm the first house on the left. Look for a white pickup. Kick your feet up a little."

After Rob drove off, I wanted to forget him but I heard my dad's voice ringing in my head, *It's about the people, Tom. That's how you learn a place.*

I thought of the blood on Rob's arm and did my best not to make assumptions. Maybe he had a medical condition. Maybe he picked his scabs. His racism was repulsive, but if my aim was to know the world, then I couldn't ignore the unsavory. I was just beginning my adventure and I had spent my upbringing in an idyllic town in the wealthiest country on earth; if I was filtering the world already, then how could I expect to know it honestly?

But my gut was telling me something different. I had no interest in seeing Rob again. I didn't like him. I didn't trust him. I was tired and ready for a spigot shower, dinner, and sleep.

After forty minutes, I reached town. Along the back roads of Georgia, I had passed so many trailers with cider block foundations and garbage bag windows that the houses in town were nicer than I expected, brick and manicured.

While I walked, I scanned for the white pickup, hoping I wouldn't see Rob waiting for me. As the road bent left, I spotted the only stoplight in town dangling from a wire and pulsing red.

Before the light, I turned into a Piggly Wiggly. In the bread aisle, a boy stopped in front of me and began speaking as though we'd been in the middle of a conversation.

"All we have at the house is a jar of pickles. Jane loves pickles. They have a really big jar of pickles at their house."

"Oh yeah?"

From around the corner, a man as broad as a semi appeared.

"Ask the man where he's from," he said.

The boy looked to his toes.

"Where are you from?"

"I'm from New Jersey."

"We're from a small town. Our town is only this big." The boy held his hands about six inches apart.

"My town is this big." I put my hands outside the boy's.

"You hiking the railroad tracks?" asked the father.

"Not the railroad tracks, but yeah, hiking through."

"I'm the mayor of the town over. I have a guesthouse that you're more than welcome to pass the night in. My wife and I would be happy to get you a shower and a good meal. It's a big house with a white wall around it. Ask anyone for the mayor and they'll point you my way."

"How far is it?"

He consulted his wife for an answer.

"About seven or eight miles," they agreed.

"Too far for me tonight, unfortunately."

"Well, if you need anything or if you make it that far, just knock on our door."

The mayor's quick hospitality softened my thoughts on Rob's offer. Maybe he wasn't as strange as he seemed. Maybe it was custom to offer a meal and a bed to strangers in this part of the country.

As the mayor was turning to leave, I caught him with a question.

"Do you know a man named Rob? I was wondering if he's okay. He offered me dinner. He said he lives in the first house left of the stoplight."

"I don't know him, but that's a nice house, and the woman in the house next to him is good people."

Outside, I prepared to hurry beneath the stoplight without turning my head, but as I neared the light, Rob pulled beside me.

"I thought you might have moved on," he said.

The blood on his arm had been wiped clean. In the passenger seat was a toddler playing with a G.I. Joe.

"You gonna come by?"

"Maybe. It's just that the sun is setting, and I need a place to sleep."

I was trying to get out of his offer without being rude.

"Well, I know I just met you, but I can tell you're good people. Sure we could figure something out. I'll run back to the store and grab some things to cook up. I have a white pickup out front, drop the tailgate, and hold tight. I'll only be a few minutes."

Bound by my inability to be impolite, I turned left at the light and walked to Rob's house. When the woods opened, I saw a brick rancher set back from the road. I lowered the tailgate of the pickup and sat. Things were scattered throughout the yard—an open lawn mower, buckets of paint, planks of wood, and a collection of broken tools. A woman yelled from inside the house. I texted Catherine my location, then slipped my knife and mace into my pocket.

Rob drove onto the grass beside me.

"I'm real glad you stopped by," he said. "Come on."

I parked my cart by the front steps then followed Rob inside. He opened the door just enough for me to slip in. Immediately, three ridge-backs barked me into a corner. I raised my hands until Rob yanked the dogs off and dragged them to another room. A television the size of a wall cast the room in a sharp blue light. The only other light was from a lamp with a red shade. In the far corner, a woman with a blanket pulled to her chin sat in a recliner with cigarette smoke lingering above her head.

"That's my sister, Lauren."

"Nice to meet you."

I went to shake her hand, but she barely stirred. She swept her gaze over me, then returned to the television.

Rob moved pillows from a chair.

"Sit down, sit down."

As my eyes adjusted to the light, the room came into better focus and I searched for something to reassure me. The door to the back of the house was shut, toys were strewn across the carpet, and portraits of family members covered the wall opposite the television.

Rob sat on the edge of the chair beside me, moved it an inch closer, then leaned toward me and spoke about his time in the navy. His eyes were like sinking stones. When I noticed he was wearing a Stephen King shirt, my imagination slunk down its darker alleys and I began dropping hints that people knew I was with him.

"I was just talking to my girlfriend about you," I said. "I share photos throughout the day so people can track me."

Rob brushed the comments aside.

"I'm sure we can figure out a place for you to stay," he said.

He bent toward me with an interest disproportionate to the few sentences I'd spoken. I imagined waking in the middle of the night to him standing over me—I'd have to sleep with my knife in my hand.

"How many kids do you have?" I asked.

"Four."

"Where are the others?"

"One is at his mother's, the other at her grandmother's, and the oldest is at a friend's house. I'll have to pick up the last one later."

I couldn't figure out what I was doing there. I wanted Rob to cook so I could eat and leave, but he kept prattling on. If he started cooking soon, I'd still have time to make camp in daylight.

Lauren left for the back of the house and shut the door. Then Rob did the same. His son jumped on my lap and gave me a *Reader's Digest* to read to him.

When Rob reemerged, he spoke over his shoulder to his sister.

"We're going to get him. Tom will come with me. We can get to know each other on the way."

I figured he was speaking about picking up his other son, but Rob made no move to leave. Instead, he sat down and continued to talk. I tried to make conversation, but nothing I said made a connection.

"I'll tell you, I saw you on that dirt road and I thought what's this good-looking guy doing out in the middle of nowhere?"

The way he said *good-looking* stuck out.

"You have an extra Xanax?" Rob asked Lauren before she reclaimed her catatonic position.

She handed him a pill and he threw it back.

"I have PTSD. The navy. You ready?"

I found myself following Rob to his car. I remembered that it was a nice car, a clean car, but when I opened the passenger door, I saw that it was neither. Everything was lined with grime. Dirty cups were stacked in the center console, dust covered the dash, fingerprints haunted the windows, and the seats reeked of cigarettes. The disorder served as a reminder that this was Rob's space and not my own. Yet I sat down.

Rob paused, then went back to the house. A minute later, he returned with nothing new. I wondered if he grabbed a gun. I tried to tell by the way he moved and the way he sat. I slipped my hand in my pocket and clutched my knife.

"Gonna take you to meet some good ol' boys," he said. "They're good people, my brother-in-law, his friends. Just live way out there."

TRUST YOUR GUT

I didn't say anything. We were already driving. The road was unlit, and Rob carried on. He bent toward me and barely paid attention to the road.

"I saw you on that dirt path and I thought now what's this good-looking guy doing in the middle of nowhere? Not to say I didn't stop because I wanted to make sure you were all right. That's the main reason I stopped. But when I was driving away, I thought, *did God send him to me?* And so, I turned around. I know you got a girlfriend and all. And like I said, I'm good people, wouldn't hurt no one. You know how it is, when you're a kid and a man makes you feel good you want to push him off cause you think it's not right, but then it feels good and you realize what's the difference? You like it."

I tightened.

"The people in town know I'm a bit crazy. Used to be crazy, that is. Into all sorts of things when I was young. Changed my ways a while back."

"Crazy in what way?" I managed.

"Lots of drugs. Selling, doing. People probably think I'm cooking meth or smoking, but I'm not."

Rob drifted between the lanes. The sun was gone. Dark farmland swept beneath a starless sky. I imagined Rob pulling up to a moonlit trailer where his good ol' boys were waiting. A knife might help me against Rob, maybe one more of the good ol' boys, but it would be no use against all of them.

Momentarily, we entered town, but the stores flicked by and soon we were driving away from the light and into the dark again. Rob drifted into the left lane. I glanced over to see a car beside us.

"Yo!" I shouted.

The person next to us slammed on their brakes and disappeared from view.

Rob slowed and turned into a parking lot.

"Oh man, thanks man," he said languidly. "Must have been in my blind spot."

Rob slouched over the steering wheel, seemingly on the verge of dozing off. Then he gazed down the road in silence before grunting and turning the car around. We drove until reaching a grocery store with an empty parking lot. The facade of the building tilted forward, as though ready to crush us.

"I have to get wine for my sister."

I thought of running into the woods, but everything I owned was in Rob's front yard, so I followed him inside. The fluorescent lights burned like disinfectant. A haggard old man stood by the only open register.

"Hey there," he said to Rob.

As Rob and the man exchanged a few words, I caught the man's eye and he smiled lecherously.

Rob looked back to me.

"Boy, you are damn good-looking, though."

I stayed at the front of the store while Rob shopped. I looked at my phone but could think of no one to message. There was no point in worrying my parents or Catherine when they were powerless to help. And besides, nothing had happened. Rob hadn't assaulted me. He hadn't touched me. We never even shook hands.

After Rob paid, we drove away and the windshield fogged. The headlights of oncoming cars were blinding as Rob slipped between the lanes. The tires howled on the rumble strip. Rob didn't notice. He stared at me and spoke incessantly.

I fiddled with the dials until the fog dissipated and I saw that we were back in town and pulling into Rob's driveway. My cart was beside the front steps and my backpack was still inside. I followed Rob into his house and convinced myself that everything was fine by remembering that no one had forced me to do anything. Still, I was starving and wired, and I needed to splash some water on my face to clear my thoughts.

"Can I use the bathroom?" I asked.

"One second!"

Lauren shot out of her chair and across the room. She slammed the door to the back of the house behind her. Rob followed, then after five minutes returned with a feigned nonchalance.

"She was getting a bath earlier and wanted to clean up."

In the back was a small kitchen with a checkered linoleum floor. Lauren stood over the stove stirring hotdogs in a pot.

"Where's the—"

"Straight back!" they said in unison.

In the hallway, I glanced to either side and saw there were two dimly lit bedrooms. In the bathroom, mold climbed a turquoise tub and grew into the grout. I shut the door, went to the sink, and threw water on my face. I wiped it off, then looked at myself in the mirror. Upon seeing my strained expression, I finally recognized the divided voices within me. The conscious voice was telling me to be open to the world, to be unbiased and curious about everything. My gut was screaming, "*Get out of here, you idiot.*"

When I returned to the living room, Rob was waiting by the door.

"We'll get John now," he said. "Come on."

"It's too late, man. I have to set camp. I usually go to bed at nine thirty. I'm usually asleep already."

"No. No. Come on."

Unable to shake my agreeableness, I followed Rob to his car. As I sat in the passenger seat with the door open and a leg out, the feelings I had earlier came rushing back. I was certain we were going to the good ol' boys this time.

"How far is it to your son?"

"Fifteen minutes."

"Fifteen minutes total?"

"Either way."

"That's too far. I'm tired. I have to go."

"No. Stick around. Or wait on the porch and I'll be back in an hour. I haven't been falling asleep until four. I could use the conversation."

"I'm falling asleep as it is."

"I just wish I could have helped you. I saw you on that dirt road and I thought I had to help you. Why don't you wait in my backyard, and I'll be back in an hour?"

When I noticed a bead of sweat running down his forehead, I stepped out and hurried to the house to grab my backpack.

"Nice meeting you," I said to Lauren as I reached inside.

She came at me from the back of the house like a specter. As I slipped out, she slammed the door and turned the locks.

"Where will you sleep?" Rob asked.

"I'll find a spot in the woods."

"I feel terrible. You can't sleep in the woods."

"It's what I've done all the way here."

"Stay here. I'll be back in an hour."

"I have to go."

"But the woods? There are two churches on the left. Stay at one of those. A Baptist church and The House of the Lord. I go to The House of the Lord."

My stomach dropped. The House of the Lord wasn't far from Rob's house, but it was still my plan for the night.

"I'll be fine," I said.

I pushed my cart to the road, then stopped to look at the map to find somewhere new to sleep. My options were limited; there was nothing but farmland. On any other night, camping in a field would have worked fine, but now I worried my tent would stand out like a beacon. At the very least, I wanted to be hidden from the road. The mayor's house was an option, but that was eight miles away and my legs didn't have it in them to run that far. If I walked, I wouldn't arrive until after midnight. But then I noticed a church just off the road three miles away. It had trees around it and a place to tuck my tent around back.

When Rob drove by, he honked then idled at the stoplight. I watched him in my periphery and the moment he turned from view, I started moving.

Around the corner, I came to The House of the Lord. It was ideal: dark in the back, trim grass bordered by a shallow forest, even a hose for showering. If I had gone straight there I'd be bathed and curled around a book. Instead, I stood picturing Rob tapping on my tent at three in the morning.

"Tom? I don't want you sleeping out here. Tom, come back to my place. We can sort something out . . ."

I strapped on my headlamp and started running. Fueled by worries of Rob pulling alongside me, I powered over one hill and then another. The beam of my headlamp was the only light. The tilled earth was like a black sea. Each time a car zipped by, I was relieved it wasn't Rob.

After twenty-five minutes, I saw the church on a hill. It was illuminated by a blaze of floodlights, so there was nowhere to set my tent unseen. I slowed to a walk to catch my breath, then bent over to vomit. I was covered in sweat and I still hadn't eaten.

Around the back of the church, I placed my tent in the only part of the stone driveway that wasn't directly lit. I boiled water for a dehydrated meal, then took off my shirt and hung it from my cart. After that I pulled off my shoes and hung my socks.

A single line of oaks serrated the farmland. Their branches groaned. I searched for the stars above them, and eventually that helped me relax. Everything had been in my head. Rob wouldn't come looking this far. After dinner I could pass out and sleep until the sun filled my tent with the heavy heat of summer.

But as I dug into my meal of chicken and rice, headlights flashed against the side of the church. I leapt to my feet as a pickup rolled into view and two men stepped out. One of them was shirtless.

"Hey buddy."

The shirtless man slipped in front of the headlights, causing his shadow to sweep across my feet like a sickle.

I glanced into my tent to where my backpack rested in the corner with my knife and mace. The men probably had guns, but they were out of shape, so if it came down to it, I could abandon my things and make a run for it.

"What are you doing back here?" the man asked.

"Just passing through. Walked from Jersey. I figured a church would be a safe place to sleep."

I couldn't see the men's faces. They were backlit and in the shadow of a tall bush that blocked a floodlight.

"All right. Some neighbors saw your light and thought we'd better check it out. Be careful. Have a good night, pal."

I almost dropped to the ground. Both men held up a hand then climbed into their pickup, backed away, and drove off.

In the morning, I woke at seven thirty and stayed staring through the mesh of my tent for a long time, wondering why I found it so difficult to extract myself from a situation I didn't want to be in. As a kid, I had never known trouble. I had never been in a fight or even in a bad neighborhood. And unlike every woman in the world, I never needed to deal with lusting men or develop the ability to listen to the alarm bells ringing below the conscious mind.

I knew the world wasn't only Mr. Eds, but I was surprised at how ill-prepared I was for it. If I hoped to make it another five years, I had to be smarter. In a few months, I would be out of my country, in a new culture, and learning a new language. I couldn't take chances on people I didn't trust.

A truck pulled into the driveway and jostled me from my thoughts.

I crawled out of my tent to see two men stepping out of a blue pickup.

"What are you doing out here?" they asked.

"Just camping. Walked from Jersey. I'll be gone in a few minutes."

"No problem. We just got a call and figured we'd check things out."

"You aren't the first."

They laughed.

"It's a small town so when someone sees something out of the ordinary, we like to see what it is. We're glad you're all right."

One of the men tipped his hat. I took a step forward.

"Do you know a guy named Rob from the town back?" I asked.

"Rob?"

"Yeah, turn at the light and he lives in the first house on the left. He invited me over last night, but once I was with him, I realized something wasn't right."

"Don't know him, but I'm glad you're okay."

After the men drove off, I packed and returned to the road.

I walked fast and spoke with Catherine about everything that happened.

"Tom!" she said. "No good person needs to say they're a good person; they just are. You knew you didn't trust him from the beginning. You need to listen to yourself."

An hour later, the same blue pickup rolled off the side of the road and the two ranchers walked over to me.

"I'll call you back," I said to Catherine.

"It's a good thing you didn't stay with that Rob guy," the rancher said.

"You found out about him?"

"Yeah, we asked around. Turns out he's a drug addict . . . heard he's messed with some youngins' in the past, too."

LOU-LOU

On each chain-link gate hung a laminated name tag—ROCKET, ANGEL, DUKE, PIPER, and BENJAMIN. Beside each name was a summary of the dog's personality and health. Most had mange, some couldn't live with cats, and almost all of them had kennel cough. Over two hours, I looked at the thirty dogs three times each, but I never felt a connection. I asked a volunteer to say hello to Rocket, a three-year-old pit who appeared to be in the best health, but once we were together, he charged at the fence to bark at the other dogs and kept at it until I called for a volunteer.

After two hours, I was hot and ready to leave, but I decided to take one last lap.

After my encounter with Rob, I thought of adopting a dog every time a twig snapped in the night or I met someone I was uncertain about. The next section of my walk, Central America, was the most violent region of the world aside from active war zones. El Salvador and Honduras ranked first and second in violent crime rate. Mexico, Guatemala, Nicaragua, and Panama were each in the top fifteen. I had managed my way down the United States, but in places where I didn't speak the language or know the culture, I thought a dog would serve as a strong deterrent to anyone looking to take advantage of me.

As I strolled the outer square of Austin Pets Alive! a final time, a volunteer appeared from a back door holding two freshly showered puppies. She sat the puppies in a kennel, and they huddled together in a corner. One of the puppies was purple black. The other was the color of dry grass. Neither appeared to be in good health. Mange had turned the spine of their backs hairless.

"Gorgeous, aren't they?" A woman with dog hair clinging to her black shirt crouched before the cage. "They're Australian shepherds," she said. "I can tell. I have two of my own, best dogs in the world. Full of energy and very smart. You should see their eyes. It's like they're talking to you."

"Yeah?"

I crouched beside the woman to get a closer look.

"Do they get big?"

"Not too big, about thirty-five pounds. They're good, medium-sized dogs—not so small you'll step on them, but not so big they'll knock you to the ground. She's not mine obviously, but I'm looking at the black one. I just have to adopt her. Who can resist?"

I turned my gaze to the tan puppy with hazel eyes. She was in worse shape than her sister.

"Can I see her?" I asked the volunteer standing behind me.

The puppy, Lou-Lou, was heavier than I expected. She had a fat pink belly and paws that were white like she was wearing socks.

"Where did you find them?" the woman beside me asked.

"On I-35, poor things. We received a call this morning that two dogs were found against the noise barrier and taken to a kill shelter."

"How terrible."

I lifted Lou-Lou to look her in the eye—they were speckled with gold. By the weight of her, she seemed like she'd grow into a stout adult. When I held her against me, she rested her head on my shoulder. That endeared me to her more than any of the other dogs, but I couldn't adopt a puppy on my first day in Austin, so I handed her back to the volunteer.

On my way out, the woman with the dog hair on her shirt stopped me.

"You know she'll be adopted," she said. "Puppies never last."

"You don't think she'll be here tomorrow?"

"No chance. They'll be out of here in a few hours. It's sad for the other dogs, but that's the way it is. Everyone wants a puppy."

If I had any chance of reaching Uruguay next winter, it wasn't by adopting a puppy. It might take her months to get into walking shape. She would need to be trained. Her vaccines and spaying would add weeks to my time in Austin. And adopting any dog would introduce a web of hurdles. At every border, I'd have to wrangle new paperwork. Hotel managers would deny us. We'd be forced to sleep on park benches in strange cities. Dogs would attack us. She'd have to fly and that would mean paying extra and buying crates. I'd need to carry additional food and water too. At some point, she'd get sick. And who knew how she would handle the sun or the snow? But better a puppy than an adult. After a few months, Lou-Lou would be perfectly adapted to life on the road because she had known no other.

How big of a deal was paperwork anyway? An extra day or two at each border was a good excuse for a break. And if a hotel didn't accept us, then I didn't want to be staying at that hotel. Lou-Lou would be a great protector, even if she wasn't—simply being a dog at nighttime would be enough to scare off most things. I'd sleep better with her beside me. That ancient part of my brain that was always scanning for danger could finally rest. I looked back to Lou-Lou pressing herself against her sister. She was terrified and looked worse for wear, but I could tell she was tough and that she would make it as far as she needed.

I waved down a volunteer and minutes later I was sitting in the office with Lou-Lou in my arms.

Other than the tens of thousands of dollars of debt I took out to attend college, I had never willfully undertaken such an immense responsibility. Lou-Lou's well-being now depended entirely on my competence. The moment I signed her adoption papers, the weight of that fell on me.

My cousin, Cat, picked us up once she was off work. Lou-Lou had her paws over my shoulder and Cat swooned at the sight of her.

"I can't believe you adopted a dog."

At Cat and her husband Steve's apartment, I laid out puppy pads and hoped Lou-Lou knew what to do with them. For three weeks, until she received her vaccinations, she was confined to the apartment. Thankfully, Cat and Steve thought nothing of having me and a rambunctious, messy puppy for as long as necessary.

The first thing I wanted to do was change her name. Lou-Lou held none of the grace or grit I hoped she would develop.

I thought of changing her name to Philly. I enjoyed it as a homage to my home city but after using the name for a couple days, I found I didn't enjoy the way it rolled off the tongue. After Philly, I tried Savannah—a city I loved and a nod to her coat being the same color as the African savanna. The name had a pleasant sound to it, too, like the flourish at the end of a signature. That was reason enough, and so it was settled. Her name was Savannah.

Savannah's mange required daily baths with a specific shampoo but she was terrified of the water. After her first shower, I came away bleeding from Savannah latching her claws to my chest. Even after a week of showers, she held to me as though the water was burning her. But, for however much Savannah hated the shower, the shampoo was working. Her mange receded and gradually her fur thickened.

During those weeks, Cat, Steve, and I made a few outings to Austin's downtown; we bar-hopped Sixth Street, played mini-golf, and sampled different food trucks. When Cat was at work and Steve was at the library chipping away at his PhD, I hid in the air-conditioning to watch television or read a dog-training book I found in Steve's floor-to-ceiling library.

As two weeks turned to three, the anticipation of returning to the road gave me a knot of anxiety. The idea that I would be spending the next seven months walking the length of Central America was incomprehensible. The first five months of my walk had been a relentless education. Every time I learned a new trick to make my days smoother it exposed ten more ways I needed to improve. I changed carts, tossed half my gear, and developed effective strategies for finding places to sleep. I learned what roads to walk, how I needed to stretch at night, and when to listen to my gut. The learning curve was steep, and now my thoughts were filled with visions of being woken by thieves in El Salvador.

To keep from becoming overwhelmed, I took to meditating twenty minutes every day. I reminded myself that there were people walking everywhere, and even though the places I would soon be walking were new to me, the locals called those places home.

When the time came to begin again, Cat and Steve dropped Savannah and me where I had left off in Houston. After they wished me luck and departed on their drive back to Austin, I stood in the suburbs watching Savannah sniff the air. She never seemed so small—a meaty twenty-five pounds, sat on her rump, teeth too tiny to puncture the skin, and years of walking ahead of her.

When a car rolled by, she darted for the gutter and cowered.

"Okay, Savannah. Time to go."

I pushed my cart and tugged her leash, but she refused to move.

"Savannah, come on."

She was shaking and her hind legs were collapsed in fear, so I sat on the curb and rubbed her back. When she finally returned to her feet, I attempted to guide her beside me, but when another car passed, she sank to the grass and dug her claws into the dirt.

After fifteen minutes, we made it the length of two houses. I didn't know how to convince her to walk on the leash or overcome her fear of cars, so I moved everything from the back basket of my cart and stuffed it in the main compartment. With the added battery, camera, and rain gear inside, the main compartment bulged. I lifted Savannah and slid her into the basket. She fit as well as any puppy in a basket ever had—her chin on the rim and her paws by her cheeks, gazing out to the world. She would outgrow the basket soon, but I had bought myself some time.

South of Houston, the suburbs withered, and I entered the flats where progress was impossible to feel. I spotted a church on the horizon, and it remained exactly the same size until it was right beside me. On our fourth night, under a vast red sky, Savannah and I came to Pierce, a small town that consisted of a few houses, a grain silo, and a post office in a trailer. The new highway bypassed the town and the old highway, weedy and forgotten, ran through it.

Off the old highway was a church with grass growing tall around it. It wasn't the ideal place to sleep—I wouldn't be hidden—but the town was small enough that I felt confident I wouldn't be bothered.

I brought my cart to the porch and sat against the double doors. While I unpacked my stove, Savannah rolled in the grass. Down the street, a mother was walking with her son and daughter. The mother smiled and waved and helped assuage my worry about being somewhere unwanted.

Since we left Houston, Savannah hadn't made any progress. When I took her out of the basket, she either ran in circles, wrestled the leash, or froze at the faintest sound of a car. I couldn't get her to walk more than twenty feet and each time I failed, I grew more indifferent toward her. If she wasn't walking by the time we reached the border, I'd have to return her to the shelter.

I called my mom to talk it over.

"I shouldn't have adopted her," I said. "I can't get her to walk more than an eighth of a mile. I couldn't even get in eighteen miles today. I was trying to have her walk on leash, but it was just back and forth with her all day. She fights every step."

When Savannah heard me, she poked her head out of the bushes in front of the church. I found a twig and flung it into the grass for her to chase.

"She's a puppy, Tom. You can't expect her to walk all day and you can't expect to walk the same amount you were walking before you adopted her. Things change when you undertake responsibility. You knew this. You signed the papers. Now you have to focus on training her. The miles you walk are secondary."

When Savannah found the twig, she leapt around it and nipped the air in front of it.

"You're only four days into walking again. You spent three weeks with family. It's hard to leave, but you'll be fine. Just focus on getting her to walk a little more each day. That has to be your priority. Buy some Slim Jims or beef jerky. If she doesn't take to those, then find something else. You have to be patient. She has to be walking with you by the time you reach Mexico. You can't push her in the cart forever."

"I know I can't push her in the cart forever, but she doesn't listen. She hates the leash. She gets paralyzed the moment she hears a car."

"She's a puppy, Tom. You knew you'd have to train her. This is it. This is the training."

That night, Savannah didn't want to sleep inside the tent, so she slept in the grass. In the morning, I drank a coffee on the porch, then began Savannah's training in earnest. I clipped the leash on her then we paced up and down the empty street. Her attention was pulled by everything: pebbles, birds, crickets, each new smell. But occasionally, maybe incidentally, she seemed to grasp what I wanted.

As we made one tedious lap after another, I put it out of my head that the day was growing hotter. I tempted Savannah with jerky, but after a few pieces, she turned her nose up at it. I tried to make the leash fun by running and cheering her on. She tripped and rolled into a little ball, but after a break, we tried again, and after an hour, we were walking an entire block together.

After Pierce, my days passed in clips: walking an hour, then spending thirty minutes tempting Savannah forward with pieces of Slim Jim. Within each day, she made little progress, but from one day to the next she improved by leaps. It was as though she needed to dream in order to understand what I was asking of her. Each morning, she walked farther than the morning before. Gradually, her terror of cars faded, too. After a week, they no longer caused her to cling to the ground. Instead of being frozen for a minute, her paralysis lasted twenty seconds, then ten. Within two weeks, she paid no mind to the cars and we were walking side-by-side for an hour at a time.

A month on, Savannah was taller and stronger. Her pink belly was flat. Her legs were long, and the muscles in her thighs were pronounced.

A few days from the Mexican border, I slipped her into the basket to give her a break from the midday sun, but she jumped out. An hour later, I sat her in the basket once more, but again she jumped out. Savannah decided that if I was walking, then she would be walking, too.

LESSONS IN FORTUNE

With an index finger, the man raised the cowboy hat from his brow.

"You walked from Reynosa?"

"Yes."

"You walked?"

He made two fingers walk on the reception desk.

"Yes."

"I don't walk here."

My Spanish wasn't strong enough to come up with a clever response.

"Do you have rooms free?" I asked.

"Nothing," he said before saying something I couldn't understand. "Look. All police." He gestured to the parking lot packed with police cars.

Outside, I untied Savannah from the cart, then we passed under the hotel's stone archway and returned to the road. To my right, a white tent sheltered a dozen police officers. Beyond them a line of cars stretched further than I could see. On the opposite side of the road, a rainbow of tarps snapped in the wind like gunfire. I could smell the beans, rice, chicken, and tortillas that the shops were selling. Beside me, a police officer in a stiff green uniform leaned against the hotel wall.

"What passes here?" I asked.

He shifted the rifle hanging from his shoulder so it was behind his back.

"Border police."

"But nothing dangerous?"

"No. Very secure. Very, very secure. Many police."

"Thanks."

I walked toward the checkpoint. There was no obvious way for me to pass through on foot, so I walked beside the southbound cars until someone stopped me.

"Hey," an officer said in English. "*Pasaporte.*"

I swung off my backpack and withdrew my passport. Savannah sat in the shade of the cart.

"*Toe-más?*"

"That's it."

He flicked through the pages.

"Where's your visa?"

"That's it."

I pointed to my passport—I knew from reading ahead that US citizens received a visa upon entry into Mexico.

"There is no visa here. You need papers. Your visa, where is your visa?"

"I believe that the passport is everything."

He shook his head and handed it back to me.

"You can't pass. You need your papers."

"I walked from the border. No one says nothing."

"You need your papers."

"Can I find the papers here?"

"No. You have to return to Reynosa. You have to go to the border."

"I can't. I walked four days from Reynosa to here."

The officer shrugged.

I took a step back. My first instinct was to find a way to sneak by—a reckless idea on many levels, but especially so because there were officers everywhere and the fields bordering the road were shrubby and open. There was no way to skirt the checkpoint unnoticed.

I wasn't sure what else to do, though. The area immediately beyond the border was the most dangerous section of the country, and now I had to walk it twice more—there and back again. During the four days it took me to reach the checkpoint, locals warned me constantly that I shouldn't be walking and each night I tucked myself as deep as possible in the thorn bushes off the road.

"There's a bus at five thirty," said the officer in front of me.

"To Reynosa?"

"Yes."

If I caught the bus to Reynosa, I'd have to navigate my way from the station to the border, then from the border to a hotel at night. There would be more dogs like the pit bull that attacked Savannah and me when we first passed through, more rebar and concrete, an overwhelming busyness, and a city I didn't comprehend, but a bus was my only option.

I cut between the cars still idling at the checkpoint to cross the street, then spotted a coach with a glowing sign: REYNOSA. I hurried to the coach and knocked on the door.

"Can I buy a ticket?

The driver sighed and reluctantly lifted himself from his seat. Once the driver was outside, I noticed the back of his shirt was dark with sweat. He inspected my cart then stopped when he saw Savannah.

"No dogs."

"No dogs?"

"No."

Two border officers appeared beside me.

"I need to go to the border. She's a good dog. Please, I need a visa."

"No dogs." The driver tapped the solar panels draped over my cart.

"I can put her in here."

I threw open the back basket and removed everything.

"Come here, Savannah."

I picked her up, put her hind legs together, and slipped her into the basket. She fit, but just barely. Unlike a month before, when she could curl to sleep in the basket, Savannah now pushed out the sides just by sitting in it. I knew the moment I left her unattended she would jump out.

The driver and the border officers laughed. The driver clapped, then said something to the officers that made them laugh harder.

"Okay."

"Yes? Thank you!"

I followed the driver with my cart to the storage area. Toward the back of the bus, he opened a door to a narrow staircase that led to a space about two feet high that was packed with luggage spanning the length of the bus. The female officer looked in and shook her head. She pointed to the cart and said something I couldn't understand, but I knew meant "it won't fit."

"Yes. Yes. Yes," I said, pulling the tires off the cart. "See?"

I climbed the steps and lay on my side at the top of the staircase. The driver lifted the back end of my cart, while I tugged on the front. We tried maneuvering and forcing it in, but it was a few inches too long, so I shuffled around the cart and tried to free it from where it was catching.

Savannah, seeing my struggle, ran up the staircase and pawed at my back.

"It doesn't work."

The driver released the cart and stepped back.

I put my feet against the wall and pulled the cart as hard as I could, but it wouldn't budge. The driver leaned in, waved me down, then helped me free the cart.

"I need to go to Reynosa," I said.

He shook his head, then shut the cargo door.

"I have to go," he said.

A minute later, the bus rolled through the checkpoint and was gone.

I brought my fist down on the cart's handle.

Without a bus, I'd have to backtrack four days to the border, then walk four days south again. I couldn't afford a cab, but even if I could muster up some money and convince them to take Savannah, fitting my cart in one of the small boxy cars was difficult to imagine. I'd have to walk. Not only did that mean putting myself at a greater risk of being mugged, but it meant I'd have to tell Philadelphia Sign and everyone following me that I walked four days into Mexico without a visa. I told everyone I was going to walk around the world, but I couldn't even make it into a single foreign country.

One of the border officers patted my arm.

"Calm yourself, my friend."

I was too frustrated to look at him.

"You're okay, my friend."

When the officer knelt to place one of the tires back on my cart, his kindness returned me to the moment, and I lifted the cart to help him. Once both tires were on, I bent over the cart and covered my head.

Eight more days.

The border officer put a hand on my back.

"My friend, how much money do you have?"

I straightened and took in the officer for the first time. His skin was rough, likely from years of acne, and unlike most of the other officers, his hair was spiked rather than brushed to a combover. He had a crooked nose from a break too.

"Huh?"

I had to be sure I understood what he was getting at.

"You have?" He rubbed two fingers together. "How much money?"

I couldn't afford much. I had two hundred dollars' worth of pesos in my backpack and only a few hundred more in my bank account. On top of that, I didn't know how far it was to the next ATM and I needed cash to see me through. If I gave the officer too much, there was the potential I'd run out of cash while on the road.

"Two thousand pesos," I said—a little more than a hundred US dollars.

"Okay, okay."

The officer pinched his thin beard and peered across the street.

"Come."

"Of course."

Among the cars on the southbound side, the officer stopped and turned to me. Most of the border officers were either looking into vehicles or chatting in the shade. Under the police tent, an officer played on his phone.

"Wait. My boss." He nodded to a man sitting at a desk in the shade. We waited until the boss shifted some papers, gathered a stack, then strolled into the hotel.

"You need to go to Ciudad Victoria."

"Okay."

"Go to the airport. They will give you a visa."

The officer's eyes were wide from scanning for his boss over my shoulder.

"Thank you."

He hit me on the arm. "Go!"

"Money? Do you need money?"

"No. Go now! Fast! Fast!"

"Thank you, brother."

I held out my fist and he pounded it. I slipped between the cars and didn't look back. After a mile, I was beyond the line of cars. After two miles, I reached a field of yellow grass that seemed a promising place to camp. I turned off the road and bowled through the field with Savannah in my wake. We pushed through until we found a dirt path that we followed to another field where the land was fallow and there were no houses and no roads. I parked my cart, set out my tarp, and sat. Savannah rested beside me.

I should have been walking north. I should have been paying for my oversight, retreading the steps I'd already taken. And maybe I still would. Maybe I'd bear consequences far worse than an eight-day walk. But I had made my decision and now I had to make it five days to Ciudad Victoria. That was a long way without a visa. There would be police and at least one more checkpoint, but I couldn't turn back. My fear of appearing incapable was too great.

Beyond the checkpoint, short black brush, guajillo trees, and the occasional Texas sage shrouded the land between villages. Great swathes were fenced by barbed wire that was only disrupted by the entrances to access roads. Sometimes the access roads were open, but more often they were closed by gates of four vertical sticks bound by four rows of barbed wire. Most of the time, I tucked myself in the thorn scrub at night. Occasionally, I camped on the access roads, certain to shut the gate behind me to ensure no livestock escaped. When I did, I lived with a perpetual anxiety that headlights would appear in the distance, force me to tear down my tent, and explain to a rancher why I was on their land. But perhaps because the properties were so enormous, this worry never came to pass.

Whenever I stopped, the locals warned me of gangs. At a restaurant, a group of mothers held my hands to pray for me. They told me not to be out at night. Maybe it was my limited Spanish, but they made it seem that gang members might abduct me at any moment. Every hour was filled with dread. I worried about the gangs constantly, but my only exposure to them was indirect. Police and armed military passed me every day. At a mezcal factory, I got drunk with the owner and he told me to trust no one. He said the military was corrupt, only the navy was honest, and that it was a shame I wasn't sailing around the world. A little while later we came to the realization that on the same night a tourist bus was robbed at gunpoint, I had been camped in the brush less than a quarter mile away.

On my third day from the checkpoint, the police stopped me. Their car pulled over and two men wearing yellow sunglasses that warped the sunbaked land approached. They loved Savannah and that she was wearing booties. By the grace of some unknown savior, they didn't ask for my passport but instead handed me ten dollars of pesos and a cold bottle of water.

"Buenas suerte," they said. "Bendigate."

I didn't understand what they had said until I was farther down the road and the Spanish clicked.

"Good luck. Bless you."

Soon after that, I stopped at a sign on the side of the road.

MILITARY INSPECTION. 3 KM.

Police stopping to say hello was one thing; it was another to pass through a military checkpoint without a visa. I wondered if the border officer at the first checkpoint knew about the military inspection and didn't tell me, or if he just didn't know. Either way, it was me who had walked through the checkpoint and not him.

After seeing the sign, I walked at half-speed as though I could think my way out of the bed I made. At the next military inspection sign, my left tire popped, so I sat on the side of the road to fix it. Savannah hid beneath the cart to escape the sun and I used the pump Mr. Ed had given me to inflate a new tube. Cattle mooed unseen in the pale bushes set back from the road. Their bells clanged and once I had the thorn pulled from the tire, and a new tube installed, I scoured pixelated images on Google Earth to find a way around the checkpoint.

All the roads were service roads that carried miles into private land without the promise of an exit. If I followed one, I could be stuck back there for days. So I continued on the main road, knowing that in forty minutes, I'd be in a van with caged windows on my way to the border for deportation. The World Walk had barely begun and I had already failed. Not only would I have to skip the first foreign country on my route because of a simple oversight, but I would lose all credibility. I dreamed of my adventure for eight years and read every travel and hiking book I could to prepare myself, yet at the first real world test, I failed.

After three kilometers, the military site appeared on a hill.

It was worse than I expected—a brutalist, earth-tone complex cornered by two guard towers. The top of the barracks peeked over an imposing wall.

Outside the main gate, soldiers in tan body armor patrolled an inspection site and rummaged through multiple vehicles.

As I pushed uphill, the road split. The left lane turned to the inspection site and the right lane continued unobstructed. Typically, I followed the shoulder against traffic, but now I stayed as far to the right as possible with the cars passing on my left. Off the road, a family of four was eating a lunch of tortillas, pork, and beans in the trunk of a minivan. They smiled.

At the top of the hill, soldiers were stopping vehicles in the right lane, too. A soldier standing on the shoulder was blocking my way. Another was turning over an ID.

As I neared, I tried not to look at any particular soldier for too long, but I also made sure I didn't look away either.

When I reached the man on the shoulder, he stepped aside to let me pass. I nodded and he nodded back. Beyond him, I kept my eyes straight and prepared to feign deafness. After a few minutes, the hill started down and the inspection site shrank behind me. A half mile on, I came to a lonely taco shack across from a gleaming metal ranch gate. I ordered three tacos and a mandarin Jarritos, then I sat on a wooden bench and sipped my soda from a trembling hand.

At Ciudad Victoria, I tried to get a visa at the airport, but I was told that because I didn't fly in, I needed to return to the border. In my hotel room, I booked the earliest bus possible to Reynosa: 2:10 in the morning. I paid for two extra nights at the hotel and told the receptionist I would pay to have her mind Savannah if I wasn't back the following afternoon.

If everything went smoothly, I would only be away from Savannah for half a day. If I was deported, I knew Cat and Steve would drive to Ciudad Victoria to get her. My standing in the family would be demolished, but at this point I had dug myself too far in.

The next day, I woke at one, filled Savannah's bowls, brushed my teeth, splashed water on my face, and hugged Savannah goodbye. As I left, I was hollow and lightheaded with nerves.

I took the hotel shuttle to the bus station, then found a window seat on the second level of the bus to Reynosa. For a while, my thoughts circled as to how I would go about asking Cat and Steve to drive to Mexico or how I would tell Philadelphia Sign and the people following my journey that I had been deported.

As I watched the city lights give way to the darkness of the country, I drifted off.

What felt like a moment later, I was woken by a soldier. We were at the military site I walked through a few days earlier.

"Bring your bag," the soldier said.

I hurried outside and joined the line of passengers putting their bags through a metal detector. My bag rolled through without incident, but at the bus an officer was checking identification and when I handed him my passport, I knew it was over. He flicked through every page more than once then looked at me and searched my eyes.

"No stamp?"

The bus driver leaned over the officer's shoulder to look at my passport.

"That's why I'm returning to Reynosa." I said. "I need the stamp."

He flipped through my passport again until settling on my picture.

"Tomás?"

"Yes."

The officer glanced from me to the passport photo.

"You're going to the border?"

"Direct to the border."

He folded my passport then rubbed his thumb over the embossed American seal.

"Okay."

He handed me my passport and I hurried onto the bus.

Within minutes, the darkness put me to sleep until once more I was woken a moment later. The bus came to a stop, and I moved the curtain aside to see that we were at the first border inspection site and that there were only three officers outside. One of the older officers boarded the bus. Making his way down the aisle, he asked each passenger for their ID. When I handed him mine, he used a penlight to illuminate the pages. He went through the pages five or six times before looking at me like a child looks to a teacher for an answer.

"You have a stamp?"

"That's why I return to Reynosa."

"Okay. Come with me."

I slipped on my backpack and followed. I felt the eyes of the other passengers against my back.

In the warm morning air, the older officer handed my passport to a scowling young officer standing beneath the white tent in the middle of the road. The young officer was fit, though not muscular, and seemed to have chosen a uniform a size too small in order to demonstrate he was bigger than the role he'd been assigned.

"What's this?"

His lips were pinched to the size of a needle.

"My passport," I said dumbly.

The bus was the only vehicle on the road, the rainbow of tarps was still and quiet.

"Where's your stamp?"

"That's why I return to Reynosa."

"No."

The officer's finger cut through the air in front of me. He pointed to a van with caged windows parked beside the hotel.

"You should be in that."

"To return to Reynosa?"

"To put you in jail."

"I'm sorry."

"You should be in that car. You should be deported, and you should not be allowed in my country for ninety days."

I envisioned being taken away in a rattling, caged-window van. Ninety days wouldn't be the end of The World Walk, but it would be the end of my credibility and my failure to care for Savannah would crush me under an unbearable weight of guilt.

"I'm sorry. I'm sorry. I'm an idiot. I'm returning to the border now. I will have a visa. Never another time. Never another time."

The severe young officer squeezed my passport between his fingers. In the long shadows from the hotel, his features were extraordinarily sharp. He yelled at me, but I couldn't understand him. The best I could make out was "I don't have enough men to drive you to the border. You're lucky I don't."

He handed me my passport.

"Leave before I change my mind."

I didn't need another word. I ran to the bus.

This time I knew I made it. I had walked the road we were driving; there were no more checkpoints.

When we pulled into the city, the rising sun was hazy from the dust raised by the harried activity of a new day. I replayed the conversation with the border officer a thousand times. I imagined being thrown into the van parked across the street.

Off the bus, I jogged nine blocks to the border. I waited in line before being screened by a steroidal American who had undoubtedly been selected with the intention of projecting the might of the country he was keeping. Once through, I made a loop back to the Mexican border, entered the office that before I didn't notice, and paid thirty dollars for my stamp. I ran to the bus station and managed to buy a ticket to Ciudad Victoria three minutes before departure. As I stepped onto the bus, I held up my passport to the same driver that had driven me in the morning.

"I have it," I said.

The driver smiled.

"You have luck," he said.

"Too much."

"Enough."

In my seat, I looked over the stamp.

People drained their savings, trudged through jungle, and risked being kidnapped so their children might one day possess what I carried so lightly—over a hundred miles and multiple checkpoints into a foreign country without a visa and I barely received a slap on the wrist. I always knew I was fortunate to have been born in the United States, but it wasn't until that moment that I understood it.

THE PATH TO FLUENCY

Central America was the beginning of my unraveling. In the same way that my thoughts were changing around a new language, my understanding of myself and the world was shifting as well. Never before had I been so overwhelmed on a daily basis. I was knocked back to the fundamentals of existing. Even the smallest interactions, entering a shop to buy water, were acts of growth. Eyes were on me everywhere—I was gangly, white, and pushing a massive red baby carriage. I needed to be comfortable with my strangeness. I masked portions of my insecurity with stern glances and timely scowls, but I also developed the ability to retreat within myself and hold a calm confidence even when I didn't feel it.

People were friendly. That was the first thing I learned, and it was my primary reassurance. Even though a paranoia about being kidnapped stalked me like a jaguar, my actual interactions were nothing but warm. I was given pineapples, coconuts, and free meals constantly. Occasionally, a fisherman would walk with me on their way home and show me an admirable amount of patience as I stumbled along our conversation.

Abuelas guided me through their menus as though I were their own grandson. I was a fool in a foreign land, but that hardly seemed to bother anyone except me.

I was burning with the desire to prove to myself. Every day, no matter how hot, Savannah and I covered twenty-four miles. When needed, we rested in squares, beneath underpasses, or on corner store stoops. Mostly though, I bludgeoned forward without nuance. We walked regardless of the midday sun or the pouring rain.

When we crossed the Sierra Madre Mountains, it was through four days of thunderstorms. It rained when I broke camp. It rained when I set camp. The rain sprayed us when we napped in the bus stops. It rained so much that I ran out of things to dry Savannah with at night. My pack towel was soaked, then my spare shirts, then my socks. Thankfully, on the western side of the mountains, there was a steady thirty-mile-per-hour wind and no rain. Wind turbines stretched from the eaves of the mountains to the Pacific somewhere beyond the horizon. In just a day, my things were dry, and I could think again.

But the weather was the least of our concerns.

Mexican cities never ceased to amp me with adrenaline, even the smaller ones. They felt impossible to navigate. The sidewalks were unreliable, the streets were busy, and the centers were hurricanes of indecipherable activity. Every neuron was put to use. I worried about being followed, Savannah being struck by a car, or someone taking advantage of us. In the busier cities, I would hastily stock up at a supermarket, then flee to the countryside.

Yet, for all the stress, the cities in Mexico were what forged Savannah and me into a unit. The hours spent navigating the moto-taxis, pushcarts, and crowds of people were what honed us. We learned to glide through the madness. I kept her leash tight around my hand so she always stayed close enough that I felt her ear brushing on my calf. When I passed the leash behind my back, she knew she needed to switch sides and have her other ear brushing against my other calf.

Twenty-four miles was no longer enough for her. In the mornings, she jumped on me the moment she heard the leash. At the end of the day, she needed a good sprint to burn herself out. The days when Savannah cowered at the sound of a car or refused to walk were long gone.

When I went into stores to resupply, I kept her tied to the cart outside. Since most people were afraid of dogs, she offered good protection for our things, but I worried someone might steal her. Compared to the street dogs, Savannah was regal in appearance. I was always relieved to see her tail wagging at the sight of me when I returned.

My love for her crept up on me. Through most of Mexico, I didn't think of her at all—I was only trying to keep us alive. But once I had a moment to breathe, I realized how much we had gone through. We'd been attacked by strays, battered by weather, and hewn to efficiency. She was more resilient than I could have hoped. One evening, while we were camped in a field near the southern border, I looked over to her and thought: *I love this little bugger.*

After three months in Mexico, Savannah and I were welcomed by the sheer green mountains of Guatemala. Our first day in our second foreign country was spent pushing our ninety-pound cart up a mountain in 90 percent humidity. After two weeks of climbs and descents, we reached Lake Atitlán—a lake in the caldera of a super-volcano with a jungle, three volcanoes, and a smattering of towns at its rim. When we crested the road and the forest opened to our first view of the lake, I howled at the beauty of it. A guard at his station smiled and gave me a thumbs-up.

In San Marcos La Laguna, I found a room for forty dollars a night. It was out of my budget, but I needed the rest. Although each day I felt myself strengthen and grow, my walk down Mexico had been the most stressful and demanding three months of my life.

Thankfully, San Marcos La Laguna was the hotbed of new-age escapism that I needed to reset. Yoga studios, meditation centers, and tarot readers were tucked in every cranny. Tourists were Scandinavians and Australians on extended gap years. Hostels were by the water, while the locals lived on the hillsides.

At night, the cobblestone streets were empty, but during the day, the piazza was alive with vendors. Most Guatemalan women wore traditional *trajes*, colored dresses held by equally colorful sashes. Men wore palm leaf hats and shirts with bold prints. Initially, I planned on staying for three days, but after those three days I found the place so endearing, and myself so exhausted, that I extended my stay another two weeks. When I discovered a poster advertising private Spanish lessons for ten dollars an hour, I signed up immediately.

I took six hours of lessons each day. Savannah and I fell into a good rhythm. We woke at six to stroll through town and take photos, I ate breakfast at the hostel while I went over my homework, then at nine I walked to a fancier hostel with stone walls, fountains, and private bungalows under a shading of palms. There, I worked with my teacher, Nicolas, until four in the afternoon while Savannah dozed at my feet.

With private tutoring, my Spanish improved rapidly. Soon I was holding extended conversations with Nicolas and when I found myself having a conversation with a street vendor about Christmas mass, I knew I was getting somewhere.

I would have liked to have stayed in San Marcos La Laguna forever, but my bank account was nearly empty, and I needed to keep moving to reach Uruguay the following winter. So, after two weeks, I caught a ferry across the lake and continued for El Salvador. The moment I left San Marcos La Laguna, I missed the English speakers and the ease of my days. Save for those couple weeks, my introduction to walking abroad had been one hard-earned lesson after another, and with the first and second most dangerous countries in the world in my immediate future, I knew there would be no relief ahead.

THE MAN WITH THE
MACHETE

I saw the bodies side-by-side in a field, but the grass was overgrown enough that I could only see that it was a man and woman—and they were facedown. I stared at the bodies until the police noticed me, black masks obscuring their identity, then I walked away as fast as I could. A truce had just collapsed between the country's two major gangs: MS-13 and Barrio 18. El Salvador was now the most dangerous country on earth by a wide margin.

Down the road, I stopped beneath the imperfect shade of a morro tree—green fruit clinging to the branches like tumors. Savannah and I had been walking since five in the morning and hustling from hotel to hotel since entering El Salvador. In front of us, a car pulled over and a man in a safari outfit jumped out, ran over, and was speaking to me before he planted his feet.

"Do you speak Spanish?" he said.

"Enough."

"Where are you walking from?"

"New Jersey."

"And where are you going?"

"Uruguay."

"Fantastic. That's perfect. My name is Manuel. I'm a reporter for Channel 26. That's my cameraman, Javi." He pointed to a man lumbering out of the car.

"You'll make a great interview. Just keep walking and Javi will get some shots of you. I'll interview you up the road. Do you want to do the interview in English or in Spanish?"

"I prefer English, but it's probably better for the people that I do it in Spanish."

"Good. That's good. Your Spanish is good, you'll do fine. I'll see you up the road in a minute."

Manuel jogged to his car. Javi and I shook hands, then he settled the camera on his shoulder as I walked toward him. Only once I started moving did it occur to me that I had agreed to an interview. Manuel had spoken so fast and with such assurance that I agreed to everything without thinking. After ten minutes, Savannah and I settled under another morro tree and Manuel reappeared alongside two new men with notepads and voice recorders.

"How's your dog?" asked Manuel.

Savannah was beside the cart with her eyes closed and her chest heaving.

"Better now."

"She must be happy we're not in the sun."

"I recognize you," I said to the men with the recorders. "You were at the scene."

I noticed that one of the men had thick eyebrows crawling over the rim of his glasses.

"The scene?"

"About three kilometers behind . . . I don't know the word. . . . with the police."

"Ah yes," Manuel said in English. "The murder."

"Was it gangs?"

"That's what they're trying to figure out, but they think that it was, yes. It was a husband and wife, shot in the head. Executed last night. They had a big family, many children. Eight, I think. There's a gun problem in El Salvador. Aren't you worried about that?"

"Of course. I mean a little, but it's within the gangs, isn't it?"

"The majority. I doubt anything would happen to you. We don't see gringos walking through our country. There are some cyclists, but you're the first walker I've seen. That's why we had to stop and talk with you. It'll be good for the people to see there's a gringo here. It's strange, a novelty, you know? Are you ready for the interview?"

"I don't know if it'll be good in Spanish."

"Your Spanish is good. You'll do fine." He turned on the microphone and tilted it toward me. "What's your name and what are you doing?"

I was far from fluent, but answering questions about my walk was easily my most-developed Spanish. Down Mexico, I had hundreds of conversations in restaurants, hotels, and tiendas that consisted of exactly the same questions. *Where are you from? Why are you walking? Where are you walking to? Where do you sleep? How does your dog like it?*

For the interview, I did my best to expand my answers more than usual, but about halfway through I lost focus when I caught a glimpse of myself in the reflection of Javi's lens. My face was edged with salt, my temples were sunken, and my cheekbones protruding—the sight made me think of the grandmothers sitting at home laughing at the dirty white boy speaking Spanish worse than their three-year-old grandchild. But then I thought of the other grandmothers that might be defending me, saying, "Look at this boy, at least he is trying to speak Spanish!"

When the interview ended, Manuel returned to English.

"It'll be on Channel 26 at seven tonight. I'll send you a link. There'll be a write-up of you in Monday's paper, too."

"That's great."

"Good luck and be careful."

The reporters dispersed as quickly as they came together.

Without them capturing my attention, I realized what little shade was over Savannah and how hot the sun felt. The air above the asphalt was wavering. Savannah was panting. The brush around us was leafless and thorny, and it occurred to me that I had just told all of El Salvador that I was on my own, following Route Two, and that everything I owned was in the baby carriage I was pushing.

As I pressed my foot against the tire to catch my breath, sweat dripped from my nose. Sunset was two hours away. I might have kept walking, but we had already covered twenty-one miles and on the rocky hillside our options for good camping were limited. The open-aired wooden structure across the street was promising—it resembled a treehouse without a tree, and it was attached to a cattle pen where a single calf was so tightly kept it could only move its eyes and tail. At the base of the structure were chairs and a wooden wire spool that served as a table. I dropped into a lounge chair made of rubber strings and Savannah jumped onto the detached bench of a minivan.

Before us was the valley we had walked in the morning. In the distance stood the scorching city of Choluteca—one of the hottest cities in the Americas. Our walk across Honduras had been barren and burning, not as lush as Guatemala or even the El Salvadorian coast, but we were near the end of it. Tomorrow afternoon we'd be in Nicaragua and on the other side of our blistering sprint.

I put my hands behind my head and shut my eyes. My thighs pulsed and my calves strained. We covered no less than twenty-five miles a day since entering El Salvador. Some days we walked thirty. Each night we stayed in a hotel, and each morning we woke at five so we had enough time to reach the next room. I was tired of staying inside. Even though we were safe, hotels were dull and repetitive. I missed the adventure of sleeping outside.

I reached back and rubbed Savannah's head.

"Another tough one, eh?"

Savannah pressed her forehead against my hand.

In Mexico, I strapped Savannah's booties on her during the worst of the heat, but she flicked her paws deliberately until they flung off. After that, I tried to goad her into wearing them by offering treats but the only food she cared about were the chicken wings she found on the side of the road. After a dozen attempts, I gave in and accepted that she was content going barefoot. For a week, I checked her paws every night, but they were always more calloused than the day before—like stones that hardened as she went.

Soon Savannah was asleep and my reluctance to leave caught up with the dwindling day. The structure wasn't the perfect place to spend a night, it was too exposed, but the next town was nine miles away and I hadn't come across anything better.

From my dromedary bag, I poured water into my Nalgene. Then, as I was stuffing the bag back into my cart, a pickup stopped uphill and reversed back to me. A man leaned over his son and called out.

"Where are you from?"

"New Jersey."

He gave a thumbs-up, then hurried around the truck and over to me.

"Come on," he said to his son.

The son, grinning and doe-eyed, jumped out to join his father.

"We saw you walking in Choluteca this morning."

Savannah went to the man with her tail wagging close to the ground. He gave her a pat and she sprang to her hind legs and put her front paws on his stomach.

"No, no, no." He nudged her back.

"She is American, too?"

"Adopted in Texas."

Savannah went to the boy, and he crouched to meet her. She pushed her head against his chest, and he fell over laughing.

"It's good you have a dog. Very good. They can feel things; they know when a person is good or bad. They're guardians, they say."

He pointed from his eyes to mine.

"That's why I have her."

"How much farther are you walking today?"

"I don't know. I'm tired now."

"In San Marcos there's a hotel. I live there, in San Marcos, it's a beautiful little town, expensive, but very precious, a town very precious. It makes twelve kilometers from the border and eight kilometers from here."

I had looked at the map enough times to know that San Marcos was nearer to twenty kilometers than eight—too far to reach before nightfall. I gestured to the structure behind me.

"This isn't yours?"

"No, but I know the owner. He lives around the corner. You'll see it. It's a beautiful house on the point of a hill. He's a friend of mine. He owns the ranch. Sometimes he's not here, but almost always he is here."

"Do you think I can sleep here for the night?"

"Of course, but sleep up there, it's more secure."

I looked back to where he was pointing and noticed a built-in ladder to a second story that I hadn't seen.

"Your friend won't mind?"

"No, no."

We spoke for a while longer. I told him the same things I told everyone. He told me about Honduras and how it was safe even though the police were kids with shotguns who could be bribed with ten dollars. After he and his son said goodbye and were in their truck, he called to me again.

"You like pizza?"

The son held a box of Little Caesar's from the window.

I laughed and went over.

"It's my favorite," I said.

"Take it all."

In my lounge chair, a view of the Honduran savanna sundering before me, I did my best to savor every bite of the three slices of lukewarm pepperoni pizza. When the sun reached the Pacific and the eastern sky darkened, I unpacked what I needed for the night, climbed the ladder of two-by-fours, and deposited my things on the second story. Then I hid my cart behind the minivan seat, slung Savannah over my shoulder, and brought her up with me.

On the second level, there were two rooms—one large and empty; the other small and with a pile of tarps and a stack of wood. Around the rooms was a wall that was high enough for me to sit against and not be seen. The wind swept over it, though. I pulled on my jacket and set my tarp with my things on the edges so it didn't fly away.

When night came, the temperature plummeted. Savannah slept on the tarp beside me. I tugged my sleeping bag over my shoulders and curled around my Nook to read *Brief Encounters with Che Guevara*.

By mid-evening, fantasies of Nicaragua were dripping into me like a sedative counteracting the intensity of the previous months. As I was drifting to sleep, I heard a motorcycle grumble up the road and stop outside. I sat up to listen. For a minute, the bike idled, then turned off. Then a man yelled in my direction.

"Donna?"

I stood and looked out to the road. A man standing on the far shoulder was veiled by distance and the moonless night. I thought it might be the man from earlier and that I had misunderstood what he said, but I wasn't sure.

"Donna?" he called.

"Donna?" I said.

"Donna?"

"Not here."

He said something else, but I couldn't make out what—only that he was annoyed.

I watched as he went back to his motorcycle and rolled down the mountain in neutral. I wondered why I had stood to answer him rather than staying hidden.

In Mexico, the idea that someone might know where I was camped would have kept me from sleeping, but after half a year of sleeping in strange places, I developed the ability to turn off my worry. It was only practical. Once I picked my spot for the night, there was nothing to do but sleep. I wasn't willing to walk a dark road in search of a new campsite.

On my mattress, I once again teetered on the cusp of sleep. Then headlights hit the structure, and I threw off my sleeping bag and jumped up.

As though appearing by way of hidden hatch, a man as powerful as a bull manifested before me. He blinded me with his flashlight, I held a hand over my eyes, and gradually, I made out the silhouette of a machete at the man's side.

I could think of nothing to do. I was in my underwear. The man was twice my size.

He lowered his flashlight and stepped into the glow of the headlights. The orange made his edges soft like a watercolor, but even blurred as he was, I could see the man had labored in the fields most his life—the wrinkles in his face were gorges and his hands were large as skillets.

He raised his machete and swatted the broad side against the top of the wall.

"It's a gringo!" he yelled.

Another man howled with laughter below.

The shoulders of the man with the machete dropped half an inch and the shape of him changed entirely.

"Is this place yours?" I said, anxious to correct any misunderstanding.

"Yes."

"A man said I could sleep here, a friend of yours. He had a son. He had twelve years, maybe. He was driving a red truck. I asked him if it was okay that I sleep here."

"There's no problem."

Savannah went to the man with her tail wagging and sniffed his boots. He glanced down then ignored her.

"You're sure?"

"Yes. No problem, relax yourself."

The man walked past me and inspected my things with his flashlight. Then he went to the smaller room, waved the flashlight about, and returned. He spoke as he walked.

"I was worried because last night someone stole a cow. When my friend called and said someone was here, I came as fast as I could. I wanted to catch them. It's not the only time they have stolen my cows."

The man spoke fast. I caught most of what he said but not everything. *Kill*, I heard. He mimed a gun to his head.

"I hope," he said.

"Do you think they'll come back? Tonight?"

"No. You're fine, you're fine. Relax yourself. Sleep."

He pointed to my bed with the machete, then disappeared down the ladder. I peered over the wall to see him talking with a younger man about my age before climbing into the cattle pen. He worked his way through the pen, then returned to search the first story of the structure.

I laid down. For twenty minutes there were flickers of the man's flashlight. Then he climbed the ladder and I sat up.

"Relax, relax."

He set his machete on the ground in the smaller room then stretched and twisted with his hands behind his head.

"Staying the night?" I asked.

"I must."

He unfurled the pile of tarps and it transformed into a bed with a blanket and a pillow.

"You have a bed."

"I'm ready."

"I want some cookies? I mean, do you want some cookies? I have Oreos if you want."

"Cookies?"

He held out his hand, so I dug through my things until finding a pack of Oreos, then handed them over. He opened the pack and shoved a cookie in his mouth. He ate the remainder while staring at the wall and standing beside me in silence. When he finished, he slipped his machete beneath his pillow and laid down.

"Relax, relax," he said in the dark. "Go to sleep."

Strangely enough, I did.

THIEVES IN THE TUNNEL

On either side of us, the highway ramps ascended, cutting off the sunlight, and squeezing the sidewalk until we were walking a dim narrow path. Ahead of us, two men rested on a tattered sofa. A third reclined in an office chair, polishing an eight-inch shard of glass.

"Buenas," I said as I neared.

"Buenas."

"You have water?" asked the man polishing the glass.

I handed him the bottle I kept on the back basket of my cart. He poured water onto a rag then handed the bottle back to me. One of the men on the sofa inspected the burn of his cigarette then took a draw.

"Thanks."

I squeezed my cart between them and continued. Eventually, the highways curved away and the sun came through again. Around us, colorful but dingy apartments towered. In the intense humidity, mold had fused with the buildings so that none were free from blotches of discoloration. At an empty intersection, a few suitcases worth of clothing were flattened into the asphalt. The air reeked of trash and roadkill.

Through a tangle of streets, Savannah and I made our way to Panama City's main artery, Calle Principal. The sidewalk there was enclosed by a tunnel of shops. Bodegas, clothing stores, and restaurants were on either side of us.

Frantic like always in Central American cities, I hurried on, but especially so because it was our last day of walking in North America. We only had six miles to our Airbnb and three days until our flight to Bogotá.

After a while, I slowed as I felt the most unmanageable section of the city was behind me. We had walked nine miles, but I still hadn't eaten, so I stopped at a corner shop. Across from the bodega, on a raised platform, was a sitting area made of school chairs with desks attached to them. I parked my cart, tied Savannah to it, then went into the shop. I bought sweet bread, an Adrenaline Rush energy drink, and two boxes of chocolate milk. It was enough sugar to put my diabetic sister into a coma, but the proper amount to satisfy my aching body. At one of the desks outside, I ate the sweet bread, sipped the energy drink, and texted my dad. It was March 14th—his birthday.

"I'll call you later!" I wrote. "Enjoy the day! Also, made it to Panama City and man is this place chaotic."

"Thanks. Traffic chaotic or people crazy?"

"Well, came through a pretty sketchy area earlier—"

Then I felt something cold against my neck. I looked to my right and saw a man stretched over a desk to reach me. He had bloodshot eyes, a face drawn like a rat, and a sore on his upper lip. He snarled and I leaped up and stepped back.

"What the hell, man?" I said in English.

The rat-faced man slipped between the chairs, and I noticed the shiv pinched between his fingers. I touched a hand to my neck to see if he'd drawn blood, but my hand returned clean.

"Back the fuck up, dude!"

"Shut up!" he yelled in English.

I threw my hand in the air in a feeble attempt to wave the man away, but he came at me quicker and raised the shiv to eye level. I looked to Savannah tied to the cart. She was at attention, but unsure of what was needed.

As I backed into the bodega, a tiny woman sidled beside me and shooed me with both hands.

"Outside! Outside!" she said.

Upon hearing her Spanish, I realized I'd been speaking in English and so I said "he's got a knife!" in Spanish. The woman noticed the shiv and yelled "outside!" at the man, but then she stepped away.

As I continued backward, ancient survival instincts creaked to life. Time slowed as I weighed what in the shop I could use to defend myself. On the right wall were refrigerators of soda, but I was moving away from them. Beside me was a table of baked goods and below the table were stacks of toilet paper. I shifted so I could step through the opening of the shop counter. When my back hit the wall of cigarettes, the man with the shiv stopped a few feet in front of me.

Beside me, the woman's husband was yelling.

"You can't be here!" he said to me. "Outside!"

"He has a knife!" I yelled back.

"Outside!"

"Knife! Knife!" I pointed to the rat-faced man.

When it clicked for the husband, he began shouting at the rat-face man along with his wife. Now the three of us were yelling, "Outside!"

The rat-faced man bent forward as though preparing to lunge at me. His pupils were huge. I glanced down the counter for something to shield myself with but there was only bread.

Then suddenly, as though remembering something immeasurably important, the rat-faced man's gaze retreated and a moment later, he took off running.

I ran outside after him and watched him sprint down the tunnel of shops until he disappeared. A crowd gathered around me. They pointed down the alley to where a man was being thrown against a brick wall and my backpack was lying on the ground.

I looked to Savannah still waiting for a command.

"Watch her!" I said to the crowd.

I ran down the alley and snatched my backpack. A police officer cuffed the second thief and stood him in front of me. The thief tilted his head to the sky and ranted about the injustice of what was happening.

"Is this the man that attacked you?" the officer asked.

"No. That's not him. He ran in that direction."

"You see! You see!" exclaimed the thief. "I didn't do nothing!"

The police officer looked between us, apparently thinking he had the wrong man.

"He had my backpack!" I reminded him.

"No, no, no! I didn't have nothing!"

The thief whined, but the officer smiled and yanked him violently by the handcuffs to silence him.

"Do you need anything of me?" I asked.

The officer gazed at me blankly.

"Do you need anything?"

The question had no effect, but that worked fine for me. I wanted to be out of there and into my Airbnb as soon as possible.

At my cart, I looked through everything to make sure nothing had been stolen and while I did, the crowd apologized.

"I'm so sorry."

"This isn't our country."

"He's crazy."

Once I saw my passport and Savannah's paperwork still in my backpack, I turned to the crowd.

"It's fine," I said.

"I saw everything," one man claimed, stepping forward. "I'm a police officer. I called the police."

"You're a police officer?"

"Yes."

"And you saw everything?"

"Yes."

"So why did you do nothing?" I yelled.

"I'm off-duty."

I threw up a hand and charged off. It was a miracle the man was there to call the police, but I was too angry to acknowledge that. I tried to isolate the incident and banish it from my thoughts. I didn't want one malicious moment tainting my view of the good people I had met during my walk down Panama—the construction workers who gave me water on the Pan-American, the people that stopped to give me food, the girl that walked with me in La Concepcion.

"Tom! Hey Tom!"

I turned around to see a man in a suit jogging over to me.

"Hello, Savannah," he said as he neared.

The man didn't spark any recognition, but he must have seen that on my face.

"Fernando." He gestured to himself. "From outside David, my wife and I stopped to give you water and an apple."

"Oh, yes. Yes. I'm sorry. Thank you. Sorry, I was just robbed, almost robbed, a man with a knife. Only a minute ago. Back there. A man touched a knife to my neck."

"Here?"

"Three blocks behind."

"This is a bad block. Better to walk across the street."

"Across the street?"

"Yes. Just there. It's safer there." He pointed across the street, then bent down to pet Savannah. "I have to go, but I wanted to say hello. Good luck with your walking!"

After Fernando left, I crossed to the other side of the street and discovered that he had been right. On the opposite side of the street, the city was transformed. Sunlight illuminated a wide walkway. Skyscrapers glistened. Men and women hurried by indifferently.

Further down Calle Principal there were more trees and the moldy apartment buildings were supplanted by immaculate foreign hotel chains. Among those silver towers was a veterinary office where Savannah and I had an appointment to receive the health certificate that would grant her entry into Colombia.

The next day, I took the subway to a mall to buy new shoes. By the time I returned to my neighborhood, it was night and I was relaxed, so I sat at the bar of an outdoor diner and had a drink. The city was calm and the bar was small, so I felt a part of the place. As the crowd died, I ordered another beer and the waiter asked where I was going.

"To Colombia then to Uruguay."

"Why?"

"For the adventure, to know the world."

"And to know yourself, no?"

"I haven't had time for that."

For nearly a year, I received my education of the world like an assault. Each day I was dressed down and knocked back. In the United States I learned the basics of surviving on the road and in Central America I received my masterclass. I slept in graveyards, orange groves, palm plantations and jungle. I learned a new language. I adapted to new cultures. Every hour was packed with lessons. A single year of walking expanded my understanding of the world further than my previous twenty-six. I discovered that foreignness was a facade, a mask hiding the universal experience with different names, clothing, and paces. The challenge, I realized, was learning to distinguish the superficial from the deeper currents shaping each place.

I was getting there, though, a mile at a time. If often only by the fraying threads of fortune, I survived.

After a third beer, I ambled the last few blocks to my room. Savannah's tail whacked the bed in greeting, but she didn't get up. The air conditioner, I noticed, was blasting right on her. I dropped onto the bed, placed her head in the crook of my arm, and scratched her side.

Surely, it could only get easier.

THE NOTE IN THE DESERT

"Espiga?" I asked.

Beams of dim light came through the nail-sized holes in the roof. The shopwoman, who could have been thirty or fifty, cupped a hand to her ear.

"Espiga?" I repeated.

"I don't know."

I looked around in disbelief. I was certain I was using the right word. I'd asked people for a spigot a hundred times.

"And you don't have bottles of water?"

"No."

"But where do you encounter water here?"

"Not here. I don't have."

"Is there another shop?"

"There isn't."

"And you don't have a spigot."

"Espiga?"

"For water, you know? You turn it like this."

"I don't know."

Like many other buildings, the floor was sand, the walls were bamboo, and the roof was made of tin. The goods for sale were alarmingly limited—rice, pasta, coca leaves, and small bags of choclo. I thought I had done my due diligence before leaving Ecuador—I had looked ahead on the map and saw there were villages, and I figured if there were villages, there were people. And if there were people, there had to be water. Still, I couldn't find any.

I stepped out of the shop and into the cloud-muted sun. The village seemed on the verge of being overtaken by the desert. A fine sand swept into every nook and covered the sidewalks and the trees. Large thorns littered the ground, but because they lay in inches of sand, they disappeared when stepped on.

Savannah was under the cart, but she scurried out once I was beside her. We had three liters of water and more than a day of walking to the next city. Winter on the Pacific softened the heat, so three liters could last us a day and a half, but it would be tight and water wasn't something I enjoyed being tight on. I wanted to drink as much as I wanted—whenever I wanted—and for Savannah to do the same.

Looking for another shop or sign of water, I paused at a path marked by white stones leading to a home off the road. The home had a three-foot-high bamboo fence, two towering mesquite trees, two moto-taxis and a diminutive Peruvian flag flying at the edge of a long-rusted roof. I considered approaching but didn't. There were too many people for there not to be water nearby—I had to be missing something.

As I neared the end of town, a boy with a donkey appeared from behind a house. The donkey was strapped with thick plastic jugs that *thunked* as it walked.

"You're getting water," I said.

"What else?"

"Where?"

"A well." He pointed ahead.

A kid behind us called to the boy. The boy looked at me and laughed, then he called back to his friend and said, "A white giant!"

"Can you show me the well?"

"It's ahead."

I walked with him for a half mile. Another boy riding a donkey joined us. Eventually, we reached the well. Ten women and as many children were chatting at a concrete slab where a metal pipe came out and bent toward the ground. Only one person could fill their jug at a time and there were a hundred empty jugs, so I stood to the side and smiled when people looked at me.

It was hot and the well was under the sun, but the group seemed like good company for practicing Spanish. Even though I still had a burning need to prove that I could walk around the world, after the trials of Central America, I found that need had calmed ever so slightly. More often than before, I considered lingering in places.

After a minute, a woman at the center of the group with a pink shirt wrapped neatly on her head called to me.

"Come here, American. Bring your things."

I went over with a dromedary bag and nodded at everyone.

"Fill your things."

I didn't know the word for skip, so I said, "I don't want to pass no one."

"You're not passing no one, America. Come, fill your bag."

The women gestured me forward and I thanked them.

"How do you know I'm American?" I asked as I put a dromedary bag to the pipe.

"You're skinny and handsome."

The women laughed.

"And white," chimed in another.

That set them off. The women fell into each other, and the children offered jokes of their own from the back. The joke made me regret not waiting my turn; they were good company.

"My dog is American, too." I pointed to Savannah. She was panting by the cart in the white T-shirt I tied around her.

"A lion."

Savannah was a year old now. Between Colombia and Ecuador, we climbed and descended too many mountains to count. She managed them better than I did. All day, she traced the shade from myself or the cart, scurrying with workmanlike focus. Her puppy impulse to take off after anything exciting had been extinguished not through any conscious training on my part, but from simply having her on leash all day. In Central America, she made for squirrels, but after being caught by the leash time and time again, she gave it up. Now, the moment the leash went on, Savannah was at work.

"Does she . . ." A woman feigned biting her forearm.

"No. No. She's very kind."

"Yes?"

"Yes. She's very kind. From Texas, she. A cowgirl."

"A cowgirl in Peru."

"Yes."

"Doing what?"

"Walking."

"Why is a cowgirl and an American walking?"

"To know the world."

"Well, this is Peru. What do you think?" The women laughed.

"I like it. The people are very kind."

"And in America?"

"There are good people, too."

"And good money."

"Yes, and good money."

After filling my dromedary bag, I was able to stop thinking of water all the time. I thanked the women for letting me cut in line then continued out of town. Down the road, I looked over my shoulder to see a cyclist rolling across the lane. As he slowed, he removed his sunglasses to reveal a wiry blond beard and a face smeared with sunscreen.

"Buenas," he said.

"De dónde eres?"

"Inglaterra."

"A Brit, you speak English then."

"That's right. And you?"

"From the US."

It had been nearly a month since I'd had a conversation in English. My Spanish was strong, but unless the conversation was predictable, I still needed to consciously translate my English thoughts into Spanish words. In Macará, a town on the Ecuadorian border where hammocks hung in the corners like cobwebs, I spoke with a professor for an hour about writing, but it was rare to find conversation of that depth. Most people grew bored once I began reaching for words and stumbling on new phrases. I missed the ease of speaking in my native tongue.

The cyclist introduced himself as Joe. I moved my cart to the edge of the pavement so he wouldn't be forced into the road while he pedaled beside me. Around us were a few single-room brick houses. Behind the houses, the desert was cruel, and it would forget you in a moment if you gave it the chance.

"How long have you been on the road?"

"About fifteen months. Yourself?"

"Fourteen. I came down from Alaska and followed the fault line. Then it was through Central America before flying into Bogotá."

"I did the same. Fly into Bogotá, that is."

"I love that city."

"Me too. Colombians hate it, though. They say Bogotá is hideous—banks and politics—go to Medellín or Cali where the women are beautiful, and the people dance in the streets. Apparently, we should have landed somewhere else."

As we followed the lane line and bore the tempered sun, Joe and I exchanged routes and figured our paths intersected at Lake Atitlán. He said he didn't like it there, that it was hazy and that he couldn't see across the lake. I told him it was the most beautiful place I'd ever been.

"You know, when friends ask me what it's like in Ecuador or Peru or Colombia, part of me wants to say, bugger off, I don't know a thing about the place. I spent three months in Colombia, but I don't know a thing about it. I saw some mountains and a few cities, so what? That doesn't mean I know it. There isn't a tourist who knows anything. Especially me."

"I know what you mean," I said. "It's always being the stranger. Sampling places but never really knowing them."

"There are eleven million people in Bogotá. There are eleven million Bogotás."

Joe lowered his head to protect himself against the gust thrown by an eighteen-wheeler.

"Where are you headed now?" I asked once he picked his head up.

"To Piura. I have a flight to England on Tuesday for my best mate's wedding. I'll be home for five weeks. Three weddings in five weeks."

"Have you been back?"

"No. First time. And yourself?"

"My family visited while I was in the US, but they haven't been able to visit since. I'm hoping they can make it to Uruguay."

"You miss them?"

"Not really. I'm sure you know how it is. Once you're on the road, it becomes your life. You get into a routine. It's tough, of course; things are new, the days slip by. But it was only when my axle broke and I was stuck in La Plata, Huila, this little city in the mountains of Colombia, that I was lonely. I was there for a month, and I didn't know anyone. I had a routine: I'd buy coffee for myself and a couple of old guys in the piazza each morning, then I would write in a café, but after that, I had nothing to do. Cities are tough if you don't know anyone."

A row of cars moved into the other lane to avoid us.

"So, if your flight leaves from Piura, are you taking your time right now? Piura can't be more than a few hours on bike."

"Yeah, taking my time," said Joe. "I'll probably get in tomorrow around eleven and find a hostel. That's what I usually do—ride for a week then when I come to a city, I get a room in the morning, stay one night, then get on the road again."

"That's smart."

"What's your plan?"

I looked down the stretch of road ahead of us. For a little while, brick and bamboo homes lined the sandy asphalt, but in the distance, the road turned to the right and made for a desolate horizon. Since Ecuador, most of my days had passed without a stir of emotion and most nights, when I tried to write, I found I had few thoughts to put down.

But my conversation with Joe was enlivening. He was full of opinions. I asked him about Brexit, and he asked me about Trump. When he said he was interested in behavioral economics, I told him I was a psychology major. Two hours of walking slipped by until we stopped at a side road so Joe could change into a shirt that wasn't soaked with sweat.

"How about a spot of tea?" he asked. "It sounds a bit mad having tea on a hot day, but I think it's a nice way to break up the miles. Every day I have some tea around four."

We pulled under the shade of a bamboo awning beside a house, and I set out my tarp. Joe started water on his stove. Kids spotted us and spied from behind the bushes.

"Could you imagine doing this in England or the US?" Joe asked. "Sitting beside someone's house like this?"

"I know. My past self would have kicked us off. *Look at those bums.* People here are much nicer; less suspicious, maybe."

"Have you ever had a problem camping on someone's land?"

"A guy in Costa Rica yelled at me, but it was five in the morning, and I was already packing. After he wrangled his cows, he came back and apologized. What about you?"

"Never."

"I don't know how people are so trusting."

Joe shook his head in disbelief.

"You have a cup?"

"I'll use this." I poured the water remaining in my Nalgene into Savannah's bowl then passed the Nalgene to Joe. Joe hung two tea bags in the bottle, then filled it halfway.

The kids spying on us grew more confident. They worked their way from the bushes and now stood a stone's throw away, staring at us in the open. There were three boys and a girl, the oldest boy was about twelve.

"I bet they're family," I said, waving to the kids.

The oldest waved back. When he walked toward us, the others followed. Soon they were at the edge of my tarp marveling at Joe and his stove. The smallest boy, maybe six, crouched in front of the stove and poked its windshield.

"What's this?" he asked.

"A stove," answered Joe in heavily accented Spanish.

The kids surrounded the stove and examined it.

"For water?"

"For water, for tea."

I took my Nalgene and put my face over the steam drifting out of it. As Joe said, it was a bit insane to be having hot tea on a hot day, but it felt good to have an excuse to break up the miles. Since Quito, my days had been relentlessly repetitive—wake, walk, camp. I might stop for lunch or breakfast at different times, but that was the only variance. If I hadn't met Joe, I would have never taken the time to sit and have tea. In my mind, there were always miles to walk, especially in the desert.

"Is there a store here?" Joe asked the kids.

"Yes!" The oldest boy sprang to his feet and pointed down the street. "There's a shop there and another there."

"Do they have cookies?"

The kids nodded.

"For the tea?" I asked.

"Yeah."

"I have something."

I dug through my food box until finding a pack of graham crackers that I picked up a few days earlier.

"What's tea without biscuits?"

"Have as many as you want. Thanks again for the tea."

I raised my Nalgene to Joe then attempted to take a sip, but only managed to burn my lip.

The kids sat across from me and Joe in a row. Sometimes the girl and the oldest boy whispered to each other, but mostly they just watched us. I thought it strange that they could sit across from us in silence. I couldn't imagine kids in the States doing the same. Their parents would wave them off for bothering strangers, or warn them of strangers, or the kids wouldn't be outside without an organized event in the first place.

"No school today?" I asked.

"No."

"Are you on vacation?"

"No."

"In Mexico, there were always kids in school uniforms walking somewhere. It seemed like every hour of the day there were kids out walking, but I don't think I ever saw them walking into a school."

Joe turned to the kids.

"Are you brothers and sisters?"

They shook their heads.

"Cousins?" I asked.

They stirred with excitement. The oldest boy swung his arm around the neck of the girl beside him and announced, "We're all cousins!"

"No, we're not," said the girl, pushing him off. "I'm your sister."

The boy grinned. "She's my sister."

"But we're cousins!" said the youngest.

"They're always cousins," I said to Joe. "Everyone is a cousin."

"No school, exploring the desert all day with your family; seems like a good life."

The tea was great once it cooled. I usually didn't have caffeine after ten, so the two bags of tea had me wired. Once Joe and I turned our conversation to each other, the kids watched us and occasionally prodded the stove or knocked on the tires of my cart. Savannah slept in the sand with her back against the brick.

"I feel so civilized," I said.

"Sorry the tea isn't better. Colombia had great tea, but there aren't many tea drinkers here, are there? It's all coffee. At home I would have tea, biscuits, and some salted cashews at the same time every day. The only thing missing is the cashews."

I went to my cart and pulled out a bag of salted cashews.

"Now we're doing it," Joe said.

"They're my favorite—also, the cheapest."

After a while, Joe finished his tea and packed his stove and I feared he was preparing to leave.

"Hey," I said. "I don't know if you were planning on riding further today, but I only need to walk two more hours to reach my quota, I could shorten it if you'd want to camp together tonight."

I felt like I was asking out my crush.

"The desert has been killing me," I added.

"Yeah, sure. I'm in no rush."

Up the road, we found a trail through the shrubs that took us to a clearing. We set our tents, and I laid out my tarp for us to sit on. Joe made pasta with his stove, and I had three peanut butter jellies. A man came through with his donkey. We were on the path he took home, but he only nodded and kept walking.

The next day, Joe walked with me to the periphery of Piura—my route was shorter if I skirted the city. We found a narrow restaurant for breakfast. Everything was served with an orange chili paste. Sand blew in a few feet from the doorway.

I stretched our breakfast to two hours because I dreaded entering the solitude of the desert. There was a village a day's walk from Piura, but after that, Savannah and I had nothing to look forward to but ninety miles of sand. Eventually, Joe said he was going to find a hostel, so I paid and we left. Joe rode into Piura and I continued down the road on the city's outskirts.

Hours later, after passing the intersection south of Piura and making my way into the emptiness, I looked back to see a cyclist crossing the lanes over to me. He didn't have sunscreen smeared on his face and his panniers weren't stuffed, but he was smiling.

Joe hopped off his bike and from his panniers withdrew two gallon jugs of water.

"You're my hero," I said as Joe pulled beside me.

"No problem at all."

"You saved me half a day of walking. I should have filled everything at the well instead of just a bag."

"I can't believe you're about to cross this desert on foot. Make sure you get more water in the village before the worst of it begins."

Fueled by empty hours and coca leaves that numbed my lower lip, I managed one stretch of desert after another. Savannah and I covered a minimum of twenty-seven miles a day. Sometimes we walked thirty miles or more to ensure we made it to town before running out of water. During the stretch of desert after leaving Joe, we walked thirty-six miles in a single day. After that, when we arrived in Mórrope, I found us a twenty-dollar room where Savannah slept fourteen hours and I stayed in bed listening to my legs throb in my ears.

In the north desert, the road was flat, but as we moved south, the Pan-American was nudged to the coast by the last ripples of the Andes as they descended into the Pacific. Beside the coast, the air was salty, and the towns were tucked into narrow valleys. The desert became drier and more lifeless, too. Sometimes I didn't speak to anyone for days. With no internet, I listened to old podcasts just to hear someone's voice.

I blared Sam Cooke, The Black Keys, and The Beatles on my speaker. I sang with uninhibited passion, often pushing my cart ahead so I could conduct with my hands.

When I grew tired of singing, I talked to Savannah. I wasn't delirious enough for full conversations, but I was bored enough to make comments throughout the day.

"What a view."

"At least it's cloudy."

"Peanut butter, peanut butter, peanut butter."

My fraternity brother and native Peruvian, Arturo, was waiting to host me in the capital, Lima. That made the desert more challenging. I had nothing to do but fantasize about the plush days that waited ahead—his parents' vineyard, their beach house, ceviche in the city. Thoughts of a bed and a shower were poison for my happiness, but that didn't stop them from coming; in fact, I welcomed them. The desert was numbing. Each day, I felt less and less, but at least with visions of Lima I had something to hold on to, some reason to push through the never-ending sand. I was increasingly dull, empty, lobotomized. What I was doing, I could barely remember.

One morning, I sat in an abandoned house tapping the back of my head against the wall to knock some life into myself. By looking at the map, I knew I wouldn't encounter a thing for another two days. I dreaded it. My boredom would turn each mile into five.

With the length of the days increasing, I should have been enjoying a morning coffee, but I left my stove in Bogotá. I knew water would be scarce in the desert and by leaving my stove I could save some weight, so instead of sipping on a hot coffee, I washed down a caffeine pill.

"Come here, Savannah."

I pulled her head to my chest and rested my head against her side. I closed my eyes and focused on how her fur felt on my cheek, how her chest rose and fell, but Savannah wasn't one for affection. The moment I let go of her collar she walked off and sat by the steps to tell me she was ready to start walking.

At noon, I rested on a rock off the side of the road. I didn't feel like making a sandwich or having mixed nuts, so I ate peanut butter with a spoon. After enough scoops, Savannah and I resumed walking.

The miles passed slowly, but in the early evening we stumbled upon a restaurant that I hadn't seen on the map. La Balsa was at the intersection of the Pan-American and a dirt road that led to the fishing village of La Gramita.

For a restaurant in the middle of nowhere, it was surprisingly busy. I took a seat at a table along the wall and tucked Savannah by my feet. I wondered if I could convince the owner to let us sleep inside for the night. They would open early, which meant I'd have to leave early, but spending another night in the desert was as appetizing as a mouthful of sand.

"From where do you come?" asked the waiter.

"The United States."

"On bicycle?"

"On foot."

"We've had only one other walker." The waiter pointed to a collection of photos on the far wall. "Look."

I dropped Savannah's leash and walked over to the collage. On the wall was a familiar photo—Karl Bushby, my idol, hands to his chest, face wrapped against the sand, standing in the Peruvian desert. It was the very picture that had been burnt into my head since seventeen. Surrounding the photo of Karl in the desert were framed clippings from Peruvian, Chilean, and British newspapers.

"I know him," I said to the waiter across the room. "I spoke with him before I left. That's Karl Bushby."

The waiter came over and stood beside me.

"He started walking in 2000."

"No, it was more early, '98, I think."

"Ah yes, that's right. He was here in 2000."

I leaned closer to the articles. Even though I'd seen the photos before, they held new meaning now that I was walking the same road Karl had walked sixteen years prior. I wasn't as tough as Karl—I wasn't an ex-paratrooper. I skipped the Darien Gap while he crossed it, and I had no interest in swimming the Bering Strait like he had, but we were of the same cloth. The club of world walkers was few. Although I'd spoken to him only once, I felt I knew him. I understood what it meant to leave, to be a stranger, and to have the insatiable need to *be out there*.

THE GOLIATH EXPEDITION
A WORLD-RECORD WALK AROUND THE WORLD!

I inspected Karl in the desert, two-wheel cart attached to his waist. He was covered head to toe, only his hands were bare. If I hadn't seen this photo at seventeen, I would have never bought a bike trailer then gone to The Factory to have it modified. I would have never met Tom Marchetty and he would have never held a press conference. Without a press conference, I wouldn't be sponsored by Philadelphia Sign. I was connected to this photo by a straight line, and looking at it I understood how one thing leads to the next and the next thing leads to all others. I wasn't an individual set apart in time, but a continuation of ideas; not the brush, but the paint; not self-governed, but guided by greater forces.

The photo brought me to the photo.

"Bring your cart in."

I turned to the waiter.

"Bring your cart in so nothing is robbed."

"Oh yes. Good. Thanks."

With the cart, the waiter led me to an area behind the register where an old man wearing a surgical mask sat at a table going over four tomes of handwritten notes. I parked my cart and the waiter gestured for me to sit across from the old man.

"This is Clemente," he said. "The Angel of the Desert."

"Good afternoon."

"Your friend."

Clemente turned one of the tomes and slid it to me.

Scrawled on the page was the drawing of a man in hiking boots and patched pants with a cart attached to his belt and a British flag flying behind him. Above and below the drawing was a note:

ON FOOT FOR THE WORLD RECORD!!
GOLIATH EXPEDITION
Punta Arenas – London. No Planes, no ships, no cars, no buses,
no train and . . .
NO BIKE !
36,000 miles / 57,000 kms (-7,300 km)
11 years (-1 year 4 months)

Alone in a bad ass world, chin straight with just enough money in my pocket to rub two pennies together, little food or water. Then, stumble out of the desert into this place and find the kindest man on Earth, Clemente. God bless you dear old chap! Fed me like a king, restores my faith in humanity, pay your respects to this man, people!

Karl had drawn a map, too, marking points of interest—NICE AND GREEN, BAD ARSE DESERT, LOTS OF FUN, CUTE GIRL.

I put my head in my hands and cried.

Other than my parents or Layla, Karl was the only person who could have written a note that cut to the core of me. I knew he was only a man, but he was also an idea that had fossilized in my soul over ten years. He was adventure, discovery, perseverance. He had written a note in the desert sixteen years before and now I was reading it—reaching Clemente and his restaurant while experiencing the same relief as Karl himself.

"Where is he now?" asked Clemente.

"Russia, I believe."

"It's been a long time. It makes ten, fifteen years. When was that written?"

"It makes sixteen years. He's been walking for more than sixteen years."

I read the note a dozen times and with each pass I felt color returning to my thoughts. The desert didn't seem the burden it had a few hours before. Karl had walked it when it was even less developed. At least I had abandoned houses to sleep in and podcasts to listen to.

"There's more."

Clemente moved a blank sheet of paper which was covering a page I assumed was empty. On it was a final note:

WHATEVER YOUR PLANS, GO FOR IT! KEEP ON THE ROAD.
DRIVE HARD. LIVE IT!
RAGE ON YOU CRAZY MOTHERS YOU!
—KARL BUSHBY—

EMPTYING OUT

Maybe it was my exhaustion, but as I descended into the valley, the village looked like a collection of toys in a sandbox. Savannah pulled hard. We were eager for shade. At a restaurant, I parked my cart outside the stone wall bordering the patio, then passed through the saloon doors and tied Savannah to a table and poured her a bowl of water.

"I'll be right back."

Inside, the thick stone walls kept the restaurant cool. The concrete floor, painted the color of moss, seemed to grow inward from the light of the entrance. A few cracks reached into the restaurant like roots. Against the walls were white plastic tables and red plastic chairs with Coca-Cola printed on them. At the far end, the ceiling above the kitchen door was stained black from smoke. The air smelled of chicken soup.

To my left, three truckers bent over their plates. Their hats sat in a pile at the end of the table. While I stood near the entrance, one of the men nodded to me before returning his focus to pulling apart the chicken thigh before him.

A woman, whose cheekbones appeared to have been sculpted by the tireless wind, stopped by the table of truckers to set down a pitcher of lemonade. I watched the pulp drift as the woman drifted to me in the same easy manner.

"Do you have a menu?" I asked.

"We have chicken, fish, rice, beans, and soup."

"Chicken is good. A plate of rice, beans, and chicken, thank you. And soup also, please. Can I sit outside?"

"Of course."

"And can I have that as well?" I pointed to the pitcher of lemonade the truckers were pouring.

"A glass or a pitcher?"

"A pitcher. I have much thirst. Do you have ice?"

"No, no ice."

"Okay."

"You came on bike?"

"On foot."

"From where?"

"In Chile, from Arica, but I walked from the United States."

The woman made a soft click of approval with her tongue.

"Seat yourself." She nodded to the door.

Outside I sat facing the street and Savannah curled beneath the table and went to sleep. The concrete was cold and so was the shade. A warm breeze ran over the low wall and the napkins beneath the plastic salt and pepper shakers fluttered.

As I looked across the Pan-American, a plastic playground offered the only note of color. Next to the playground, a municipal building was pressed into the sand like a brick. A crest of two crossed rifles marked the entrance, but otherwise the building was undecorated. The modesty was a good fit for the valley. This outpost of a dozen buildings was the only civilization for seventy-five miles.

In northern Chile, the Atacama desert transitioned from three-thousand-foot plateaus to sea-level valleys. The plateaus were long, and the only shelter on them were the occasional bus stops. The bus stops usually marked a road leading to a copper or lithium mine in the mountains. Whenever I came to a bus stop, I took a nap, but on the previous plateau, Savannah and I walked sixty miles without finding a single structure to rest in. The restaurant awning was the first meaningful shade we'd had in days. Under it, a profound relief crawled into me.

After Bushby's note, the desert had been much less a trial and more akin to a months-long meditation. Never before had I dove into my life and my influences with such clarity. As always, thoughts came and went, but in the desert, like nowhere else, I had the quiet to examine them. Sometimes a topic stayed at the top of my mind for days, but usually thoughts appeared, disappeared, and didn't resurface for weeks. Life before the walk felt untethered from the one I was now living. As memories cropped up, I looked on them without emotion—curiosities to be turned over and examined against the light of the sun.

The waitress set a pitcher of lemonade on the table and broke me from my stillness.

I poured a glass and drank it in one go. The sweetness rushed to my head and down my neck. I poured another glass and finished it as quickly as the first. By the time the food arrived, my stomach was rumbling and the pitcher was empty.

"Can I have another?"

"Of course."

I dug into the food. Finding satisfaction in the simple meal was effortless; all the exercise and peanut butter jellies I'd eaten over the previous months did the work for me.

Savannah perked up at the smell of chicken. She poked her snout beneath the armrest, and I pulled apart the chicken breast to give her the bone. She crushed through the bone then poked her head under the armrest for another.

"That's it for now, baby. That's all there is."

She looked away, then flopped onto her side to savor the cool concrete.

The truckers stepped out of the restaurant, and the man who nodded to me earlier stopped at the saloon doors and turned to me. His beard was a mottled gray and he moved thoughtfully like a monk. He was someone's grandfather or someone's great-grandfather—he radiated the softening a man gets from seeing successive generations of potential realized.

"You're the walker," he said. "I've seen you for weeks on the road to the north."

"You're driving to Lima?"

"Ilo. You passed there, no?"

"I remained there for a night. It was a beautiful place. The colors on the ocean were fantastic. There was good ceviche in the market. I wanted more time there."

"It used to be a big fishing port, but now they mine copper in the mountains, so there are ships from Europe and Asia. Where are you going?"

"I have cousins in Uruguay, but for the moment I'm walking to San Pedro de Atacama."

"And over the mountains?"

"That's the idea."

"The altitude is dangerous. It's cold there."

"Have you passed there?"

"You can only pass in the summer. There's much snow in the winter."

"But it's summer now, no?"

"From what I've heard."

"There's nothing there, yes? Without water, without towns?"

"Without everything. But the desert to San Pedro is dangerous, too. You need much water, much food. There's nothing here. There are drivers if you need help, but the desert isn't easy."

"Yes, of course."

"Take care of yourself."

"And you."

"Take care of him, too." He gestured to Savannah.

"Of course. Enjoy the road, brother."

The man held up a hand. The other two truckers nodded and turned. A few minutes later their eighteen-wheelers roared to life and rumbled out of the valley. A breeze poured over the outpost, and again it was quiet. Savannah was asleep. On the concrete by her nose was a triangle of perspiration.

After I finished the food and the second pitcher of lemonade, the waitress came to take my plate.

"It was fantastic. How much do I owe?"

"Already it's paid."

"Already it's paid?"

"Yes, the man has paid for you."

"How good. Good people."

"Yes, he's always here."

It wasn't customary to leave tips in Chile, but I left a purple bill beneath the empty glass anyway.

Savannah and I returned to the sun, and I pushed our cart down the street to a market. I bought twelve liters of water, a loaf of bread, jam, a liter of ultra-high-temperature milk, lemon cakes, five bars of chocolate, raisins, a loose bag of cashews, and two kilograms of dog food. The next town was three days away.

As I pushed our cart, Savannah trotted eagerly beside me. Her fur was short; I had her trimmed and pampered in Lima. But that was a month ago, and neither of us were ever clean anymore. I washed myself at night with baby wipes, but a perpetual mix of sand and sweat stayed stuck to my skin. Savannah was so dirty that whenever I patted her a plume of dust wafted into the air. She also had a streak of some tar-like substance on her side from rolling in a pile of liquified fish remains.

As the road wove between the plateaus, Cuya disappeared, and the valley tightened like a stone corset. As the walls grew, the wind built.

Savannah moved behind the cart and walked with her head pressed against the basket. I put on my sunglasses, pulled down my hat, and tucked my chin to shield my eyes. Every step was challenged. Whenever a truck passed, it threw a vortex of wind from its tail that knocked me back.

"What a battle," I said to Savannah.

But Savannah didn't mind. Her tail was high, and her legs hurried on. She was a professional. She'd done this her whole life.

For two hours, the wind blew against us. The persistent roar made it so I couldn't think. Dark stones smattered the valley, but none were large enough to take shelter against. It wasn't until the valley widened that the wind died and I was able to relax.

Eventually, our path forked. To the left, shrubs and short trees followed a dry riverbed. To the right, a low bridge stretched over the riverbed and the road escaped to the plateau. To ascend from the valley and reach the plateau would require another two hours of walking, so I turned off the road and made for open land.

I unhooked Savannah's leash and she darted ahead. I followed the foot-deep riverbed until I found a bend where the land was flat and shrubs with olive-colored leaves acted as a natural curtain. After I set out Savannah's food and water, I lowered to my hands and knees and searched the area for thorns. I found a few and tossed them to the side, then I spread my tarp out and rested against the wheel of my cart.

A truck engine groaned as a driver shifted. The sun was behind the plateau, and it cast the valley in an orange intensified by the sand. I stretched to fight off the worst of my muscle aches. Savannah sniffed at a bush, unfazed by the twenty-five miles we had walked that day.

"Come here, Sav."

She trotted over and her tail wagged erratically, as though she'd never been taught how to do it properly. When she pressed her head against my chest, I massaged her hind legs with my palms.

"You stink, chica."

She pressed her head against me harder.

"Yeah, you stink. Had to roll in that fish, didn't you? Come here."

I pulled her closer and sniffed the black streak on her side. It didn't smell anymore. I picked at the fish tar, and she yelped and jumped back.

"I'm sorry, baby. Come here."

I kissed her forehead.

"It's all right. It'll fall off eventually."

I gave her a pat and she wandered off.

When night fell, Savannah dug a hole in the sand and curled inside it. I read *Life and Death in the Andes*.

*"Somewhere during Darwin's long journey, however, his ideas about
the world shifted and he began peering at it freshly, from
a different point of view."*

After a dozen pages, the failing light caught me, and I grew tired. I turned
on my back. The stars were out as they always were in the Atacama, but
in the valley, they weren't as impressive as on the plateau. There were
thousands of them, but the bush over me and the mountains of sand
around us trimmed the sky. I turned on my side and watched Savannah
sleep instead.

In the morning, a sharp pain at the center of my lower lip woke me.
I touched my finger to the pain and discovered my lip had split open.
I noticed the lines on the back of my hands were parched white and a
cuticle was cracked and bleeding, too. Not only was the Atacama the oldest desert in the world, it was also the driest. There were sections of the
Atacama that hadn't seen rain in a thousand years and though the median
humidity was about 30 percent, at night the humidity approached zero.

Savannah eyed me while I shuffled but didn't leave her self-made bed.
It was only once I looked at her that she rolled on her side and pawed at
the air. I went over and rubbed her belly.

"Good morning, baby."

The pre-dawn had a nip to it, so I slipped back into my sleeping
bag. With a camp stove I bought in Lima, I boiled water for coffee then
tapped a bit of Nescafé into my aluminum mug. A finch flitted across
the riverbed. There were hares, mice, and lizards in the Atacama, too,
but I hadn't seen any. After a coffee and a few granola bars, I packed the
cart and we returned to the same road we'd been walking since southern
Mexico.

We crossed the bridge and began our ascent. Semis stormed into the
valley in low gear. One shuddered to a stop beside us and a man in a
Yankees cap peered out the passenger window.

"My friend!"

I stopped at the door and looked up.

"For you, my friend."

He passed me a sleeve of crackers and a joint that he held in place on the crackers with his thumb. I considered telling the man that I didn't smoke, but I took what he offered.

"Thanks, my friend! Everything helps!"

We had to yell to be heard over his engine.

"The desert is boring, friend!" He touched pinched fingers to his lips. "But a little music helps!" He winked.

"Thanks!"

He gave me a thumbs-up. "Good luck, my friend!"

I put the crackers in the back basket and sat the joint in the top pocket of my backpack.

An hour later, the road flattened as Savannah and I reached the plateau. A restaurant that wasn't on the map was to the right. Inside, I had fried eggs, potatoes, and two cups of coffee. I forced down a liter of water and bought another to bring with me.

The rest of the day was empty. The highway was a black arrow through the lifeless void. When the sun was setting, I turned into the desert and put my tarp somewhere. I ate more peanut butter jellies and watched the delicate hues of the desert descend into the ocean. The sky was blue, orange, red, and indigo, then the sheets of color were relieved, and the sky went black.

In the darkness, stars ripped the abyss asunder.

To let in as much light as possible, I kept my eyes relaxed and unfocused. Every second, a hundred new stars appeared. They burst through in such numbers that the only break in them was the purple Milky Way. At the seams of the galaxy, a bright silver highlighted the deeper blacks and blues. Near the top, the stars crowded together. Soon there were so many that I felt the weight of them on my chest, crushing me, hinting at a wisdom too vast to comprehend.

Lying there, flattened by the multitude of stars, I realized that after a year and a half of walking, I had turned over my life, my influences, and my idiosyncrasies for so long that I had nothing left to resolve. I was at peace with my choices, my errors, and the things beyond my control. Just as when I was young and trying to imagine death, I lost feeling of my body. The stars poured through me, shredding the self and annihilating the ego.

You are nothing, they said.

You are nothing.

You are nothing.

You are nothing.

It wasn't antagonism. It wasn't fact. It wasn't anything.

As the desert went on and there were no edges in my thoughts to wear smooth, I considered smoking the joint the trucker had given me. During my freshman year of college, I smoked too much and developed a paranoia, so I stopped. Over the years, I tried to smoke a few more times, but the paranoia always returned.

Now, I could think of no good reason why I wouldn't enjoy it. Savannah and I had walked months without incident. My cart was loaded with more than enough to eat and drink. The road was empty, descending, and I had learned to embrace the calm demanded by the desert.

When we came to a concrete median on the side of the road, Savannah and I rested in the short shade it provided. I pulled out the joint, took a few puffs, thought of stopping, then took a few more until I felt something. I pinched the joint where it was burning, licked my fingers, pinched it again, then set it in my backpack. Gradually, the world warped as though I were drifting underwater, and I considered my favorite line from my favorite poem:

I exist as I am, that is enough, / If no other in the world be aware
I sit content, / And if each and all be aware I sit content.

My months in the desert had brought me to the nearest approximation of Uncle Walt's tranquility. I was master of myself and my world. No thoughts dyed my soul without permission; no trial was made undue by wild emotion. The challenges of my first year readied me for the quiet of the second. I unearthed the self, held it to the fore, and under the stars discovered it was only an illusion.

Now, I sat in the shade, residing without critique.

I watched Savannah step into the sun, raise her head, and shut her eyes to the light. The Andes were far off and faded behind her. She took a step forward, sneezed, and flecked blood across the sand.

I jumped up—reverie made unimportant against the immediate. "Savannah."

I ran over and tilted her head back. Blood was pouring from her nose like water, running down her chin, and dripping off my hand.

"Okay, baby. Come here, come here."

I pulled her into the shade where she stood with her tail curled between her legs.

"Stay there," I said needlessly.

I flung open my cart, found my first aid kit, and withdrew a patch of gauze. Then I sat with my legs around Savannah and put her chin to my chest with her snout tilting up. I wiped her cheeks clean then held the gauze to her nose. She gagged on the blood pouring into her throat and tried to wriggle free, but I kept her in place.

"I know, baby girl, I know. We have to stay like this, though."

After a few minutes, the bleeding slowed and gradually, it stopped.

"Good girl, Sav. Good girl."

She swallowed once more. I let go of her collar and fell back against the median. The sand rippled like waves against the shore. Pebbles marked the crests. Savannah looked into the desert as though expecting something to appear. I could see she was bracing herself. Then she sneezed, and the blood began again.

For as far as I could see, there was nothing around. The earth and the sky were separated only by the cut of the Andes. The Pan-American remained an empty gash. No sound of civilization made its way to our lonely huddle.

My mind was dull and uncertain from the joint, but I attempted to assess our situation as best I could. Savannah was in the shade. Her chin was raised. In my first aid kit I had gauze, Neosporin, burn cream, ibuprofen, bandages, melatonin, and a tourniquet. I could see no use to any of it beyond the gauze.

I rubbed Savannah's back to calm her and slow her heart rate, but after ten minutes the bleeding never slowed, and so I stood and looked down the road for answers.

Only a few dozen cars had passed since morning, but the Pan-American was the only way north or south so someone would pass again. We had to be ready when they did. I jammed everything in my cart and wheeled it to the side of the road. Then I picked up Savannah and cradled her in my arms.

"It's okay, baby."

I kissed her forehead and walked to the middle of the road. Blood was falling onto her chest and even in my clouded state I knew this was something much worse than a nosebleed. The driest desert in the world wasn't enough to give blood the consistency of water. I scolded myself. I had taken the desert too lightly. Repetition had lulled me into a false sense of security, and now Savannah was paying the price. We had to find help. We had to reach town.

"It's okay, Savannah. Someone's coming soon. It's okay."

ROAD TO ARICA

From out the back windshield, I watched my down jacket fly away. It flicked, tumbled, then vanished in the distance. The kid was flooring it. He and his four friends were the first to find us. They hurried us into their Jeep and strapped my cart to the top. Occasionally, one of the teens turned to say something, but I was finding it difficult to concentrate on anything aside from Savannah.

We were laid in the trunk with a jumble of auto parts. My back was against a muffler, my feet on an axle, and Savannah was on top of me. I had a wad of toilet paper to her nose, but it was already soaked to the point of futility. Blood was falling onto my shirt.

My heart ripped looking at Savannah. Her eyes held the resigned gaze of a sick child. I couldn't figure out where I went wrong. I provided as much water as she could drink, she ran circles at the end of each day, and we always stopped at noon to avoid the worst of the heat. Maybe we should have been walking at night when it was cooler, but she had walked through worse and handled it easily. Texas was hotter; Honduras was hotter; Costa Rica was hell.

The monotony of the previous months had led me to forget what an absurd task we were undertaking. I'd forgotten that crossing hundreds of miles of desert wasn't common not because it wasn't peaceful, but because it leaves you untethered from care. There was no vet or pharmacy around the corner. I didn't even have cell service to look up ways to stop a dog's nosebleed.

"Forty minutes, my friend." A teen tapped his wrist despite not wearing a watch.

The car couldn't go fast enough.

The girls in the back seat put their heads together to watch Savannah. "Poor baby . . ."

I stroked Savannah's back, painting it red as I did. Her face was somehow pale.

"It's okay, baby girl. We're almost there."

By the time we reached Huara, a town that on Google Maps was only visible when fully zoomed in, the heat had worsened. We stopped at a police checkpoint—a single booth beside the road. I slid out and set Savannah on the asphalt with my hand under her chin. Savannah snorted loudly, swallowed, and gagged. As I looked around, my hopes of reaching a vet plummeted. Huara was little more than a rest stop.

One of the teens spoke to the police.

"There's a vet in town," he said upon return.

"Good." I scooped Savannah into my arms. "Let's go."

The teen slapped me on the shoulder. "Let's go!" he called to his friends.

We bounced along the back streets, rolling over broken concrete and into divots. We asked a man for directions then stopped beside a wide corrugated metal garage door. Out of the trunk again, I hurried Savannah to the shade of a tamarugo tree. The wispy branches sheltered us as well as a moth-eaten blanket.

"This is it?" I asked.

There was no sign that we were anywhere other than someone's home.

The teen banged on the door. When no one answered, he jumped to see into the yard.

"There's no one here," he said.

"You're sure this is it?"

"It's okay. You'll be safe here for the night."

I noticed the others unstrapping my cart and went into a panic. If Savannah and I were left in Huara, she would die. I was certain of it. There was no vet in town, no hotel, and there was no bus or taxi that would accept us covered in blood.

The best care nearby was in Arica, the largest city in northern Chile, but Arica was four hours north and at present we had no way to get there. The teens were headed west to the coastal city of Iquique. Iquique likely had a vet, but the city was so removed from every other that if we drove there and found the veterinarians were inadequate or closed for a holiday, we would lose at least two days until we could reach another city.

For the moment, our only solution was Pozo Almonte, a town twenty minutes south that was slightly larger than Huara. There wouldn't be a vet, but there would be a pharmacy and a hotel where we could clean up and find a way to Arica.

"Can you take me to Pozo Almonte?" I asked.

The driver looked to his friends. My cart was already on the ground. One of the teens was folding the straps that held it to the roof and setting them in the trunk.

"Please," I said. "We can't stay here. That's not a veterinarian. There's nowhere to sleep. There are no hotels here. There's no pharmacy."

The driver ran a hand through his hair and smiled.

"Don't worry, my friend. We won't leave you. We're going to Pozo."

"Thank you."

"We're going to Pozo!" he announced to the others.

The teens strapped my cart onto the roof once more, and I reclaimed my place in the trunk with Savannah in my arms. I had known my love for her had grown, but it wasn't until that moment that I realized how deep it ran. I would do anything for her. If it cost me every cent, if I needed to run through the desert, if I had to block traffic and beg every person in town for a ride. We had been through too much. She was my home, and I was hers. We were each other's only constant.

When we reached Pozo, the Chileans dropped us at a health center. I thanked the driver, and he wished me luck. The employees of the health center came outside to meet us. They told me there was nothing they could do for a dog, but they showed me to a spigot and handed me a rag.

For the moment, Savannah wasn't bleeding, but her fur was matted and damp. As I scrubbed her, blood swirled onto the concrete and into the drain by her paws. Her tail was down and her gaze was far off. There was no vet in Pozo, the buses had stopped, and no taxis ran this late, but there was shade and a pharmacy that I could use to stabilize Savannah before we did anything else.

Once she was clean, I removed my shirt. Her blood had dried to my chest. I wiped myself clean, then pulled on one of my two other shirts. It was the first time in weeks that any part of me was free of grime. I threw an extra splash of water against my face just to feel the relief.

Down the street, we came to two hotels across from one another. Savannah was holding herself together, but the first hotel didn't accept dogs. At the second, the receptionist told us they wouldn't take Savannah, but with some cajoling I convinced him to call the owner. The owner didn't answer immediately so the receptionist suggested I sit and wait until he called back.

I sat on a sofa and Savannah put her head on my foot. When the receptionist came over to pet her, I did my best to appear unnerved, but each second was excruciating. I waited for Savannah to sneeze, start bleeding, then accept that we'd be on the street for the night.

"She's very calm," the receptionist said.

"We've stayed in many hotels."

I reached down to rub Savannah's back. She glanced up at me without moving her head. Her eyes were bloodshot.

After twenty minutes, the owner returned the receptionist's call.

"My boss is a good man."

"We have a room?"

"You'll have to go in the back, in case your dog barks."

"That's perfect. She won't bark; she never barks. Thank you. We would be on the street without you."

The receptionist handed me a key then pointed down the hallway beyond the common area.

"You're upstairs."

I brought my cart inside, nodded to the receptionist as I passed, then headed toward the back patio. I left my cart at the bottom of the steps and made my way to the room with Savannah. After three steps, she sneezed and blood began dripping onto the stairs. I cupped my hand beneath her snout and we ran.

Outside the door, she sneezed again. Blood shot between my fingers and hit the tile.

I shouldered the door open, nudged Savannah inside, then ran downstairs to haul up the cart. I went as fast as I could, but by the time I returned Savannah was already standing over a small puddle of blood.

"Stay there," I said.

I grabbed a roll of toilet paper, ran outside, and cleaned the tiles before the blood could dry.

Back in the room, I tossed my shirt onto a table to keep it clean, then I put my arm around Savannah and held a wad of toilet paper to her nose. After a few minutes, the toilet paper was soaked. As I swapped it for what remained in my cart, an idea struck me—the shower. I ran to the bathroom and swung the tap open. Steam billowed forth.

Minutes dragged by, but gradually steam filled the room and Savannah's nosebleed receded. Once I was certain the bleeding had stopped, I released her from under my arm and she hobbled into a corner and slumped to the ground.

While she slept, I ran to the nearest pharmacy and asked the pharmacist if she had anything to relax a dog. She yawned, nodded, then slowly rummaged through the glass cabinet behind the register. After an eternity, she returned with a vial the size of my thumb. I didn't recognize any of the ingredients, but the medicine was labeled as a central nervous system relaxant for dogs, so I bought it and a large box of gauze, then I sprinted back to the hotel.

Savannah was where I left her, but I saw with fresh eyes the disaster we had created: spots of blood speckled the tile, the bedsheets jammed in the far corner, the contents of my first aid kit strewn across the table. The room was humid, though. Steam was rolling from the bathroom and into the main room.

I cracked open the medication and put half a dozen yellow drops on Savannah's tongue.

After twenty minutes, the medicine had knocked her into such a state that I put my cheek to her nose to be sure she was breathing. Her chest was rising and falling, but just barely. Gently, I picked her up then set her on a makeshift bed I fashioned from the room's extra blanket and my tarp. Looking down at her, I was reminded of our first day of walking together when she had appeared so small.

The only thing I could think to do was set to work scraping the blood off the floor. I picked at the dried flecks with my knife for hours until the room was clean, then I showered and lay down.

In the night, I woke in a panic. I turned on the lamp, and saw a stream of blood flowing from Savannah's nose down the tarp and onto the floor. I raised her head and set some gauze beneath her snout. For a while, I watched her, wondering how I could possibly walk around the world without her by my side. She wasn't even two. So much still waited ahead of us.

I fell back asleep with my hand rested on her side. At first light, I walked to the transport office at the center of town. The manager told me no taxis would arrive until ten. That might have worked, but I didn't trust that Savannah could make a four-hour ride through the midday sun without incident, so I reserved a taxi for seven the following morning.

Back in the room, the medication had done a number on Savannah. She could hardly stand. She had four or five fits through the day, but they were brief. The following morning, we went outside at six so she could go to the bathroom. We turned the corner, Savannah sniffed at a patch of grass, then began bleeding as freely as when we were in the desert.

In seconds, my arms were streaked with blood. When a woman stepped out of her house, I waved her down.

"Can you bring us paper?" I asked.

The woman backed away and shut the door.

If the cab driver arrived early and saw us, we'd have no ride to Arica and he'd tell the other drivers not to take us either.

The neighbor reappeared with a thick wad of toilet paper. I put it to Savannah's nose while the woman watched us with a dull expression.

"She your dog?"

"Yes."

"It's too dry here for dogs."

"Is there a spigot?"

"I don't know. I only have cats."

After ten minutes, the nosebleed stopped. Savannah looked like a lion that had just finished gorging on a gazelle, and I appeared to have just finished open-heart surgery, but we still had forty minutes before the taxi arrived. We hurried down the street until we found a spigot, then I doused Savannah and wiped my arms and wrung my shirt.

When the taxi arrived, we were standing dry and clean outside the hotel. I was wearing the last bloodless shirt I owned. The driver's name was Juan. He had a few wind-blown hairs and a kind smile. He helped tie my cart into the trunk, then I dropped my backpack onto the back seat and sat in the front with Savannah. As we left Pozo, there were no stores open and no one on the street. Juan played cumbia on the radio.

"He won't go to the bathroom?" Juan asked.

"She knows we're traveling. She'll wait until we stop."

Juan nodded. "There aren't a lot of taxis that will bring dogs."

"The buses don't accept them either. It's difficult to find a ride with her."

"Do taxis in the United States accept dogs?"

"Some, but not all. The same as here."

"I used to not accept dogs. Years ago, a dog bit me from the back seat on the cheek."

Juan snapped at his cheek with his hand, then looked at me and widened his eyes. Then he frowned and shrugged.

"But now I look at the dog and I look at the owner. I look them in the eye and I think, how is this person? How is this dog? Sometimes I won't take them. Sometimes I do."

"Well, thank you for driving us to Arica. I don't know what I would have done if we didn't find a taxi."

"You seem very calm."

Juan tapped his fingers to the music. Savannah shuffled until she was curled with her snout tucked between my arm and chest. Other than a few deep valleys, our ride would be a straight shot through the Atacama. After an hour, we passed the place where Savannah's nosebleed began—it was more desolate than I realized. I tried to turn up the air-conditioning, but even at full strength it did little more than blow lukewarm air.

"Why are you returning to Arica?"

"I need to take her to a veterinarian. She's sick. She's has blood from her nose."

Halfway to the city, we came to a section of road that was being cleared of construction rubble. Juan turned off the car and I opened the door to let in the breeze. The heat was concerningly high. The sun blared through the windshield. Savannah curled in front of the passenger's seat where it was shaded. I fixated on her, searching for any sign that a nosebleed was about to begin. But she never sneezed. Not a drop of blood left her nose. We were waved on and the remainder of the ride passed uneventfully.

With Savannah flopped on the metal table between us, the vet in Arica told me he believed it was ehrlichiosis.

"If it is and she's showing early symptoms, then she'll be okay. There's medication that will work. But if she's had the infection for a long time, the medicine may not be effective. We'll test her blood. We'll have the results in twenty minutes."

We waited in the reception room until the vet poked his head in and gave me a thumbs-up.

"The test came back positive," he said in his office.

"What does this mean for her?"

"It means her red blood cells and platelets are close to zero, and her blood isn't coagulating because of that. The good thing is that she's in the early stages. This is treatable. She probably contracted the infection from a tick in Peru. You said you were there a month ago?"

"But I've been using tick medication."

"The tick only needs to latch on for a few hours and in the south of Peru the infection is very common."

The vet wrote four prescriptions: three of them for vitamins and minerals, the fourth for an antibiotic. At the front desk, I bought a month's supply of everything.

"She will be feeling better in a few days," the vet said. "In a week she'll be able to do everything she was doing before and in a month the infection should be totally terminated."

The next day Savannah slept twelve hours and didn't eat. I stayed in the room with her and only left to get food or water. She had nosebleeds for two more days. She bled on the walls and on the floor, but my host told me not to worry.

"Paint's cheap," he said.

A week later Savannah was on the beach, running in circles like nothing ever happened.

THE TOP OF THINGS

When Savannah and I left the small oasis town of San Pedro de Atacama in the early morning, my cart was weighed down with as much water as it had ever been. The first day I pushed the cart up nine thousand feet of elevation. As we ascended to the altiplano, shrubs and cacti became simpler and more scarce. At fifteen thousand feet, the world emptied and leveled. We saw vicuñas, the wild cousin of the alpaca, but they were skittish and never anything more than a mirage.

On our second night, I wore every piece of clothing I owned, and Savannah slept in the sleeping bag with me. In the morning, our tent was covered in frost, but there were no clouds, and the sun cut cleanly through the sky. Savannah trotted to the salt lake beside our campsite. The lake was shallow; salted tufts of grass, silver with frost, carried into the water from the shore and a flock of flamingos gathered at the far end of the lake like a blotch of bright paint. Savannah barked and the birds took flight. Their wide wings labored, then they rose slowly and soared tight overhead like an immense living puzzle.

By the end of our third day on the pass, we reached Salar y Laguna de Tara—a wide valley that was cupped like a hand reaching for the sun. Inside the valley were two salt lakes with water calm enough to put the sky at my feet. Around the lakes, the mountain peaks were hills. When the wind suddenly hastened, it pelted us with sand and marred the reflection on the water. I put Savannah's goggles on her and pulled my buff over my nose, then we turned into the wind and walked as fast as we could in search of shelter.

Far off in the shimmering valley, I spotted a glint of metal. We turned from the road, and I leaned forward to push the cart through the soft sand. It was impossible to make a straight line. Sand slipped from beneath the tires and under my steps. Savannah stayed beside the cart to hide from the wind. After twenty minutes, we reached a chain-link fence bordering a gas pipe sticking up four feet from the ground. It wasn't much by way of shelter, but it was the only man-made structure in sight.

I tied my tent to the fence, staked the corners as deep as I could dig, then kicked sand onto the sides of the tent to keep it stable. When the wind blew off the sand, I piled on more until the tent was halfway covered and I only had room to squeeze into a coffin-sized space inside. I pulled Savannah in with me, but she fled the moment I let go—inside was far too loud.

The tent slapped the side of my face all night. By the time morning limped over the mountains, I had only slept two hours. I dragged myself outside and was surprised when Savannah wasn't there to greet me. I stood and called for her. A few feet away, sand cascaded off her back as she rose from the ground. She was the same color as everything else. I filled her water bowl and when she finished drinking, we only had a liter and a half of water remaining and twenty miles to the border. We were drinking more than usual. The thin air demanded it.

I packed as well as my tiring body would allow—not rolling the tent neatly but shoving it into the cart. Then, once we were packed, I began pushing the cart along a groove in the sand where someone had once driven. Mercifully, there was no wind, but the sand was loose, and I needed to lean parallel to the ground to inch the cart forward.

When the cart slipped to the side, I lost my footing and fell.

I did nothing to catch myself. My chest hit first, then my face. Sand flew into my mouth and up my nostrils, but it felt good to be facedown and not moving, so I stayed like that.

After a lifetime or two, I turned over and Savannah came to sit beside me. The temperature was perfect, the sun was gentle and beside us was a hill covered in fantastic yellow tufts of grass. I felt Savannah's back against my ribs and suddenly I imagined us like a painting from above.

When we began together, I was indifferent, even annoyed by her, but my feelings for Savannah had moved beyond care, beyond love, and transformed into something nearer to awe. How many times had I looked down at her and marveled? *She must be some form of God.* She wandered from scent to scent as though in a state of eternal joy—showing no reluctance to face the challenges ahead, never complaining, and not once lagging behind. She was a beast. She drove us on, perpetually pulling the leash, forever curious.

We had walked eight thousand miles together, always each other's shelter, and now we rested at the top of the earth changed from who we were. We faced our fears side-by-side and discovered they were born of inexperience, and that adventure was really just an education. Somehow I knew that we had walked the earth already, that we would walk it again, and that we would be walking it forever.

THE RAPID DESCENT

When I unzipped the tent, wind blew off the lake and kicked snow against my chest and down the back of my shirt. Lexi glanced at me from her sleeping bag, pulled it tight over her head and rolled to her side. I pressed my camp stove into the snow and started a pot of water. The next town, Reykjahlíð, was across a stretch of volcanic flats that would be difficult to navigate even on a clear day. In a snowstorm, the crossing was near impossible.

Once the water was boiling, I poured coffee for Lexi and me.

"You up?" I asked.

"Awake," she said to the wall.

Our tent was thumping in the gale.

Lexi sat up, pricked her finger, squeezed a drop of blood onto a test strip, and dosed her insulin accordingly. After that, I passed her a cup of coffee and she withdrew the fifth of whiskey she bought at the airport and poured some into our mugs.

"May as well," she said.

"May as well."

Our attempted crossing of Iceland wasn't going to plan. The weather was harsh and fickle, and the route we hoped to follow across the center of the island was cut off by early-melting glaciers. Lexi opened a pack of cards and set them on the floor to play rummy.

"So what do you think?" I asked. "Is it everything you imagined?"

"Definitely colder and slower."

"And we're here in June."

"Have you talked to Mom and Dad about the house?"

"Not really. Dad won't talk about it. I can't imagine they'll be able to keep it much longer."

"It's been years already."

"You definitely moving to Denver?"

"I can't stay in town. There's too much drama. I can't even enjoy hanging out with my friends anymore. Everyone is so petty. It drives me crazy."

For as much as Lexi wanted out of town, my dad wanted her out, too. He knew the value of leaving to come back and he knew Lexi needed that. I worried about my mom, though. With Lexi gone, it would be the first time both of her children would be living far from home simultaneously. I felt partially responsible, as though my walk around the world had spurred Lexi into leaving.

The next day, the sun was shining, the snow was melting, and we scrambled boulder to boulder to escape the wind blaring across the flats. Lexi's blood sugar was unsteady, so we stopped often, but eventually, we made it to town and rented a campsite. From there, Lexi hitchhiked to the Nature Baths and spent a few hours relaxing in the hot water. I stayed by the tent and read. Occasionally, a stomach cramp caused me to wince and lose focus.

After Iceland, Lexi and I would return to New Jersey and Savannah's EU paperwork would be ready. Savannah and I would fly to Ireland, and I wouldn't see my family for another three years. I dreaded leaving everyone. It wasn't that I wanted to stay, I couldn't imagine that, but after the Americas I understood how taxing and isolating the walk would continue to be. When I tried to imagine the years ahead, I could only see the challenges. I would be alone, tired, and searching for a long time.

But I had family in Europe at least—a hundred cousins in Ireland, a first cousin in London, and a dozen relatives in Croatia. That would soften things. The rest of Europe, I imagined, would be a far different adventure than surviving the jungles and desert of my first two years.

While I stood with Savannah on the road, Colm, Margaret, and Michelle stepped from the jetty and into the frigid waters of Muir Éireann. After a twenty-minute swim, they climbed out with their skin red and their eyes clearer than when they entered.

"Aren't ya going in, Tommy?" asked Colm, my father's first cousin, a teacher in Dundalk.

"As appealing as it looks, I think I'll stay dry this morning."

"If you want to feel alive, there's nothing better in the world," said Margaret, a woman with more energy on her average day than I had at my best.

"You do this every morning?"

"Winter and summer, rain or shine."

A dozen swimmers came and went. Margaret and Colm knew everyone. Most swimmers were middle-aged or older, Michelle, their daughter, was the only person near my age.

"You should jump in, Tommy," she said. "We have towels. Just drop in for a minute. It's as good as a coffee."

A year or two before, I might have gone in for the thrill of it, but my interpretation of what it meant to seize the day had changed since then. No longer was seizing the day about packing my hours with things to do or doing things for the sake of novelty. The more time I spent with myself the better I knew where I derived satisfaction, where I found meaning, and what I desired from the world. Seizing the day now meant maximizing the time I spent doing the things I valued. And currently, after walking ten thousand miles through nearly every climate, I valued being warm, dry, and comfortable.

After an elevenses of scones and tea at a nearby café, Colm and I dropped Margaret and Michelle at their house, then we drove from

Dundalk onto the peninsula to the northeast. We followed a single-lane road, passing cattle ranches, white houses in green pastures, and Carlingford Mountain, which shielded Northern Ireland from view. Eventually, we slowed into a driveway shrouded by thick bushes and tall crooked birch. At the end of the lane, we reached a stone house with a field in the back that opened to a view of the Irish Sea.

"Your great-grandfather's home, Andrew Murphy. We visit with Liz and Bob whenever they come. Imelda and Pádraic's kids live here now: Peter, Aileen, and Ray. You may not see Ray, but Peter is here. He's another one of the teachers in the family."

From out a squat wooden door, Peter met us in the driveway.

"This is Liz's brother's son, Tommy," Colm said to him.

"Pleasure to meet you," said Peter with a nod.

"Thank you for having me. I've always wanted to see the homestead."

"Well, it's one of them, I suppose," said Peter, hands in his pockets, turning carefully to look at the house. "My grandfather stayed. Your great-grandfather left."

"It's beautiful. It seems like a peaceful place to grow up. I can't imagine how empty everything was when they were here."

"It's not a working farm anymore. Aileen and I make our living as teachers, but we do what we can to keep up the land. We used to have cattle in the barn if you'd like to see."

We followed Peter into a long stone barn where the air was cool and musty. We stood at the end beside a wall piled with rusted farming equipment. The other two-thirds of the barn were stables. Savannah sniffed at the corners for a minute then ran outside and into the field with Peter's dog chasing.

"Used to have all sorts of livestock—chicken, sheep, cattle. Just storage now. It was never big, even in Andrew's time. I hear the Lindens have a big place in the heart of things, though. Haven't visited."

"Peter just graduated with Sustainable Agriculture," said Colm. "Bright lad. Doing his father's head in with all the changes he wants to make."

I peered into one of the stables. Hay was matted on the ground. At the far end was a small square cutout that a breeze came through. The tightness in my stomach, like a balloon being pumped with too much air, was close to its breaking point. The anticipation of pain covered me in a chill and caused the hair on the back of my neck to stand on end. When the spasm came, it came in an instant. My muscles constricted like I'd taken hold of a live wire. I pressed my forehead against the wall and crumpled.

After ten seconds or so, I regained my vision and Colm helped me to my feet. He swept the hay from my side.

"It's okay," I said, out of breath, to Peter. "I've been getting them since I returned home from Uruguay. They've been getting worse, but Colm and I went to the doctor. He thinks it's irritable bowel. I have some probiotics and mebeverine that should help."

"I still don't like the looks of it, Tommy," Colm said.

We went inside for tea and biscuits and so I could sit down. Around a small table by a window draped in lace, I met Peter's girlfriend of twenty-five years, Eilis, and Aileen, Peter's sister, who my cousin Aileen was named after. Everyone was friendly but once we were together the conversation felt more like a formality than a naturally flowing spring. I wasn't helping matters. The discomfort from my spasm lingered. My mind was foggy. I drank a few black teas in an attempt to liven myself, but they had little effect.

Colm spoke about when he was twenty and visited the States and how my dad picked him up from the airport and showed him around New Jersey that summer. Peter said he'd never been Stateside.

After an hour, Colm and I said goodbye and I thanked everyone for allowing me to see a bit of my history. Driving away, I thought it a strange experience. I was glad to have seen my great-grandfather's home in a check-the-box sort of way, but I felt more connected to Ireland by my living relatives: Colm and Margaret, the Lindens, Ronan in Dublin, and Deklin, Angie, Ana, and Owen in Galway. Though I was tied to Ireland by history, and my blood was the pretense for everyone I knew there, my warmth for the place was more alive than Andrew Murphy's childhood home. Ireland was Guinness by the sea with Colm. Music in a basement bar with Owen. Talk of modernizing the farm with Peter.

What might have been a week's walk across a tiny green island was instead a month-long jaunt from cousin to cousin, just the way I wanted.

Two days after leaving Colm and Margaret's, I spent the night with a friend of a friend outside Belfast. When I looked in the mirror, I wondered if I was losing weight. My ribs were showing more than usual, and my cheeks were strangely withdrawn.

Belfast was gray and industrial. I stayed at an Airbnb, then the following morning, I walked three miles to the ferry. On the ferry, Savannah had to be in a kennel by the cars. I left one of my shirts in the kennel to reassure her, but she barked the moment I left, and she was still barking when I returned to check on her a half an hour later.

After two hours, we took our first steps in Scotland. I had hoped there would be a restaurant in Cairnyan when we landed, but instead we were met by a thick drizzle and a dozen minuscule houses. We followed a narrow road between the village and the sea until connecting with a path along the water. After three miles, the rain stopped, and the path opened to a glen where the grass glimmered in the sun. I set out my tarp and sat against the cart. Savannah stayed with me for a minute, then walked off to prowl the tall grass around us.

Even at the beginning of my walk, when my legs cramped and blisters beset my feet, I never walked less than fifteen miles a day. But seated in that glen, after six miles of walking, I couldn't go a step more. My muscles weren't aching, my eyes weren't bleary, and my mind wasn't tired from overstimulation. Ireland and Northern Ireland were the easiest walking I'd done, but I was more hollow and exhausted than after my longest weeks.

I found a level area for my tent and ate two bowls of pasta in hopes that the extra food would revive me. The next day I followed a back road through a forest where the ferns rose three feet high to pack the space between the trees and the clouded sun gilded the tips of the pines. Occasionally, a cottage could be seen nestled deep within the darkness like a forgotten rhyme.

I would have cut my day short on that pristine back road, but a follower offered me a place to stay in Dumfries, a town that was three days away, so in anticipation of a bed, I willed myself forward.

Off the back road, I connected with the EuroVelo: a network of bike paths that crisscrossed Europe. The walking was ideal—flat, secluded, and paved—but my spasms were stopping me six times a day. Sometimes it felt like I was walking on my bones and not muscle. My steps were heavy and sent shocks up my leg. I had to fold my pants at the waist and tighten my belt.

A few days later I stayed in Dumfries and shared a hearty meal with the family that hosted me, but I could barely enjoy it for fear of a spasm. I sat unmoving at their table. Beyond Dumfries, I fell into a bus stop to escape the rain and called my mom.

"It feels like I'm pregnant," I said. "Like my body doesn't belong to me. I've always been able to will myself through my discomfort until I adjusted, but now I'm just getting weaker. I can barely make it fifteen miles. I'm taking naps twice a day. The spasms are lasting longer and becoming more painful. I had one a minute ago. I couldn't see at all. I couldn't see a thing. And I'm just so tired. The rain is killing me. This freaking rain never ends."

"I'm not sure that's exactly what pregnancy feels like, but I get your meaning. You can catch a train to London from there, can't you? It's probably time to head to Monica's. I know you don't want to pause the walk, but it seems like you've tried to push through for a couple of months, and you aren't getting better."

"I know, but I'll feel like a failure. I just started walking again."

"You can't walk around the world if your body is failing. You have to get yourself right."

I only walked a few more miles. The rain grew heavy and when I sheltered in another bus stop, I decided to call it a day. The bus stop was at a corner where cars turned for a town on the water a half mile away. I would have preferred to hide in the woods or a field, if only to keep from being bothered, but I couldn't bring myself to continue. I inflated my mattress, pulled Savannah so she was beside me, then moved my cart to block the light from the turning cars.

In the evening, as I was drifting to sleep, a car paused with its lights on us. I rolled over to ignore them and the car drove off. A half an hour later, the same car returned, and I looked over my cart and waved. A woman lowered her window and asked if I was okay. I told her I was fine, but at midnight, the cops woke me.

"You're fine, you're fine," said an officer walking over as I stood to greet her. "Just wanting to check on you, make sure you're okay. Oh! You've got your friend by your side. Isn't she a bonnie?"

I showed her my passport and explained my journey and why I decided to sleep in the bus stop.

"There's a field two kilometers down the road that would make for lovely camping," she said. "I'm sure you'd get a better sleep without lights passing over you all night."

"I wish I had known a few hours ago, but I'm so tired now that I'll sleep through anything."

In the morning, Savannah and I were a few hundred yards from the bus stop when a police car pulled beside us, and a different officer said good morning.

"Better than yesterday, eh? No rain at least. You sleep okay?"

"Well enough," I said. "Once I knew it was okay to sleep there I slept better."

"Our land is your land, my good lad. Here, brought you a wee breakfast." The officer handed me a paper bag with two sausage sandwiches inside. "Good luck with your walking. Let us know if you need anything."

I carried the sandwiches to the train station in Carlisle, then ate them with Savannah sitting between my legs and the hills of North England zipping by. In London, a room at my cousin's home was waiting.

Me and the family before the send-off.

First day of walking together.

Savannah on the high pastures of Ecuador.

Sand sweeps across the road in north Peru.

Eye protection in the desert.

There's no better camping than desert camping.

An ayahuasca meloka in Iquitos, Peru.

The descent from 15,000 feet in Argentina.

Kayaking among crabeater seals in Antarctica.

Algerian escort copying my passport information.
Eventually, I learned to just give them a photo of it.

The ideal Italian campsite.

NORTH
AND
CENTRAL AMERICA

WINTHROP

BONNIE

TOWNER

AUSTIN

HADDON TOWNSHIP

SAN MARCOS

SOUTH AMERICA

THE PAN-AMERICAN

RESERVA
LOS FLAMENCOS

WESTERN EUROPE
AND
NORTH AFRICA

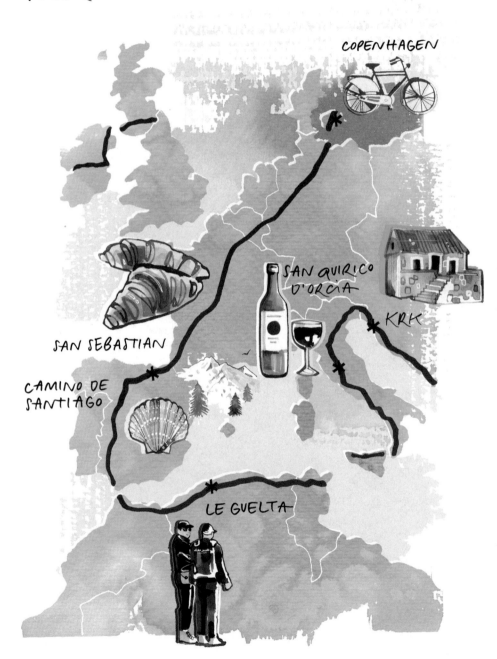

COPENHAGEN

SAN QUIRICO D'ORCIA

KRK

SAN SEBASTIAN

CAMINO DE SANTIAGO

LE GUELTA

EASTERN EUROPE

ISTANBUL TBILISI

KAŞ

ASIA

BAKU ARSLANBOB

Island-hopping in Croatia.

Hot air balloons in Cappadocia, Turkey.

A man prays in an Uzbek madrasa.

The most beautiful valley I've ever seen, Kyrgyzstan.

Under the stars in Kyrgyzstan.

Savannah in her down jacket on the plains of Kansas.

Crossing the finish line.

A DYING DREAM

The day after arriving at Monica and Dave's, I walked from their home on the Isle of Dogs to the nearest private doctor I could find. That doctor happened to be in Canary Wharf. In the basement floor of a tower brimming with marble, I watched panic grow in the doctor's eyes.

"I don't want to alarm you," he said. "But these are serious symptoms. The spasms, the blood in the stool, the weight loss. It points to stomach cancer. Or ulcers. If it's ulcers, you can't fly. If an ulcer bursts on the plane and you're over the Atlantic . . . well, it might be the end."

"You think I might have stomach cancer?"

"We'll do bloodwork and an ultrasound, but you realize I'm a private doctor, right? This will run you thousands. If this is as serious as I think it is, it's probably best that you go to the Royal London Hospital. Patients come to me with heartburn and anxiety. This isn't my expertise. I can direct you if you want, but I don't think I'm who you should be seeing."

"How much would an ultrasound cost?"

The doctor called another office then jotted down a number greater than what I paid for my flight from Philadelphia to Ireland.

A few days later, I followed the doctor's orders and caught a cab to the Royal London Hospital. I stood in a waiting room until I was told to sit in a smaller waiting room with ten rooms branching off it. Monica appeared just before my name was called.

"What are you doing here?" I asked.

"I'm here to make sure you get admitted. I can't have you dying in my house."

Monica was the first in my generation of Turcich cousins. Her blonde hair and blue eyes belied a decidedly harsh personality. Because I'd grown up with her, I knew her sarcasm and dark wit had little to do with who she was at the core, but I was certain there were many people who met her that could have used that insight.

In the next room, I sat on the bed and Monica sat in a chair in the corner. The nurse entered, looked at me once, then hunched over my chart and fired off questions.

"About four months ago," I said. "They started after I returned to the US from Uruguay."

"And how was the pain then?"

"Mild. Barely anything. Like I drank bad milk. A stomachache here and there, but that was it."

"And how is it now?"

"When I get a spasm? A ten out of ten."

"A ten out of ten?"

"Yes."

"Would you mind lying down and lifting your shirt?"

The nurse pressed my stomach with one hand on top of the other. The doctor in Canary Wharf had done the same and it sparked a spasm. I feared another.

"Not much pain?"

"It's uncomfortable. I'm bloated, but it's really only painful when a spasm happens."

The nurse stepped back. I sat up and reset my shirt.

"I'll get you some paracetamol. Is that what you want?"

"Paracetamol?"

"A painkiller. You want painkillers, is that it?"

"No. I can stand the pain. I want to know what's going on."

"I see no reason to admit you. I haven't seen a spasm and you're not reporting any pain."

Monica leaned forward. "He just finished walking the Americas for two years, he's not faking stomach pain for some Tesco paracetamol. He's on my floor writhing in agony four times a day. He's just acting like a stoic. He's saying he's not in pain, but he's dying."

The nurse considered Monica.

"Okay," she said eventually. "Someone will be in to bring you to a bed."

After the nurse left, Monica said, "They're trying to save money everywhere. I should have come with you from the jump."

I was brought upstairs for an ultrasound, then given a bed at the end of a long hall where a nurse put a needle in my hand and an IV filled me with warmth.

That afternoon, that evening, and the following morning, I didn't have a spasm. The few times I felt one approaching, the bloating didn't snap like usual.

"That IV is magic," I told the doctor who had checked in on me half a dozen times since being admitted.

"Well, you don't have a hernia or inflammation in any of your organs. Your bloodwork came back normal, but because you've been abroad for the past couple of years, I'm going to refer you to infectious disease where they can run some more obscure tests. You can head there now if you like."

At Infectious Disease, I was brought to a vast room with two computer desks and two beds in it. I sat on a swivel stool with a doctor whose first question was if I had seen anything crawling in my eyeball.

"My eyeball?"

"Yes, is there any movement in there? Worms? Anything of the like?"

"No. Does that happen to people?"

"What about in your skin?"

"Worms? No, nothing."

I ran my fingers along my forearm.

"Nothing moving about in your feet?"

"No."

"When was the last time you were tested for HIV?"

"You think I have HIV?"

"We screen everyone for HIV, but no, I don't believe you have it. Could you list the countries you've spent time in during the previous three years?"

I rattled off my route.

"We'll have your blood drawn, see what comes back, then go from there. Let's follow up next week."

When I returned a week later, two pages of tests returned negative, so they drew more blood and ran more tests. They were looking for everything from giardia to yellow fever and river blindness. Over a few weeks, I had so much blood drawn that I came to learn which nurses were best at inserting the needle, but after a month, none of the tests returned positive. They could pinpoint no parasite, no STI, and no common bacteria. They had no certainty as to what was causing my spasms, but they knew from my internal bleeding that my body was attacking itself.

My symptoms worsened rapidly. I began throwing up after almost every meal and at least once an hour, a spasm would knock me to the ground and leave me sweating. Eventually, Monica suggested it was time for me to head home.

"If you died on my floor, your mom would kill me."

She was right, not about my mom, but that it was time to go home.

I had been staring at the painting for hours. It was of South Point, Hawaii, and it was illuminated by the growing dawn. My dad's Hawaiian friends had given him the painting three decades earlier. When he was a caterer, it hung in our garage over the chest freezers. When he was a solar developer, it hung in his office at our house. Now, it hung in the office of my parents' apartment. The window opposite the painting looked out to King's Highway, Haddonfield's main avenue. The sound of passing cars whirred about the room. I could barely sleep anyway. I couldn't lie on my stomach, that put too much pressure on it, and when I lay on my back, it felt like my stomach was being stretched to the breaking point. It was only in the fetal position that I could contain a spasm, but by morning, my air mattress was deflated, and my shoulder and hip were touching the floor.

Even when I was able to fall asleep, I woke frequently to sit on the toilet. A recent CT scan revealed I had developed colitis, but the colitis couldn't be treated until I received an endoscopy and colonoscopy to determine which type of colitis I had. Those procedures were three weeks away. Until then, I had to survive.

When I could no longer ignore the churning in my stomach, I pushed myself off my deflated mattress, then walked to the bathroom and stared at the toilet, testing how long I could resist the urge to sit. With my foot, I slid a scale from under the toiletries basket. The numbers flashed zero, I stepped on, and the scale showed 141.6. I slipped the scale back then looked myself over in the mirror, turning my face to see how it changed in the shadows.

To say I was gaunt would have been an understatement. Every rib was defined, my biceps were as thin as my wrists, and my temples were deep valleys. I was withering. My underwear barely held to my waist. Bags darkened my eyes. My skin was bone-white, and my hair was thinning.

I tried to depress a cowlick, but I grew tired of keeping my arm up, so I sat on the toilet to catch my breath. I dressed in shorts and a hoodie then walked to the fridge and removed a nutritional shake. I cracked it open and peered down at the pink liquid—two hundred and sixty calories. Eight would push me over two thousand.

Eating had become a test of will, a practice in delayed pain. I'd become familiar with the pattern. Half an hour after I drank the shake, I would want to throw it up. If I held it down, the urge to vomit would reappear two hours later. If I made it through the second test, I would be rewarded with the long torture of the food tumbling through my shredded intestines until its exit.

In a moment of fortitude, I chugged the drink.

Afterward, I slumped in a chair beside the kitchen island as though I'd come through a great battle. I pushed the empty bottle to the opposite end of the island and laid my head in my arms. I was too tall for the seats, but my back was too weak to hold myself upright. Behind me, the door opened, and Savannah ran in. Upon seeing her, I felt well enough to move. I crouched to say hello. Savannah pressed her head into my stomach, and I pressed my head against her side and rubbed her back.

"Did you have a good walk, my love?"

"She almost knocked over Fred," my dad said. "He weighs about a hundred pounds, and she jumped right on him. If she had another five pounds on her, he would have gone down."

My dad hung Savannah's leash and his rain jacket in the closet, then went around the island and put water on to boil for my mom's tea.

"How did you sleep?" he asked.

"An hour or two. Maybe three."

"I heard you up."

"How was the walk?"

"Lots of people. Savannah saw all her friends, threw up from drinking too much water like always."

I patted Savannah on the side, then returned to my seat. I lay my head on my arms and listened to my dad talk about how Fred does yoga every day and how he's been doing it for fifty years. Then I listened to how Savannah would never make as good a goose chaser as our late dog Scout.

"She doesn't have the killer instinct," he said. It was relaxing to listen to him. An old boss once told me, "Your dad could talk to a brick wall."

He slid over a piece of buttered toast.

"I had a shake already," I said.

"All right."

He turned off the gas and poured hot water into his mug to make green tea. I realized I'd forgotten to write down my weight.

"Could you get my phone from the living room?"

My dad set down the kettle, retrieved my phone, and placed it in front of me. I opened my notes.

10/19 – 143.2
10/20 – 142.4
10/21 – 142.8
10/22 – 142.0

I entered 10/23 – 141.6, then pulled the buttered toast toward me. I ate half of it, then shoved the remainder aside. The nutritional shake was ready to be rejected. Nausea was mounting. I kept my forehead to the cold granite and focused on how it felt. After a few minutes, the nausea moved from my throat to my chest, then gradually it dissipated. After that, I took another bite.

In my dad's office, I deflated the air mattress and kicked it to the corner. Savannah peeked in to check on me, then turned and trotted back to the kitchen, her nails clicking on the tile. Beyond her, I could see my half-eaten toast, so I went to the kitchen and carried it to the living room. I sat on the ground with my legs under the coffee table and stared apprehensively at the cinnamon swirl.

Behind me, draped over the cushions, was an alpaca blanket I'd sent my parents from Peru. The blanket was thin, but as warm as my sleeping bag. It was something that would have been impossible for me to obtain in my earliest days of traveling. In Cusco, every vendor had blankets labeled "ONE HUNDRED PERCENT ALPACA", but none were as soft as you'd expect given the wool's reputation. For hours, I walked the market, rubbing each display blanket between my fingers until finding one that was as soft as I imagined it should be. The vendor had the blanket over a pole. When I told him I wanted to buy it, he held out a different blanket from one of his shelves.

"No, no," I said. "I want this one."

The vendor removed the blanket from the pole, folded it, then turned his back to me and pretended to slide the blanket into a plastic bag, but instead swapped it for a different blanket of the same pattern.

"Sir," I said. "I want that one."

The vendor looked over his shoulder at me and smirked. He gave a slight tilt of the head, then set the counterfeit blanket on the shelf and handed me the true alpaca.

I pulled the blanket from the sofa and draped myself in it. Each time I put it on, that memory of Cusco played itself. It reminded me of how far I'd come: from someone whose fear of being impolite put him in danger to someone confident enough in his assessment to call a vendor's bluff in a foreign land. Every day, thousands of tourists were duped into buying counterfeits, but I was no longer one of them.

Savannah watched me from her bed against the wall. My mom was asleep, and my dad was checking his emails in the office. I clenched my eyes to the ride out the pain of digestion and a chill swept over me as I attempted to remember what it was like in the Andes when I was collapsed from exhaustion, but at the height of my power. *If I die*, I thought, *at least I lived.*

ECHOES OF ANGUISH

But I didn't die.

After the endoscopy and colonoscopy, an antibiotic won the war raging in my stomach. It was the third antibiotic we tried. My symptoms didn't subside immediately, but I regained my weight in a blink—118 pounds to 150 in two weeks.

No longer did I need to spend my days in a curl of exhaustion. I could sit up straight and walk down the stairs. Sometimes I even walked to the woods with Savannah.

When an entire day passed without a spasm, I relaxed in a way that I hadn't in months. The constant fear that captured my hours lifted, and I remembered a life beyond the narrow existence of avoiding anything that might lead to a spasm. But even though my days of absolute pain were behind me, after living through them for such a long time, a darkness lingered. My normally optimistic outlook had turned bitter.

I didn't recognize it until my sister commented on the change at the dinner table.

"Since when did you become a pessimist?"

"Since I've been in fucking agony for five months."

I hung my head.

"I'm sorry."

Once I finished my antibiotics, I started steroids to fight the colitis. The doctor who looked over my colonoscopy images said, "It's not the worst I've seen, but it does look like hamburger meat, doesn't it?"

The colitis dominated my days as much as my spasms, but the colitis was predictable and not remotely as painful. Because of that, I didn't have the same dread associated with it. And gradually, the colitis was beaten back as well.

Once I didn't need to always be near a toilet, I picked up at the gym, spending hours torturing myself on the stair stepper. The stamina I built up during my walk down the Americas had been lost, but I was determined to gain it back.

After a few months, I was in decent shape, but out of money. To restart my sponsorship with Philadelphia Sign, I needed to resume the walk. I did some yard work for a neighbor, then used that cash to fly to Denmark before I was ready.

I decided to restart in Denmark rather than Scotland because I was terrified of the Scottish rain and because I knew from Copenhagen I would be able to step onto a bike route and follow it all the way to Gibraltar. For a week, I stayed in the city with a high school friend, Marlyse, who married a Dane, Jonas. We zipped through the city on our bikes, getting coffee in the morning, taking their son to the parks and the museums during the day, then sipping drinks at the bars in the evening.

South of Copenhagen, Savannah and I crossed a few bridges then took a ferry to Germany. In Germany, when I didn't have a protected bike lane, I followed empty farm roads between villages, but even with such peaceful going, I could rarely manage more than eighteen miles a day. My legs cramped constantly. At night, I needed to drug myself to sleep through the pain. Often, I slept ten or eleven hours, but crawled from my tent in the morning as sore as though I were back at fifteen thousand feet.

I was an emotional mess, too. My thoughts were scattered and panicked. I missed my family. I missed Sunday dinner with my grandparents. I missed being able to have a beer with friends. I wanted a roof and a fridge, and to not need to search for a place to sleep each night. When it rained, all I could think was *what the hell am I doing out here?* Most nights I held a shirt to my face and screamed.

I leaned on Savannah and tried to emulate her. She was the model of stability, never fazed—not by mean dogs, long days, or icy rain. On the back roads, she ran ahead to explore new scents, waited for me to pass, then ran ahead again. When we camped, she sniffed the air and smiled. I tried to find the same wonder.

There were plenty of reasons to be grateful. Germany was as wealthy as the US, but more orderly and with better infrastructure. In Belgium, I drank a beer outside my tent most nights, and one day followed a secluded trail under a mile of blooming cherry blossoms. In France, the prospect of fresh croissants motivated me to get up each morning. I met kind people, too: a German man who hosted me in a treehouse in his backyard; a Belgian woman who gave Savannah water while I was in the supermarket; a French woman who paid for my meal at a café.

In spring, Western Europe wore a modest pastel beauty, but rather than basking in it, I complained, trudged, and threw fits over the slightest inconvenience. I was as fragile as a child. After a farmer found me on his land and offered a thumbs-up, I fumed that he had woken me. When I arrived at a village and discovered the bakery was shut for a holiday, I cursed at the sky.

"I can't enjoy anything," I told Fitz over the phone one evening. "I find a perfect campsite and I'm miserable. I have a great meal and I don't care. Every mile feels like an hour. All I can think about is that if I was back home then I wouldn't be walking in the rain, and I could get a drink with you and Julian, or I'd be having dinner with my cousins."

"Yeah, but it wouldn't be like that, though. You'd have to work. Julian works all week. I'm in New York. And anyway, you don't want this, even if you think you do right now. Life here is just life. Nothing changes. You're living your dream. You've talked about this since you were seventeen."

"Yeah, but it sucks."

"That was the point, wasn't it? To experience every aspect of yourself? To challenge yourself? To grow?"

"Of course."

"You don't want to come back and find an apartment and a job. You have it good. I'm lucky I love what I'm doing, but a lot of people don't. Right now, the walk might suck, but that happens with everything. It's like when you started, when you were cramping and didn't know where to sleep, but you'll get through it."

Fitz was right. I couldn't imagine what I would do at home to make a living. I worked in an office for a few weeks, then stopped showing because I hated it so much. The job I enjoyed most, and which paid the best, was installing solar panels, but I couldn't do that forever. The guys I worked with were ravaged from years in construction. They had back pain, swollen knees, and joints that creaked and popped with every movement.

I didn't want an apartment or furniture either. In fact, I was repulsed by the very idea of them. There was no greater bed than soft grass in the afternoon shade. A tent below the stars was more gratifying than the finest tin-press ceiling. And what was furniture, but vanity? Why spend my life striving for increasingly expensive furniture as though it carried satisfaction equal to the density of its wood? Outside was a symphony. There were sparrows and rustling leaves to move the soul. There were mountains and streams and plains that reminded you of eternity. Why work forty hours a week to afford a lesser abode?

For a moment, I remembered everything good in my life, but that was only a flicker. After three months of walking from Copenhagen, I sulked into San Sebastián, Spain. I found a cheap room on the edge of town so I could wrangle a visa extension, but after two weeks, I only had a few hundred dollars to my name. Thankfully, Karlos, my Airbnb host, said I could stay in his living room for free. I slept on a twin bed against the wall where the ceiling rained dust when the upstairs neighbor walked. Since the Spanish bureaucracy moved at a glacial pace, I knew I'd be coughing for at least another month.

To feel like I was doing something of value, I went to a café and studied Spanish for four hours every morning. After studying, I sat at the café bar with the locals and flirted with the barista. Her name was Isabella. Her blue-green eyes shifted color as often as her desire and I fell into a desperate sort of love with her that only worsened the pain I was attempting to escape.

SAN SEBASTIÁN

Whenever I could, I took a seat in the corner with my back to the wall. People-watching was easiest that way. Between sips of cappuccino, I ate my croissant then my medialuna. When I finished eating, I pored over the textbook I found in San Sebastián's center. The local Spanish was a beguiling tangle. The Basque language, Euskara, was mixed in, endings were truncated, and the dense accent offered no space between words.

One afternoon, after hours of studying, Savannah grew restless. It was nearly one o'clock, so I decided not to stay at the bar to chat. At the register, a man was talking with Isabella. I waited behind him, but then decided to say something quick to her so I could leave.

"Excuse me, I'm sorry," I said to the man before looking to Isabella. "We'll see each other tomorrow at five? We'll meet at Kayak?"

"Yes, yes." Isabella flushed and looked to the counter.

"I can't wait," I said to Isabella, then "Thank you, I'm sorry" to the man I interrupted.

Back at the Airbnb, I baked a frozen pizza and ate it in the living room while watching football highlights. After I finished, Karlos came to say hello.

Karlos was a physical therapist who had recently put his apartment on Airbnb but had never stayed at an Airbnb himself. Initially, he believed people were only looking for a place to crash for a night or two, but after some poor reviews, he began touching up his home as fast as he could. The bed frame I slept on when I first got in was bent and squeaky, so Karlos found a new one. In the second guest bedroom, he placed a few plants. He also moved his things into his Sprinter so the master bedroom was rentable, and he could live in his van.

"How are you, my friend?"

"I'm good," I said. "Working on my Spanish like always. I'm going to go to the immigration office this afternoon. It makes two weeks since I've heard from them."

"The Spanish summer. If you hear from them in two weeks, receive it as a sign from God."

"They have their own time, no?"

"All of Spain has its own time. Did you have pizza again? How do you have pizza every day? Pizza, pasta, pizza, pasta. How do you do that?"

"When it's good, it's good. And I'm an American. I love pizza."

"I suppose. No one is renting my room. There's a booking in two weeks, but nothing until then. You can stay in it if you'd like."

"You don't want to stay in it?"

"I'm enjoying sleeping in the van."

"Are you sure? I don't want to be a weight for you."

"Yes, of course. Sleep there. You'll sleep better than in here."

"Thanks, Karlos. When you drive across America, you have a home with me."

"I hope so, one day. That's the dream."

After eating, I took the train to the city center. At the immigration office, I waited until I could be seen by the same woman who took my application. She told me she had yet to hear from upstairs and that I should come back in another week.

The next day, I met Isabella at the café when she got off work. We walked to the inlet where for a dollar the ferry carried us across the water to Pasai Danibane. On the way, Isabella had me take photos of her.

"Oh! How fat. How ugly. I don't want to see those."

"You're beautiful."

"You only say that because you like me."

"No, I said it because you're beautiful."

"Stop talking like that. I don't want to hear that I'm beautiful."

"Who was that man at the café?"

"A friend. He confessed his feelings for me a few weeks ago, but he's like my brother. I told him that, and that I didn't like him in the same manner that he likes me, but then you came and spoke of our date and now he's angry with me. He came to my apartment to talk last night. I've known him for years, but now he confesses his feelings. He could have told me at any time."

"He's very old, isn't he?"

"Only thirty-five."

"He seemed older to me."

"He's very serious. He's very nice, but he's very serious."

"What a shame."

At Pasai Danibane, we held hands along the water. With the other tourists, we looked up at the laundry hanging from the balconies of the colorful houses and the cliffs behind them that seemed on the verge of crumbling.

"When was the last time you were here?" I asked.

"I was never here."

"You were never here? But you live in San Sebastián."

"I always talk with my friends about coming here, but it never passed."

"Should we take the path to the point or go to the beach?"

"Let's take the path. I want you to take photos of me."

We connected with the Camino del Norte and walked until we came to the observation deck overlooking the inlet and the Bay of Biscay. A lighthouse marked the end of a jetty and a few sailboats sailed out to sea. I stood on the concrete platform and Isabella posed below. I took photos of her with the inlet and the hills in the background, but the light was too harsh.

"We need to come back later," I said.

We decided to walk to the beach. The beach was stone, but it was busy anyway. I swam out into the water to cool off. Then I dove down so I could feel the cold on my head and the sand escaping between my fingers. Back on the beach, lying beside Isabella, I saw how her eyes changed in the light, and how her shirt hugged her waist. I tried to kiss her, but she turned away.

"Kiss me here," she said, tapping her cheek.

Over the next few days, Isabella wasn't working, but I went to the café to study anyway. In the afternoon, to get some exercise, Savannah and I walked over the mountains and down to a secluded bay where there were only ever a few people. By the time we reached the bay, I was sweating. Savannah went to a shallow cave where she could sleep in the shade. I crossed the boulders to my favorite one that was flat and large enough that I could jump into the water, then lay on my towel and read.

On Friday night, Isabella and I walked the Camino del Norte. Backpackers with headlamps passed us until we turned off the path and ducked under the trees to find a stone that looked over the sea like a balcony.

"Hold me here," she said.

I held her from behind and we watched the sun fall over the dark water. When Isabella turned around, she looked up at me and I tried to kiss her, but she flinched and put her forehead to my chest. Her fingers squeezed my back.

"Do you have fear?" I asked.

"Yes."

"Why?"

"I haven't kissed anyone in years, Tom."

"I know."

"Do you want to be hurt?"

"Of course not."

"But it always hurts."

"But that's life."

"I suppose."

She looked at me again and we kissed. I shivered. She stepped back and laughed at me.

"You're shaking."

"So are you."

"Because I'm cold."

"Me too."

"You're a liar."

"You too."

Isabella wouldn't kiss me again, but we made plans to dance *bachata* in the center the next day. She was supposed to meet me at the train station, but she never showed. I called and texted, but she didn't reply. That night, I barely slept.

In the morning, Isabella texted an apology, but she wasn't at the café for another two days, so I lost two more nights of sleep. When I finally saw her, she seemed to delight in my pain.

"Am I keeping you awake?"

"I'm sleeping fine."

"Tom."

"What."

"I want to tell you why I'm sorry."

"Why are you sorry?"

"I've had three boyfriends. Always in Colombia. When I arrived here, I wanted to save money, buy a house in Colombia, and start a business. I don't want love. I don't want love because my last three boyfriends made other girls pregnant while we were dating."

"Three?"

"All of them. They have children now."

"That's why you have fear."

"I said I did."

"I didn't know how much."

Later that day, I called Fitz. He agreed that I was putting too much on Isabella, and he suggested I not see her for a week, so I spent more time on the boulder in the bay or making friends with people at the dog park. When two girls from Lyon moved into the Airbnb, I found them much less complicated than Isabella. The first night they moved in, I was watching a football game, and Fanta came to watch with me. After an hour, it occurred to me to ask, "Do you like football?"

"No," she said.

From then on, we went to bed together every night. Fanta would knock on my door and ask to come in.

"Young and old," I said one evening, as we were entwined.

"Black and white."

"Beautiful and ugly."

"No, happy and happy."

I asked her to join me for a coffee one morning, but she said she had to get ready with her friend. They did their makeup for hours, so I never spent any time with her except at night.

"Anyway," she said. "I don't drink coffee or alcohol. Only sex."

But that was more than enough to liberate me from Isabella.

Four days into knowing Fanta, I saw Isabella outside the café.

"Where have you been?" she said.

"Taking a rest."

After a week, Fanta and her friend returned to Lyon and my visa extension came through. I was elated that the government granted the visa, but they deducted my time in San Sebastián from it, so the ninety-day visa only had forty-five days remaining. In order to reach Gibraltar before it expired, I needed to leave immediately.

I spent the next day gathering supplies. I messaged Isabella that my visa had come through, and that I would be leaving in the morning. She said she wanted to say goodbye, but that she was busy, and I should come by her apartment later that night.

She lived with her mother, grandmother, and sister. Her grandmother and I spoke for a while about Colombia, then Isabella poured me tea and we went to her room, which was pink and childish. We sat on her bed, and she was wearing a tight black dress.

"I knew you were leaving," she said.

"I don't want to, but I have to."

"It's good you're leaving. You're an adventurer. You have a purpose."

"I don't always want it."

"Maybe I'll visit you in America."

"You won't."

"Why did you say that?"

"I'm bitter. I'm sorry. Maybe you will, but I won't be in America for three years. In three years, you'll have your business and a house in Colombia."

"In my dreams."

I wanted to kiss her, but there was no point. She went to her dresser and grabbed a book from on top of it.

"Look," she said. It was a textbook for beginner's English. "I want to learn."

"How good," I said. I was happy for her, I hoped she did learn English, but I had no more time to give. My days in San Sebastián were at an end.

FINDING THE WAY

From San Sebastián, I climbed the Pyrenees. I thought the mountains would be a shortcut to the south, but instead they trapped me on steep, uneven paths. A couple of days in, I nearly broke my ankle holding to my cart as it slid through the brush off a narrow switchback. When I finally skidded to a stop, my legs were bloody, and Savannah looked to me as though wondering why I had taken such an odd way down.

Soon after, I abandoned the Pyrenees by turning west and connecting with the Camino de Santiago. The Camino was a longer route to Gibraltar, and hotter than the Pyrenees, but it was flat and well developed. Near Portugal it connected with another pilgrim route, the Vía de la Plata, which would take me south.

In some ways, the Camino revived me. For the first time on my walk, I was surrounded by people walking the same path as myself. I met pilgrims of every background—moneyed retirees, young vagabonds, widows in search of answers. In San Juan de Ortega, I met a German who wore a gold cross over his black shirt and scattered his wife's ashes as he went.

"She made me promise," he said. "She died three months ago. Three years ago, she was diagnosed with liver cancer. We went through the state health care system in Germany first, but things weren't moving quickly enough so we went to a private doctor. After a month, we owed $57,000. I didn't have the money. We didn't have that money. I sent a thousand emails to churches across Europe asking for help and do you know how many responded? Two. The first said he couldn't help. The second said he needed the money for his vacation home. So, I'm still religious, but I don't believe in the church anymore."

Halfway along the Camino, I sat in a piazza watching the late pilgrims lumber in, and realized I was happy for the first time in months. I had a coffee and a pastry, and I was hoping someone would sit nearby so I could strike up a conversation. Under the baking sun and the terracotta roofs, I found my way out of my long darkness, though not unchanged.

The lust for adventure that motivated me down the Americas had been overtaken by an obsession with what my future home would look like. I listened to architecture podcasts and bought audiobooks on design to feed the fire. For hours each day, I envisioned every detail of the home I would raise my family in. Sometimes it was a hacienda with a courtyard; other times a Philadelphia row home where I could cross the street to the park; most often, it was a cabin in the woods with land for Savannah and a porch where we could watch the summer storms. My imagination had no end. I saw myself in Colombia, Denmark, or with a vineyard in the Argentinian Andes.

The only thing I couldn't imagine in those many varied lives was who was beside me. I played with thoughts of Fanta—maybe an apartment in Lyon where I could have a croissant every morning. I remembered Layla, but she was married now, and I had long ago accepted how our paths diverged. I wondered who I would love, what made her happy, and where she was born. The only thing I knew for certain was that she was kind and intelligent, and that we would be deeply in love.

After a month and a half following the Caminos, Savannah and I caught the night ferry from Gibraltar to Morocco. I was told Savannah had to be kept in a kennel on the upper deck, but the wind was brutal.

After a few minutes of sitting beside the kennel with her, I knew neither of us could stand it. I went inside and convinced a worker to allow Savannah into a private bunk room—I had to pay for two beds and promise she wouldn't go to the bathroom.

For two weeks, we walked Morocco's north coast. I had fresh sardines with crushed salt most mornings. On our last evening, the police found us in the woods and told me we would have to accept an escort to the border.

"It is not safe," an officer said. "Young men are trying to cross the sea every day. Down there. You can see where they leave through the trees. They want more money, better jobs. They sleep in the woods here."

A week before, news had broke that a boat of teenagers hoping to make it to Spain had capsized off the shore. Similar tragedies happened often. That year alone over two thousand people died while attempting to cross the Mediterranean. Yet, in the same way that I was able to skirt the laws of Mexico to stay in country without a visa, I was able to skirt the bounds of geography with a stamp.

Since the border between Morocco and Algeria was closed, Savannah and I ferried to Spain, then ferried south again to land in Algeria. In both directions, we had a room with a view. When we landed in Algeria, the police took us into custody.

THE ESCORTS

I woke to the sound of dried leaves crunching underfoot. Then I heard them on the dirt road—the click of a car door handle and the sound of a door shutting. I listened, feeling the cold creep over my shoulders and into my sleeping bag. Savannah was asleep in the corner. I hesitated to open the tent, but I didn't want to waste the morning so I crawled outside and saw that a hundred feet away, parked among the bare eucalyptus, was a white sedan with three police officers looking at me. One of them stepped out and walked over.

"Good morning," he said.

Savannah scurried over to the man to say hello. He stepped back and looked down at her. His hands were in his pocket and a black beanie was pulled to his eyebrows.

"You've been awake all night?" I asked.

"Two hours I sleep."

"You didn't need to stay."

"The boss." He nodded somewhere.

"I'm going to pack, then let's find a coffee."

Using my headlamp for light, I broke camp, then I walked through the forest and the picnic area where tables the night before had been swarmed with families eating and men playing dominoes.

A little while on, I reached Khadra in a violet dawn. Most shops in Spain didn't open until nine, but in Algeria, everything was open before I awoke. The straight-line street of Khadra was busy. Working men boarded buses that would take them a hundred kilometers to the capital. Retired men had finished their morning prayer and now sat in the cafés to watch the light grow.

Halfway through town, the officer driving beside me turned his hand over and back again to ask when I was going to stop. We passed a few cafés, but I knew the quietest ones were on the edge of town. When I finally spotted a café I liked, I pointed to it, then crossed the street.

About a dozen men sipped from shot-sized paper cups. They were in groups of three and huddled together as though plotting revolution. At the bar, a teenage barista was serving a man in a tan burnoose. Behind them, a red espresso machine had four presses and a polished steel base— one of the better products of France's hundred-year occupation.

I put down two coins to order four espressos. The teenage barista grabbed a press with both hands and pulled on it so mightily that his veins bulged until drops of dark espresso eked from the press. After half-filling four minuscule cups, the barista was out of breath.

When the police officer appeared beside me, I handed him an espresso.

"Thanks for staying up all night," I said.

He raised the cup to me, then I carried the remaining cups to the officers outside and took a seat at a table beside my cart. The trees across the street were painted white at the base. Children in smocks and blue jeans walked to school with their mothers in hijabs.

Seeing my gaze, the police officer asked, "You know Islam?"

"Of course," I said.

"And Allah?"

"Everyone knows Allah."

The officer smiled and translated for the others.

My chair was comfortable enough that I could have stayed at the café people-watching for hours, but once I felt the caffeine, I started walking to make the most of it. With the eyes of the police on my back, I walked four hours without rest. I passed tomato fields, shepherds, and a few towns where rebar jutted from homes in aspiration of a second story. When I finally stopped, it was because I had reached the border of the municipality and needed to present my passport, so I could be exchanged from one escort to the next.

Once my information was noted, the group of three that had been with me the night before was replaced by a group of six. One of the officers introduced himself.

"Thomas the American," he said.

He grinned with smoke-stained teeth.

My climb out of the valley was slow. I could feel the previous twelve miles in my legs. Three police cars drove behind me at two miles per hour. Halfway up, I spotted a picnic area in a cluster of olive trees. I cut across the road and lay on a bench there. My escort pulled onto the gravel and the man with the stained teeth stood over me with the sun behind his head.

"Fatigué?"

"Ouí. Fatigué. Affamé."

"Thomas, you want eat? Sandwich?"

"Yes."

"Restaurant." He pointed up the hill.

"What distance? How many kilometers?"

He turned to the other officers.

"One kilometer."

"Okay. Let's go."

"We go?"

"Yes. Let's go. Je marche."

Out of the valley, I could see the Mediterranean and the horizon bound to it like a white thread. The restaurant was where the man promised. It had a large menu outside with circles where prices were supposed to be written. Inside, I was the only customer. I sat facing the kitchen because I was tired, and I knew the police officers were watching me, but I didn't feel like talking to them. I ordered a sandwich because it was the only thing I knew how to say. I received a baguette with french fries, harissa, and a smattering of ground beef. The bread was fantastic, but the sandwich had no taste, so I doused it in oil and vinegar.

The officer with stained teeth stepped in front of my table and pointed to a painting.

"Thomas." He flicked his hand down to tell me to come over. "Thomas."

"I'm eating."

"Come."

"I'm eating."

"Algeria and Morocco." He tapped the painting. "La frontière."

"Beautiful," I said through a mouthful of starch.

"Thomas, Algeria, how is?"

I glanced behind me to see four cops and four civilians crammed in the doorway. The youngest were gripping each other in laughter. The sergeant called to the overzealous officer and he left with little loss in enthusiasm. After eating, I was in better spirits. The restaurant owner gave me half a baguette on my way out.

"Bonne chance," he said.

From town, I followed the road along the rocky coastline until descending to Le Guelta, a town encircled by two rivers, the sea, and the road. After crossing a bridge over the river, I was met by another escort. I shook hands with the new officers and the youngest squeezed my hand with unnecessary force. The sergeant wore Ray-Bans and didn't smile. He tried to keep my passport and only returned it under pressure from the previous escort.

Walking again, I passed shop owners in their doorway who touched a hand to their heart.

"Salaam alaikum."

"Alaikum salaam."

The escort drove just beside me, and the young officer hung out the back window and stared. I tried to make as little eye contact with him as possible.

"Thomas, how much money do you have?" He spoke English with only a mild accent.

"Huh?"

"How much money?"

"I don't know. Four thousand dinar."

"Four thousand dinar isn't much."

"My friend told me not to carry much. I'll get more in Ténès."

"You want an Algerian woman, Thomas?"

"What?"

"You like an Algerian woman?"

He said something to the other officers that made them laugh.

"Thomas, give me your number."

I gave it to him.

"I will message you. You write me a note to come to America. I come to America, Thomas. I have no money. Americans have many money."

When the sidewalk ended, I walked on the dirt beside the road. It was bright outside, but the winter sun was weak. Beyond town, I reached a parking area where a gathering of bushes provided shade at the hem of a hill. I went to it in hopes that the escort would stay on the road, but once I sat against my tire, the young officer walked down to me.

"What are you doing, Thomas?"

"Taking a break. Lots of kilometers today."

As the officer neared, Savannah spun to her feet, growled, and put her body against his shins. The officer stepped back.

"He?" The officer mimed biting his forearm.

I wagged a finger.

"Savannah, come here."

Savannah walked over and I tucked her under my arm.

"Thomas, you get me a visa to America."

"You don't need me. You can apply. There's a lottery."

"I want an American wife."

"That's a good idea."

"You can write a letter for I go to America."

"Sure."

"How much money do you have on you, Thomas?"

"What does that matter?"

"What you said?"

"Nothing."

"How much money do you have on you?"

"Four thousand dinar."

"That's not much. What food do you have? I'm very hungry. I have no lunch."

I gave him the baguette the restaurant owner had given me.

"Nothing else? What do you have in there?"

He tapped my cart. Savannah barked and her hackles went up. Reluctantly, I stood and opened the cart. My food crate was buried among my things, but a fuet sausage I carried from Spain was in the open, so I held it to him.

"Full of pig," I said.

The young officer held up his hands.

I shut my cart and sat down. I wanted to stare into the void for thirty minutes, but the officer wouldn't leave me alone. He stood a few feet away, gnawing at the baguette and looking down at me.

"You have nothing else?" he said once the baguette was finished.

I dug my hand into the back basket until I found a tomato a farmer had given me in the morning. I tossed it to him.

"What religion, Thomas?"

"No religion."

"No, what religion do you have?"

"Christian."

"Of the book. Good."

The sergeant came down to join us and for a few minutes the two men stood in front of me without saying anything. Eventually, the sergeant patted the young officer on the back, and they returned to their car.

I unfolded my tarp so it was wide then lay with my backpack as a pillow and shut my eyes. I listened to the waves sounding against the hills and how there was no noise of cars or humanity. As I was drifting to sleep, my phone rang. It was my ex-boss, Amar. He called almost every day since I entered Algeria. His mother lived in the Sahara and wrote me the letter of invitation I needed to obtain my visa.

"Tom, how are you?"

"I'm good. Taking a break in the shade, looking at my escort and the sea." The young officer started downhill when he noticed I was awake.

"That's good, man. That's good. So, man, how is everything there?"

In the late nineties, a coup to prevent an Islamic electoral victory sparked an Algerian civil war that killed roughly a hundred thousand. Amar was granted political asylum by the United States to escape the violence. When we worked together, I asked him to tell me about the war, but he would only say that it was awful and that he saw too many bodies in the street. Since leaving Algeria, he hadn't returned.

"No problems," I said. "Lots of good people. Good espresso. Good sardines when I can find them. I'm covering more ground than I thought I would, too. I thought the short days would keep me to eighteen miles, but I've been doing twenty-four pretty easily. I should slow down, but it's hard to stop with the escorts watching and wanting to talk whenever I rest."

While Amar and I spoke, the young officer circled like a vulture. After five minutes, he finally broke in.

"Who is that?" he said.

"My Algerian friend."

"He lives in Algeria?"

"He lives in America, but he's from Algeria."

"He lives in America?"

For the first time since meeting him, the haughtiness in the young officer's voice gave way. Until that moment, it seemed that he didn't believe it was possible for an Algerian to move to America. Suddenly, he became small and childlike.

Amar's voice came through the phone.

"Tom, let me talk to him."

I handed my phone to the boy so he and Amar could talk. They spoke long enough that I leaned my head back and shut my eyes. After a while, the boy returned my phone.

"What were you talking about?" I asked Amar.

"Tom, you have to understand what you are doing is very strange. It's very strange, Tom. You know it's hard for him to believe you walked all these places when he can't leave the country. Algeria is not like America, Tom. He works seven days a week, man. His family is in the mountains and he's living with police officers in a town he doesn't know. He sleeps in a bunkhouse. He goes home two days a month, man. Give him my number. He wants information on how to come to America. I told him I would help."

"He was asking me to write a letter of recommendation. I didn't think it would do any good."

"Tom, give him my number when we're off the phone."

"Okay."

There was silence between us.

"Okay, man. I'll let you go."

"Okay, Amar. Thanks for calling."

I shared Amar's number and the boy typed out a message to him. Then the boy looked to me and snapped his fingers near his temple.

"You're a crazy man," he said.

"I know."

"A crazy man. Crazy. Crazy."

He went uphill. A pickup stopped in front of the police car. A farmer stepped out and sold the officers dates from the bed of his truck. I could hear them talking and laughing.

"Thomas, come eat."

The boy was waving to me. The older officers were chatting with the vendor.

I joined the boy over a plate of dates that he had set on the hood of the car. The dates were sweet, and the fruit slipped from the long seeds with ease. The boy handed me a vine.

"For you."

"Thank you."

"I'm going to send a message to my friend in America, Thomas."

"That's good."

"Do you think I can get a visa to America?"

"I don't know."

"I'll message you."

"Okay."

"Inshallah I make it."

"Inshallah."

I finished a few more dates then carried the vine to my cart before walking again. The police drove beside me, and the boy leaned from the window and gave me a thumbs-up whenever I looked to him. After a few miles, I was transferred to a new escort, who drove far behind me. At the top of a bend, I came to an outcrop that overlooked the Mediterranean. I was in a daze, so I sat against a boulder, and the sea was only blue and the mountains were only red. Supposedly, on a clear day you could see France.

The new escort came over. One of them spoke pidgin English.

"How are you?" he said.

"Good. Fatigué. Resting."

"Take time."

They returned to their car and milled about without looking at me. Savannah was snoring. For half an hour, I stared at nothing.

In the mountains, there were pines and houses of unpainted concrete. The sergeant who had been with me since morning stood with his hands behind his back while I peeled a prickly pear and tossed the skin over the guardrail behind me.

"There's a hotel there?" I asked. "In Tamalous?"

"Yes."

"And I can sleep there? Dormir?"

"Yes. Dormir in Tamalous."

"You're sure?"

"Dormir in Tamalous, yes."

"Okay."

My easy stroll down Spain was a fading memory. Each day in Algeria had become a sprint between hotels. After two nights of camping, my escort decided that camping was no longer allowed, and that at the end of each day I had to be inside.

The best place to seek shelter was a youth hostel in a nearby town, but it was too early to stop. If I called it a day at one o'clock, I would have nothing to do until I fell asleep. I wouldn't even be permitted to explore town without an escort trailing me. My other option was Tamalous. Only five hours of daylight remained, and we were fifteen miles from the city, but at least I'd be occupied all day.

I opened the translator on my phone.

"I'm very tired, but I'm going to walk to Tamalous. If you see a store with Red Bull, stop!"

"Red Bull good." The sergeant pounded his chest.

In town, I found a knockoff Red Bull that was little more than sugar water with taurine, which helped me over the mountains to a plateau where walking required less fortitude and swaying fields of wheat comforted my tiring mind. The open land made me miss how camping leads each day to bleed into the next. I enjoyed a hotel for the occasional shower, but I bristled at how sleeping inside truncated my days into singular, heavy, and artificial things. I knew Savannah preferred camping, too. In a hotel room, after her initial nap, she simply waited by the door to go out into the world again.

Later in the afternoon, I was transferred to my second escort of the day and while they copied my information, I went to a café for an espresso. I bought a packaged chocolate croissant to have with my drink, then I sat across from a man outside who was tapping his wooden cane rhythmically on the ground.

"What country?" he asked.

"America," I said.

"Las Vegas."

"Philadelphia."

"Basketball."

"Rocky."

"Allen Iverson."

"You're good."

He pointed inside with his cane. "Café?" he offered.

"No, thank you. Too much."

"Here." He held out some coins.

"No, no."

He took my hand and pressed the coins into my palm. "For your café."

"You speak good English."

"Militaire."

I put a hand to my heart. "Back to the road."

I set the coins in my backpack, retrieved my passport from the escort, and returned to walking.

Hours later, as low clouds washed over the city, I arrived in Tamalous. My escort guided me to a police station near the center. The station had a thick concrete wall that isolated the building from the city around it. At the gate, twenty cops came to greet me.

"Is there a hotel?" I asked.

"No hotel in Tamalous."

"A youth hostel?"

An officer shook his head.

I was disappointed, but it was my fault that I didn't speak French or Arabic, and that I didn't take the time earlier to clarify the details of exactly what was waiting for me in Tamalous.

The captain ushered me into the station and showed me to a bench in an empty hall. The bench was metal and one of the legs was bent so the whole thing leaned forward. I could only sit on it by resting my elbows on my knees for balance.

While the police made calls in the room behind me, I dozed off and Savannah fell asleep at my feet. I'd been living espresso to espresso, hotel to hotel, for over a month. In the four days prior, we had covered a hundred and fourteen miles.

"Thomas?" A police officer stood in front of me.

"Yes."

He showed me his phone: "Relax. We will find you a place to sleep."

I gave a thumbs-up.

"You're tired."

"Very."

"It's tired." He pointed to Savannah.

"Sleeping." I pressed my hands together and placed them against my cheek.

I glanced at the man and smiled, then I rested my head in my hands and closed my eyes. I might have fallen asleep, but eventually, a few officers came to tell me they had found us a place for the night.

In a police car, I watched the city flick by. A man and his son held hands outside a café. Wet trash stuck in the gutters. The neighborhood felt distant and sitting in the car made my separation from Algeria more pronounced. With poor internet and few English speakers, I had built few deep connections.

We snaked through the city and ascended the mountain on the outskirts. Eventually, we pulled into the dirt parking lot of a mechanic shop, which had a three-car garage and a three-story home beside it. At the far end of the garage, four men bent over the open hood of a Mercedes. At the edge of the property, chickens pecked at the ground. In the middle of the clearing was a flagpole with a macaque monkey chained to the base.

When Savannah and I stepped out of the car, two mastiffs charged from the garage to bark in Savannah's face. She froze while they sniffed her, but once they were satisfied, they followed her with their tails wagging as she trotted off to explore.

After the officers and I had the wheels of my cart back on, a boy and his father came out of the house. The boy was hugging two blankets and a pillow. The father wore grease-stained khakis. He reminded me of my dad. He was tan and his hands were thick with calluses.

The father didn't speak any English or Spanish, and I didn't have reception to translate, but he smiled and led me to the garage. The monkey bounced and squealed as we passed. The men working on the Mercedes put their hands to their hearts. In the back of the garage was a small room with a rug, a table, a space heater, a wooden bar, and two tattered sofas that made me wish I had stayed at the youth hostel fifteen miles back. The father lit the space heater with a lighter and the son placed the blankets and pillow on a sofa.

"C'est bon?"

"C'est bon."

A police officer poked his head in and said something I couldn't understand, then the boy, the father, and the officer left.

Savannah curled on the carpet, and I dropped onto the sofa. Sitting there alone, it occurred to me I had no real sense of the average Algerian home. I had stayed with Amar's friend outside Algiers and with a family in Jijel, but after a month in the country I should have had a better scale to judge what sort of situation I was in. My thoughts were turning to the two women recently beheaded in Morocco. Millions of tourists visited Morocco each year and I walked the country without incident, but nonetheless, the thought persisted.

When a police officer came in and sat on the second sofa, I put pinched fingers to my mouth to ask if there was anything to eat.

"They come."

"Restaurant?"

"Food. It comes."

"Thank you."

I unpacked and tried to read, but I found it difficult to concentrate with the police officer beside me. After twenty minutes, the father entered with a baguette and clay tagine of meatball, olive, and chickpea stew.

While I ate, I noticed a stain on the concrete that looked like blood. To my left, there was a hole in the wall near the ceiling that I could use to escape if needed. I would have to push the bar against the wall to reach it, and Savannah would need to cling to me in order to climb out together, but we could manage it. If we escaped that way, there was a forest behind the house we could run into. Once I found service, I could call Amar's friend, Rachid. He was three hundred miles away in Algiers, but I was certain I could hide in the forest long enough for him to reach me.

I tapped an olive in the soup and watched it bob. I was too tired to be kept awake by thoughts of being murdered.

"Cold, isn't it?" I said to the police officer.

He cocked his head and spoke in Arabic.

I pointed to the heater. "C'est bon, no?"

He smiled.

"Je marche." I pointed to myself.

The officer nodded.

"Bon," he said.

I looked to my soup. I couldn't even manage a benign conversation to put me at ease.

When I finished eating, I set the tagine on the bar and the police officer and I sat in silence until he glanced at his watch, rubbed his hands together, and stood.

"I go."

"Okay."

I followed. He turned in the garage and held up a finger.

"No outside."

"Okay."

"Tomorrow I come."

"Okay."

He left through a flimsy plastic door. The door had metal brackets where a lock could hang so I slid a pen through the brackets to hold the door shut, but there was an entire garage door that could be opened, so it was pointless. In the smaller room, I tied my cart to the door as a makeshift lock. The door could be yanked open with enough force, but the weight of the cart would be enough to buy me a minute to reach the window and slip outside.

Behind the bar, I found a chainsaw, then I inspected the stain on the wall and discovered it wasn't blood, but oil.

Savannah watched me from the sofa. The room was warm from the heater and the warmth made me drowsy, so I laid down and pulled the blankets over me. I read *The Bone Collector* until I realized what I was doing. To put myself at ease, I put on a comedy podcast and watched the flames of the space heater until falling asleep.

In the morning, my darker thoughts held no sway. Blankets tight around me, I savored the comfort of being inside and on a sofa. After an hour of relaxation, I dressed and walked outside. It was foggy and cold. A thin frost covered the pines. Savannah went to the chicken coop to steal some food while the macaque watched.

From his house, the father emerged holding a tray of coffee, hot milk, and pastries.

"Shukran," I said.

The father touched a hand to his heart.

I wished I knew how to say more than just thank you. There were so many layers to Algeria, but I could only reach the surface.

LEAVING THE MAGHREB

After forty-five days with an escort in Algeria, I planned to walk nonstop to Tunisia's capital and catch a ferry to Sicily, but the moment I crossed the border I was overcome with the profound desire to hide from everything for a very long time. In the first town after Algeria, I booked an Airbnb for a night and the following morning I extended my reservation to two weeks.

The owner of the apartment was a middle-aged man named Akrem. He spoke English, and most nights he came to my door with a tray of tea and biscuits for conversation. On a few occasions, I joined him at a tea shop with his friends who ranted about Tunisian democracy; how it was a failure and how the Arab Spring ruined their economy by opening it to Europe.

"Before tea one-quarter dinar, now tea one dinar. Everything is two, three as much. The Arab Spring is the Tunisia Winter."

My instinct was to argue on the side of democracy, but instead, I listened. And as my conversations with Akrem and his friends progressed, I considered the many ways I was inadequate to understand their plight. I wasn't Tunisian, I didn't know their scars, or even what Tabarka's weather was like in summer. I couldn't name their old kings or place a single state on the map. I didn't know the geography, the local language, or how free trade might affect a nascent democratic movement. The only thing I knew for certain was that, at the end of each day, I was shown to be smaller than the day before.

When I began the walk, I sought to understand the world by experiencing the in-between and by allowing the world to come to me without bias. For years, this allowed my grasp of the world to expand in proportion equal to my exposure. But recently, my growth had shifted into a revealing of all the things I didn't know. The lessons I learned during my first few years of walking—people are the same everywhere, people are small, and we control little of our own lives—were now so deeply ingrained that I took them for granted. What remained to consider was the confluence of circumstances determining how any one person lives. Wandering that forest of nuance, it grew ever more apparent that I knew absolutely nothing.

Thankfully, in Tabarka at least, I had a friend to see me through, and when I finally mustered the courage to leave my modest haven, that friend saw me off.

"Where are you walking next?" Akrem asked.

"To Italy and then Croatia. My great-grandfather came to America from an island there. My family might fly out to see me. Their son will only be walking around the world once, you know?"

"I hope they visit. Family is important."

Akrem and I shook hands, hugged, then I thanked him once more for being so warm.

An hour later, I reached a police checkpoint at a fork in the road. The police copied my info and allowed me to pass, but when I looked back, I saw they were trailing me. I almost ran into the woods to escape. I couldn't take another forty-five days of eyes on my back.

But there was no need to run. The Tunisian escorts were indifferent to watching me. They followed from a distance, allowed me to camp, and never asked for a selfie. Usually, they just wanted me to walk faster so I could be passed off to the next team sooner. I was with them for a week, and when I reached Tunis, they left.

In Tunis, a young couple I met on my walk across the country served as my guides to the capital. They took me to Carthage, where I passed hours attempting to resolve one small corner of my historical ignorance. We strolled Sidi Bou Said, a culturally important village of whitewashed houses and bright blue doors. Later, we went dancing and drank until the club closed, then stumbled into a restaurant for a bowl of *lablabi* to sop up our day.

I didn't know Tunisia before the Arab Spring, Akrem might have been right that times were better then, but it seemed from my brief jaunt in his country that democracy provided something autocracies never could— freedom. Freedom to dance, freedom to voice dissent, and the freedom to hold belief without fear. This subtle yet pervasive difference hinted at something else, too—the possibility that human lives weren't solely directed by chaos and circumstance but could be shaped by systems open to progress and improvement.

The allure of Tunisia and its budding hope lingered, but our walk needed to go on. The ferry to Sicily beckoned. So, with the intent to revisit this notion in new lands of contrasting perspectives, Savannah and I set sail for Europe once more.

THE PIGEON AND THE BOAR

On our first morning in Palermo, Savannah and I found a grassy area beside Teatro Garibaldi where we could stand in the sunlight to wake up. Birds whistled from the wires, stilettos tapped the cobblestone, and children made circles on their bikes. The peace of the place washed over me—until a pair of shutters clanged open and a woman shouted.

"Luigi!"

I spun around to see a woman slapping her hands together and a man jogging across the square. The man spoke to the woman from below her third-story window, then the woman lowered a plastic bucket to him, he took some coins from it, and the woman reeled the bucket back up. In all likelihood, Luigi was fetching something ordinary like bread or a newspaper, but the scene felt like a dream. I had no idea there were people named Luigi outside of video games or that a woman could call from her third-story window with such flair.

After Palermo, I stopped to people-watch, linger by the sea, and sip cappuccinos at every opportunity. Italy's grandeur was too much for me. In most countries, even though I was a gangly white man pushing a baby carriage and walking a dog, I didn't feel out of place. There were always blue-collar workers in clothes as stained as mine, but as I made my way up Calabria, then Campania, I never felt more uncivilized. While women dressed neat as a pin and men strolled to work in tailored suits, I wore the same sun-bleached outfit and the same torn sneakers that saw me across Algeria and Tunisia. Certainly I smelled, too.

But my lack of refinement was a secondary anxiety compared to the fact that I was turning thirty. Typically, I didn't acknowledge my birthday, but I felt my thirtieth looming. Even though I was living my dream, I couldn't help but feel I was behind in life. While my friends had careers and homes, I was earning twenty thousand dollars a year and living out of a tent.

My anxiety reached its peak the day before my birthday.

Savannah and I were in Tuscany, following a hilltop road where on either side of us green valleys and hills rolled in small swells to the plains in the north. It was a stunning setting, but the only thing I could think of were the ways I failed and the lives I hadn't lived. My life with Layla had failed; I should have been with her in Colorado, skiing on the weekend and raising a family. My schooling had failed; my psychology degree was useless until I obtained a doctorate. And worst of all, I had failed my family. I should have been in Philadelphia with my parents, my sister, and my grandparents, but instead I was called to satisfy some amorphous and selfish desire to *be out there*.

At night, I camped in a shallow depression and read *Meditations*:

> *"To bear in mind constantly that all of this has happened before.*
> *And will happen again—the same plot from beginning to end,*
> *the identical staging."*

When I woke on my thirtieth, I discovered my anxiety had lifted in the night. I remembered that I had chosen the life I was living—I was in Tuscany, and I had brought myself there with my own two feet.

To the east, billowy clouds were made a fiery red by the burning sun behind them. The clouds tumbled from the mountains and splashed into a dense fog that settled over the valley and rose to my toes. Rainbows appeared and vanished like the crests of breaking waves. Soon the clouds were so thick that the distant mountains and the narrow road were the only solid things I could see. For half an hour, I watched the most beautiful sunrise I've ever seen.

Once the mist lifted and the clouds evaporated, the sky cleared to a stark blue. I looked for coffee in the first village, but there were no shops and no one on their morning stroll to ask, so I sat in the crook of a cypress tree and watched the hills. Savannah rested her head on my leg.

Another few hours on, we arrived in Bagno Vignoni. I wandered the streets in search of lunch, then stumbled upon the natural springs at the town's periphery. I met an American couple on their honeymoon there. The girl was wearing a bikini under her dress because they thought the natural springs were hot springs.

The couple directed me to the Osteria del Leone for lunch and inside I ordered pigeon, artichoke, and an espresso. I had never had pigeon: small golden wings, sweet glaze, and a meat tender and lean. There were only a few pieces, but I spent ten minutes on them. When the artichoke arrived, I scooped its center and ate it like a savory ice cream. For dessert, I took my espresso with *Meditations* while waiting for the midday sun to fade.

Down the road, in San Quirico d'Orcia, the room I reserved was in a cramped but ornate hotel.

"Your reservation is for a small room, Mr. Thomas."

"That's okay, it's just for a night."

"We have a new building on the other side of town. It's the same hotel, just newer, we opened it a year ago. If you'd like, we can upgrade you to a bigger room free of charge."

"The new hotel is in town?"

"Oh yes, down the street."

"And I won't be charged for the upgrade?"

"No. The room you reserved would be tight for you and your things, you see?"

Savannah and I found the new hotel on the other end of town and were shown to a suite that was entirely white, but with a king bed and a deep tub. After a bath, I sat around for an hour then walked to the center by way of cobblestone streets between pastel houses. I thought every part of Tuscany was busy year-round, but other than the honeymooners, I was the only tourist I'd seen.

For dinner, I ate at a restaurant in a cellar. I had four spinach and ricotta ravioli and a glass of house red, then I ambled to the piazza beside the gardens and took a seat beneath the green awning of Bar Centrale.

"Something local," I said.

The waiter poured me a splash of Tuscan wine, but I was put off by the grape juice flavor.

"Do you have anything drier?"

He returned with another Tuscan that I found equally fruity.

In France, I made it a point to try wine in every region I entered. In Bordeaux, I was hosted by a family of wine vendors and sampled an array of increasingly complex varieties of Bordeaux blends. Now, by virtue of its name, I expected a similar intensity from Tuscan wines. But upon tasting my second glass, I realized that in some ways Tuscan wine was Bordeaux's counter—rather than savory and structured, Tuscan wine was almost innocent in its modesty, fruity and approachable like a box of Welch's packed in a school lunch.

Once I understood the wine, I drank one glass after another until I was good and drunk. A handful of people were imbibing inside, a soccer match was on, but I was the only person in the piazza. It was still cold. I watched a few locals walk home and listened to a man humming as he went.

Around ten, I stumbled back to the hotel playing Dean Martin on my phone.

I barely had an income, just enough for food and the occasional room, but I possessed time in abundance and most days that was a wealth beyond dreams.

I never enjoyed sleeping on someone else's land, but I had little choice. Under the pale light of a crescent moon, I turned from the road and into an olive grove. The trees were old and the branches were clipped to form a wide canopy. To the north the trees carried into the dark, but to the west was a highway and I could hear its thrum. It wasn't the perfect campsite. There was no hiding, no tucking away my tent, but I only needed to sleep for nine hours, and I would be on my way.

For a little while, I followed the olive trees into the dark and away from the provincial road, but I discovered tire tracks that became heavier and more numerous, so I doubled back in fear of approaching someone's home. On the grass beside the fence that separated the olive grove and the street, I set my tent. The fence was overgrown with vines, but the vines were thin and did little to conceal me. When a passing car illuminated my camp, I was certain the driver spotted my tent.

For dinner, I ate another heavenly meal of fresh casarecce and ragu cooked on my stove. Each day, I bought fresh pasta from the supermarket and each night I wished I had bought more. Once I finished, I used my finger to clean the side of my pot.

Savannah came over for her nightly dental chew then ran with it to the base of the nearest tree. As I watched her eat, I heard a distant grunt from somewhere in the grove. I stayed still to listen, and thought of turning on my headlamp to peer down the aisle of trees but decided against it. Instead, I went to Savannah and stared into the grove and listened. I could see as far as twenty trees. They were far apart, and the grass was white from the moon, but beyond that, the world was dim.

After five minutes of no sound, Savannah and I returned to camp and went to sleep.

In the night, I woke with a jolt of adrenaline. Savannah was growling at something huffing outside. I found my knife, held Savannah's collar to keep her from charging, then unzipped the tent. Five feet away, backlit by the moon, was a massive, hairy, blade-tusked boar. The boar didn't move to acknowledge us, but it huffed low and then high like it was whining. If it decided to charge into the tent, there was nothing Savannah and I could do to escape. I couldn't reach my cart to block it, and my four-inch knife might not even break its thick hide.

Over my months of walking in Europe, I had become adept at avoiding where boars slept. In France, after waking in a field surrounded by two hundred boars that scattered the moment I opened my tent, I learned how they tilled the land to make their bed and I never forgot it. After that, there were occasions when I walked away from an otherwise good campsite because I recognized the familiar pattern in the earth.

But I had seen no sign of boars in the olive grove, and this was the only time I'd seen a single boar on its own. They always gathered in sounders.

The boar turned its head. Its tusk was stained and curled. Its small eyes were a glint. I pulled Savannah closer because the boar seemed ready to charge, but instead it squealed and shot away from us into the darkness.

I stepped outside and swept the light of my headlamp over the grove. Savannah stood tall beside me. I could see no other boars.

"Good job, baby girl."

I gave Savannah a pat on the head, then I closed my knife and tossed it into the tent. Then I wheeled my cart in front of the vestibule as a meager form of protection.

"Come on, Sav."

I climbed inside and into my sleeping bag.

Savannah stayed beside the cart, watching.

"Savannah, come on. Get inside."

She didn't acknowledge me.

"Savannah," I said more sternly.

Her ears flicked back momentarily, but then returned to face the grove. While she sniffed the air, I shut the tent and fell back to sleep. In the morning, she was in the same spot I left her.

THE FAMILY FROM KRK

Savannah stood on her hind legs to look over the balcony. I could hear my dad's voice echoing through the walled city but I couldn't yet see him.

"Savannah!" he called musically.

Savannah yipped, then began barking and wouldn't quit. She turned to me, then peered over the balcony again. When my parents and Lexi finally came into view, I went to the stairwell and jogged down with Savannah to the patio entrance. I opened the door and Savannah ran to the only people that she'd lived with for longer than a month other than me.

She jumped and squirmed between their legs. She whined and bounced and rolled over to paw the air. I hugged everyone between the moments they weren't showering Savannah with affection.

"Flight wasn't too bad?" I asked.

"Dad was losing it, but no, not too bad."

"You know how he gets with all those people around," my mom said.

"What do you want me to do? I can't hear anything in there. It drives me crazy. And anyway, we made it. We're in Croatia with our boy."

"Welcome to the motherland. Are you hungry? Did you eat?"

"Checked into our rooms and came straight over."

"Perfect. I'm sure we can find somewhere that's still open."

I clipped on Savannah's leash and gave it to my dad. Savannah yanked his arm. We walked a few minutes through the narrow Zadar alleyways until we found a restaurant with a wooden table outside. The owner said they were closing, but that he would stay to serve us. Savannah sat beneath the table and poked her head through everyone's legs. We ordered calamari, monkfish, white fish, and a bottle of Plavac Mali. Lexi told us about moving to Denver and how she was glad to escape the small resentments that had built up over the years between her and her friends. I caught my family up on everything that had happened since I last saw them. I told them how Fitz visited me in Florence, how I saw Da Vinci's *Vitruvian Man* in Venice, and how our cousins on the island Krk were excited to meet them. My dad couldn't wait. For most of his life, it was his dream to see his grandfather's home and the island we came from.

After two nights in Zadar, we drove to Krk. For me, it was backtracking. I stayed on Krk for a month with Ernest and Margaret, family who had a home near the center of the island. Over that month I met every cousin in the area but spent most of my time with Smiljana, Edi, and their girls, Ema and Andrea. Smiljana and Edi lived in Rijeka, the city across the water.

On Krk, my dad woke early to take a walk and see as much of the island as possible before everyone else was awake. Once he found a guidebook about the stonework on Krk, he started pointing out what he learned when we were out exploring.

"The holes on the second story were for curing sausage too high to steal."

"The stone at the base is so carriages don't crash into the house while rounding the corner."

His favorite moment, other than visiting family, was when we stumbled across a fourth-century church during a walk in the woods.

"The fourth century!" he kept saying. "Sitting in the middle of the forest like it's nothing."

One afternoon, Smiljana told us there was a cemetery where most of the Turcich relatives were buried so we made our way to it by following a back road on the west side of the island. It took us a long time to find the place, but eventually, at the end of a dirt lane, we came to a stone church with a bell tower high above the trees.

Behind the church were a hundred burial plots bordered by an iron fence. The plots were familial and the headstones were marked by black-and-white portraits. There was MARAČIĆ, ŽGOMBIĆ, BOGOVIĆ, and on about a third of the headstones was TURČIĆ.

"Crazy," my dad said in a low voice.

My parents and Lexi made a slow lap around the cemetery then went to the steps out front to rest in the shade. I lingered a little longer, crouching before a headstone with a hand on the raised bed where weeds burst through the soil. I couldn't take my eyes off the name.

In Ireland, I wasn't capable of fully appreciating my connection to the place. Although I visited my great-grandfather Andrew's home and stayed with relatives across the island, the place was too alive for me to feel my ancestral roots. But now, gazing upon the name TURČIĆ carved in stone, it was as though everything I'd been told about my family was verified. My ancestors were real. I had come from this island.

The next day, we met cousins at a restaurant in Dobrinj—a hilltop village with views of the Adriatic. Smiljana, Edi, and the girls were there, as were Uncle Ivica, Aunt Katica, and cousins Ivana, Lucija, Igor, Mia, and Dora. We occupied two tables aside the piazza. Zora was one of the few restaurants that made traditional *šurlice*, a Krk pasta tediously crafted by coiling each piece of dough around a wooden stick then dousing the finished pasta in a beef goulash.

"What do you think of your motherland?" Smiljana asked my dad.

"It explains why we were raised on a river and why my dad was in the Coast Guard."

From lunch we drove to Gostinjac, the village beside Dobrinj, where my great-aunt Dusica and her husband lived. Dusica had a garden that wrapped around her house, and in the back, she had a small farm with corn and chickens.

"She's the toughest woman you'll meet," Smiljana told me as we approached. "She runs the whole place by herself. She used to have goats, chickens, potatoes, and just about everything else, but Nikola fell sick and taking care of him has taken up most of her time. Nikola was strong in his day, but he's almost ninety."

The cousins descended on Dusica's home like a swarm. In her basement, Dusica pointed to the bottles of homemade rakija and the hocks of prosciutto she'd hung to cure. I took a swig from one of the wicker-covered bottles and thought I ingested gasoline. Lexi was in tears with laughter.

"Why would she keep gasoline in there?" she said.

"I don't know, but that can't be drinkable."

After showing us her home, Dusica led us across the street and down a narrow stone-walled lane. At a bend, we came to the gate entrance of two stone houses.

"Your great-grandfather Anthony's home," said Smiljana. "The one further away. The family used to own the land, but it's not ours anymore. Someone remodeled it recently."

"It's in good shape."

"Dusica says it's a young doctor and his family."

We took the lane a little further and it tightened between the walls until we stopped at another stone house that was only three walls and a caved-in roof. A mound of stones was set beside the house as though the missing wall had been dismantled piece by piece.

"This was your great-great-grandfather's home."

I couldn't see much of it because the bushes were so overgrown.

"Gives you an appreciation for your ancestors, doesn't it?" said my dad. "How anyone managed to live here, I don't know."

"It's no wonder they came to America."

"And on the back of a pamphlet. We wouldn't be here if they hadn't."

At that moment, I wondered if my need for adventure came from my dad, or if it had been in our blood for generations. Maybe Anthony and his brothers didn't leave Krk because it was a barren island of stone and a pamphlet promised more in America; maybe they left simply for the adventure of leaving. Maybe we had both left in order to satisfy that innate need to reach into the unknown. Whatever the motivation, Anthony was successful. He made it to America. He built a life in Philadelphia and his progeny multiplied into the hundreds.

After a week on Krk, my parents and Lexi returned Savannah and me to Zadar. On our final afternoon together, we hired a boat to take us onto the water to watch the sunset. Alfred Hitchcock called Zadar's sunset the best in the world. When we came to a stop, I jumped off the side and swam out. When I was far enough away, I looked back to the boat. My dad was talking to the captain, Savannah was watching me from the stern, my mom and sister were chatting on the bow. The sunset was nearly green in the haze. I thought of my great-grandfather, Anthony—how by leaving Croatia he brought us back to it.

TURKISH WEDDING

I entered Turkey beside a Brit named David, who was loaded like a mule on a pilgrimage to Jerusalem. We met on the back roads of Greece, then again at the Turkish border. Turkey's flag, particularly the star and crescent, gave me flashbacks to my escorts across North Africa, but after David and I paid for our visas at the immigration office, we strolled into Turkey with no one on our trail. At the first hotel beyond the border, David and I shared dinner and a few beers, then parted ways in the morning. David was walking to Istanbul along the coast, and I was headed there by looping north, where I hoped it would be more peaceful.

After two days on the northern plains, I arrived in Süleymaniye, a terracotta village that rested on a yellow hilltop like a fez. At a *çay* shop near the center, I parked my cart by the concrete wall and took a seat in the corner. Savannah tucked herself behind my feet. The dozen men at the shop watched until I was settled, then resumed their chatter.

The untamed heat that followed Savannah and me through Croatia, Montenegro, Albania, and Greece had broken, but it was still too hot to walk midday. I planned on having twenty teas over two hours to take advantage of the shade. After my second tea, the man beside me slid his chair closer and stuck out a hand.

"Vedat," he said.

"Thomas."

Vedat typed into the translator on his phone. I looked around. The men were well-dressed—suits, vests, and flat caps. Vedat was in a green and black plaid shirt tucked into his jeans. His face was flat with a sharp nose and brows that cast a shadow over his eyes. I waited until he rotated his phone to me.

"Where are you from?"

"America."

I typed in my translator.

"I walked from Denmark. I'm walking to Mongolia. I've been walking for four years."

Vedat curled over his phone. "What brings you to Süleymaniye?"

"It's the quieter way to Istanbul. It's more peaceful than the coast."

"It is peaceful and beautiful here."

Upon noticing the difficulty with which Vedat typed each response, we switched to using the voice translator on my phone and our conversation hastened.

"Is everyone resting or is everyone retired?" I asked.

"Everyone is retired. I'm retired. We were farmers. We come here in the morning, return home for lunch, then return to the tea shop until dinner."

"The ringing of the spoons is beautiful. When did you retire?"

"I retired only two years ago, but my wife makes brooms and tomato sauce. I worked in the field since I was a boy. It's beautiful here, but there are no jobs. Every year, the land is bigger and there are fewer jobs. All the young people go to Istanbul. When my sons are grown, they won't be farmers. Süleymaniye is old now."

He gestured to the retirees playing dominos and the unhurried movements of town. The wall separating the patio from the street had seating like a bar. There were stools and men leaned on the wall to gaze down the street. A shepherd, his dogs, and his flock walked by. The Anatolian shepherds wore spiked collars to protect their necks during wolf attacks. A few sheep had bells. The shepherd stopped to speak with someone at the bar, then ran to catch his flock that had continued walking without him.

"Do you want to have lunch at my house?"

Vedat and I had been speaking for half an hour. It was nearly one, and I didn't care to resume walking just yet. During the long summer days, I had developed the habit of taking a midday nap in the arm of some shady tree. I was loath to miss that, but even if I had lunch with Vedat, there would still be time to reach my imagined quota for the day. And anyway, what good was my adventure if I didn't have lunch with a local when offered?

"Where do you live?"

Vedat pointed to a square white house across the street.

Tied to the gate of Vedat's rutty driveway, a scrawny white dog squirmed and barked at the sight of Savannah. Savannah darted by it along the wall. In the backyard, which was also the front yard, there was a trailer overflowing with dried sorghum and brooms at varying levels of completion in neat rows on the dirt. I parked my cart in the shade of the awning and tied Savannah to it, then I took off my shoes and followed Vedat inside.

He brought me to the living room, where I sat and enjoyed the cold air. After a few minutes, Vedat returned with his family—two boys and his wife. I stood to greet everyone. The boys, seven and sixteen, were copies of Vedat, thin and sharp. His wife was tan and demure. She shook my hand and smiled, but left immediately after.

I helped Vedat unfold a plastic table, then we sat across from each other and his wife laid out a meal of yogurt, tomatoes, white cheese, lentil soup, and sausage. I placed my phone between us, and we spoke as we ate. His father and his grandfather had been farmers, but Vedat said Süleymaniye would be gone in fifty years because there were no farmers anymore.

After lunch, we sat outside on the sofa and looked to his yard. I was squeezed between the youngest son and him. The air was hard, but in the shade it was cool.

"There's a wedding in town this evening," Vedat said through his phone. "It's between two families from the neighboring village. You can come as my guest."

"What time is the wedding?"

"Seven. It will go into the night. You can sleep in the living room."

"Can I give you an answer in a bit? I haven't walked far today. I feel bad about that."

"Of course."

Over the wall were golden hills and the occasional tractor pulling a cloud of dust. The tractors hauled a type of honeydew whose rinds were yellow and mottled with green. The day before, a farmer had given me a melon and I ate half of it as a dessert in the evening.

In our silence, I fell asleep. When I woke, the shade was touching the edge of the patio and Vedat's wife was peeling tomatoes into a large bucket. I didn't feel like walking anymore.

"I'd love to stay for the wedding," I said. "Thank you for inviting me."

We sat without saying a word and the hours fell by unnoticed. The youngest son sat beside me with a stillness equal only to his father. Their eyes were calm like they had absorbed the patient rhythm of the land.

At sunset, Vedat and I left for the wedding.

Processions of people were winding through town, converging at a bend where two roads became one. We joined them and Vedat spoke with everyone, and each person shook my hand and touched their hands to their hearts. On a back road, we reached the entrance of the wedding where a man sat at a table handing out plates. Vedat paid for me without me realizing it. He handed me a paper plate, and we went to where workers were portioning out meals of rice, goulash, soup, and beans. With our plates full, we walked toward the sun falling over four rows of tables in a field. There were a hundred men and no women.

"The women are uphill," my neighbor to my right told me after Vedat and I sat down. "The men and women will be joined later. The bride and groom will dance, then the immediate family, then the cousins, then the close friends, then the friends, and then everyone."

"But they're dancing already." I pointed to two lubricated old men snapping and bobbing to the music.

"God willing that will be us all."

Between the tables, lights were strung on tall sticks. I left for a moment to buy Vedat and me an Efes from the bar. When I returned, the men asked about my journey. There were no young people. I asked the men about Süleymaniye and their farming, and they agreed that it was doomed but that it was okay because their children were in the city living different lives.

After a few hours of drinking, we were summoned uphill. Vedat and I joined the back of the crowd and followed it to a clearing with chairs and lights strung above. At the center of the clearing, the bride and groom were dancing. Behind them, I could see the altar. Apparently they were already married, and we were well into the celebration. Just as my neighbor said, the crowd of welcome dancers grew one notch at a time. People put their arms around each other and whirled in great circles; sometimes a man showed off in the middle. An hour passed but I still wasn't permitted to join. By midnight, I was tired. I told Vedat I would head to his home and sleep. Vedat told his wife that he would walk with me then return.

In Vedat's yard, I unhooked Savannah's leash and she jumped against my legs to say hello, then ran to the door to be let in.

"The sofa in the living room is comfortable. You can sleep there. My wife and I will be back soon."

"Thank you so much. Is Savannah allowed inside?"

"No dogs are allowed inside."

"She won't do anything. She's slept in a hundred hotels, and she's never done anything. I can make sure she sleeps on the floor."

"In our culture it isn't permitted."

"Okay. I'll sleep on the sofa outside with her."

"You should sleep inside."

"I promised myself I would always sleep where Savannah sleeps."

"Won't you be cold?

"No, no. I sleep outside every night. It'll be nice on the sofa."

"As long as you'll be comfortable."

"Thank you, Vedat."

We shook hands then Vedat returned to the wedding. Savannah continued to stare at the door.

"Not tonight, baby girl. Come here."

Savannah glanced at me but didn't move. In my cart I found my sleeping bag and the clothing bag I used as a pillow. I lay on the sofa, but my legs hung off it, so I switched to one of the recliners and lowered it until it was parallel to the ground.

"Savannah, come here."

Reluctantly, she left the door and came to my side. I reached over and picked her up, then I shifted to the side so she could lie with her head on my chest. In the middle of the night, a drunk stumbled into Vedat's backyard and peed on the wall until he noticed me. He apologized and walked off.

The occasional boar, the curious landowner, or the bumbling drunk might stir me awake, but I had yet to be woken by anything malicious. That fact was wearing deep into me. With each passing night, I slept better than the night before.

THE LIGHTS OF TBILISI

Tbilisi was beautiful, especially from the hillside. Its purple and blue lights winked in the bright evening air, but the members of parliament took no notice. They were busy chain-smoking and celebrating the protests that ended in their favor. Three months before, I had seen the start of the protests, but then returned to the States to secure a Kazakh visa extension and work with the Uzbek consulate to place two visas back-to-back. Winter and the protests were over now, though, and it was almost time to return to the road. After a few months of relative relaxation, I dreaded beginning again, but it was February of a new year—2020—and Savannah and I needed to start our sprint to Mongolia. Each day in comfort was another day lost.

My host, Ika, tapped me on the arm.

"Tom, do you want some wine?"

"Sorry, yes. That would be great. Thank you."

"Red? Orange?"

"Red is perfect, thank you."

Ika found an open bottle of wine and poured me a glass.

"Only you and Giga don't smoke," I said.

"We used to. Georgians love their cigarettes."

Ika and her husband Giga had a second home in London. Their English was flawless.

"Come. Let's join them. We don't have to smoke to enjoy the night."

Ika and I stepped out to the patio and space was made for us in the circle. Everyone was speaking Georgian, so I smiled and tried to stay interested in what I didn't understand.

Two of the PMs were baby-faced. A third had the scowl of a Soviet intellectual. There were two journalists, too: one was beautiful and quiet, holding their cigarette like a secret; the second was older but had infinite energy and spoke without breathing.

Ika's husband, Giga, stood across from me. The lights of the city were reflected in his glasses. He gazed at a table as though he wasn't listening. I'd only spent a few weeks with him, but few people I met on the walk changed me more. He was raised in Soviet Georgia and after the fall of the Soviet Union, he studied business at Berkeley. Since then, he had worked as the economic advisor to the Georgian president, served on the board of multiple companies, and taught finance at the best university in the country. By talking with him, it became clear that he had a fundamental understanding of the world that I was lacking.

During my stay, I probed him with questions, hoping for an answer that would permanently make me more effective in navigating life, but instead he introduced me to a methodical and highly capitalistic thought process. His disdain for communism was as apparent as his reverence for the free market—his dog was named Milton after the economist Milton Friedman.

"And what do you think of all this, Tom?"

At the sound of English, I saw Giga smirking, and I became aware of everyone looking at me.

"I agree with everyone completely."

"It's just that we're speaking in such details," said the older journalist. "It would be too difficult in English."

"It's no trouble. I'm the foreigner. I don't mind."

Gradually, the group returned to speaking their native tongue. I stood with them for a while, but when my glass was empty, I went inside to fill it. As I stood beside the many bottles of local wine, I calculated how long it would take to cross Azerbaijan—two hundred and fifty miles from the Georgian border to the Azeri port to catch a ferry that would take us to Kazakhstan. At twenty-four miles a day, that was ten days, but Savannah and I would follow the scenic roads. That would add three days, and with a day of rest, it would probably take us two weeks to reach the ferry.

If I wanted to beat winter to Ulaanbaatar, I needed to walk the next seven months with the same speed I had walked the Americas. If everything went well, I would ferry from Azerbaijan to Kazakhstan, cross a stretch of Kazakh desert to Uzbekistan, cross a larger stretch of desert through Uzbekistan, climb the Kyrgyz mountains, descend to the Kazakh plains, walk north to Russia, wrangle a transit visa to Mongolia, meet an as-of-yet un-hired Mongolian guide, then sprint across one of the least populated landmasses on earth before winter set in.

My plan was tenuous at best. Something would go wrong—I would get sick, have trouble finding a guide, a cart axle would break, or I might get stuck at a border. Unless everything went perfectly, I wouldn't have enough time to reach Ulaanbaatar before winter. Still, I'd walk as far as I could as quickly as possible and that was the best I could do.

"I hear you're on a long walk."

The Soviet-looking parliament member interrupted my thoughts and filled his glass with *qvevri*—an orange wine made in terracotta pots buried to the snout to ferment.

"Oh yes, with that one over there." I pointed to Savannah walking with Milton on the lawn.

"Zurab." He held out his hand.

"Tom," I replied. "Congratulations on your victory."

He nodded and took a sip.

"So, what does it mean? Giga explained it to me, but I'm not sure I grasp what you won exactly. The constitution was written so the president appoints a third of the parliament, right?"

"Correct."

"But now that third will be voted on by the constituents."

"Correct. Georgia is a parliamentary republic. In theory, power rests with the parliament, but because a third of the parliament was appointed by the president, it meant that whichever party won the presidency in effect won the parliament. It also meant a large percentage of our population was having their representative selected for them, and how can a democracy function if the people's representatives aren't accountable to the people?"

"No, of course."

"Giga told me you saw the protests when you were here in December. We have a more representative democracy because of them. You witnessed change."

"And an oligarch losing power."

I gestured to the glass castle of Ivanishvili that loomed over the historic district of hot baths from which Tbilisi derived its name.

"Yes, well, the press did a wonderful job putting pressure on the government."

Zurab unbuttoned his suit jacket.

"I was thinking earlier that you look very Russian," I said. "More Russian than most."

"Do I? My politics would say otherwise."

"To be fair, I've never been to Russia. Maybe you just look like the movie version of a Russian."

"Ideas hold up better than men, anyhow."

"But you were saying . . ."

"Yes, I wrote an op-ed recently on the three things needed to topple a democracy." Zurab held up his fingers to count. "The courts must be corrupted. There will be political prisoners taken. And lastly—" He pointed to the journalists outside. "There must be control of the media. Courts, political prisoners, and the press. The first two happened."

"There were political prisoners here?"

"Yes, of course.

"I mean, members of parliament were actually thrown in jail? How does that happen?"

"By replacing independent judges with party-line judges then creating some trumped-up charges. It was almost enough to entrench Ivanishvili as prime minister, but our press did fine work. Or perhaps Ivanishvili underestimated them. Either way, our press is the only reason Ivanishvili wasn't able to take control. The press remained independent, they did honest journaling, and he was voted out."

"And he's out of power entirely now, isn't he?"

"Technically, yes, but he still has sway in the ruling party. His net worth is a third of Georgia's GDP."

"Every time I take Savannah and Milton for a walk I wonder why he built such a monstrosity."

"I've always thought it looked like a spaceship."

"He chose a terrible location. All that money and he put his house behind the hills. Ika and Giga chose much better. This is the best view of any city I've ever seen. Even better than the restaurants above the river."

"They were thoughtful."

Zurab had a manner of speaking that made you feel as though he believed your potential was both unlimited and yet never considered because he was already satisfied with who you were.

"And when are you starting your walk again, Tom?"

"Tomorrow. To be honest, I'm a bit distracted because of it. I always hate leaving. I used to really work myself up over it. In Central America, I had to meditate for twenty minutes before I could bring myself to leave the hotels. I know I'll love it once I'm out there again, but it's never easy to leave a comfortable place."

"Well, that's to be expected, isn't it? I'm sure you've left comfortable places before, though. What did you study? Did you go to school?"

"Psychology and philosophy."

"Those must be useful in meeting as many people as you do."

The others came in from the deck.

"Shall we eat?" Giga asked rhetorically as he took a seat.

Zurab and I joined the others at a table overflowing with traditional Georgian dishes. There was so much food that a side table was needed to hold everything.

I hadn't eaten for most of the day, so I dug in. Everyone was speaking Georgian, so there wasn't much else to do. I slathered a slice of *khachapuri* with *phkali*—an oily walnut spread—then I ladled myself a bowl of beef *kharcho* and dipped my khachapuri in it. I ate a few *dolmas*, took careful bites of *khinkali*, and between it all I worked on an endless flow of wine to drown my nerves. After a while, Ika started a conversation with me out of civility.

"How are you feeling about things, Tom? Are you ready to begin again?"

"Oh, yes." I was speaking to Ika, Zurab, and Zurab's wife whose name I hadn't caught. The other end of the table was occupied by a debate, so the four of us huddled together to hear one another.

"But it's difficult to leave. You and Giga have been wonderful. I love Georgia, too. I would move here if I could. I don't know if you realize this, but Georgians have a great sense of ambiance. That might be what I look for most in a country. Not every country has it. Colombia, Denmark, Italy, Algeria—the people have an understanding of what a place should feel like. Everything is taken into account and balanced: the music, the colors, the food, the conversation. Georgia is that way, too. It makes a country seem like it knows who it is."

"You should have been here before the smoking bans. There was no ambiance then."

"Tom's a photographer as well," said Ika. "He's working on a wonderful book."

Ika found the photography book I'd given them and handed it to Zurab. He withdrew his reading glasses to look it over. Ika smiled to me. I leaned back and looked beyond her to the city. For a moment, I saw Savannah chasing Milton.

ATTACK IN THE MOUNTAINS

It was cold enough that I slept with my beanie on and my sleeping bag pulled over my head, and in the morning, I could see my breath. As Savannah finished her breakfast, I leaned against a pine and gazed at the coal fires burning in the town below. A few hundred years before, the land was a desert. The temperatures still rose to unbearable highs in the summer, but forestation and agriculture had tamed the region's harshest impulses. A smattering of villages carried to the horizon—cinder blocks, tin roofs, and aboveground piping on every street.

I felt a paw on my calf and turned to see Savannah looking up at me. "You have a good meal?"

I reached to pet her, but she ducked, barked, spun in a circle, then darted away. Chased by an imaginary predator, she zipped between the trees.

An hour later, the muscles in my upper back were tense and my calves strained as Savannah and I pushed into the clouds one switchback at a time. My lungs burned as I heaved in the cold air. Eventually, the fog grew so thick that I could only see a few feet ahead of me.

Somewhere in the clouds I spotted three men crouched in the forest around a glowing samovar. The red light of the coals made them silhouettes. A stray dog fled with its tail between its legs when it spotted Savannah. Then one of the men called out, but with my buff tucked over my face and my hood up, I could barely hear.

"Baku!" I said, neither hearing the question nor understanding Azeri.

A man stood from the samovar and so I waited for him. As he approached, I worked out that he was a laborer. They were building a home or a restaurant. He spoke to me in Azeri.

"I don't know. English," I said. "Español."

"Baki," the man said, making an "X" with his arms.

"Closed? Cerrado?"

"Baki." He made the "X" again.

"Thank you."

"Today. No Baki." He wagged a finger.

After Savannah and I left Tbilisi, a lethal virus had caused Milan's hospitals to buckle under the weight of an unsustainable volume of patients. The virus was hitting the United States, too, but there were only a few cases in the Caucasus, and even if Baku was closed, it didn't affect my plans. Kazakhstan remained open, and I was five days from the ferry. Reaching the next country on my route was the only thing on my mind.

Savannah and I pressed on. We were practically running when a German shepherd materialized from the fog and charged at Savannah. After a thousand encounters, reading and fending off strays was my most developed skill. In a moment, I could assess a dog's intention and divine the best way to deal with it. Savannah spun behind me, and I pulled the leash to keep her close. Before the German shepherd got to her, I put my foot to its neck and held it back. With a few seconds to process, I realized the dog was friendly—its tail was wagging, and it was well-groomed and collared. A man appeared a few feet away and waved, then he called the dog and they disappeared.

Bundled as I was, I couldn't tell how much time had passed, but when the fog lifted, it happened in an instant. Suddenly, the world was green and bucolic, and it felt as though I were coming out of a dream. The road curved down to the left and ahead of us two men worked on the tin roof of a restaurant surrounded by a dewy pasture.

As we followed the bend, sunlight fell on my face. I unzipped my jacket and let my hood down.

Across the street, a hundred-and-twenty-pound Anatolian Shepherd, a kangal, stormed onto the road. A long, broken chain attached to its neck rattled on the asphalt. It was obvious that the kangal was aggressive, so I bent over the guardrail to my left and grabbed two good stones.

"Okay, Sav."

I wrapped her leash tight around my hand.

"We have to go slowly."

Most seemingly vicious dogs I came across were actually small and scared. Only a few times on my walk did I encounter a stray whose primary emotion was hate and not fear. This kangal was one of them. I wondered if it was a fighting dog. I could see in its eyes that if I gave it a chance, it would tear off my leg and kill Savannah.

The kangal edged closer and barked rhythmically like a war drum. I pretended to pick up a stone at my foot, but that only made the kangal bark louder and pounce forward on its front paws. Savannah was pulling wildly, digging her nails into the street, so I held her with equal force to keep us moving a half step at a time. Below the guardrail was a steep drop to the forest—there was no way out except on the other side of the kangal's territory.

When the kangal was close enough that it only needed two pounces to be at my leg, my focus trained on its teeth. It bore them with malice. I needed a car to pass to scare it and put some space between us. The stones I held were bluster. I knew that even if I hit the kangal square in the jaw, it would only serve as fuel. If the dog charged, I'd have a small window to kick it and kick it well; I'd have to hit it under the chin to knock it off balance and give myself enough time to reset.

Savannah and I inched our way down the road until we were opposite the shack across the street where the kangal first emerged and was most likely guarding. If that was correct, then we were almost to safety.

But the dog grew more confident. It strode forward until it was three feet away. I could see the skin above its snout wrinkle as it snarled; its gums and teeth glistened with perfect clarity. Suddenly, it lunged, snapping at the air in front of my ankle. I nearly kicked, but resisted instead, not wanting to expose myself or incite the dog further.

The kangal drew back, then lunged again. As its jaws clamped down inches from my shin, the severity of my situation hit home—I had years of experience fending off strays, but no framework for fighting one, especially not one nearly as large as myself. That realization came with a shock of adrenaline—a change that emanated from my chest and warmed my ears. Suddenly, I saw the kangal in slow motion, how when it pulled back from its lunge, it settled on its hind legs and was still for a moment. I had an opening to throw a stone, but I refrained.

Instead, I remembered toward the beginning of the walk when I was attacked by two dogs. They were the first aggressive dogs I encountered, and the only thing I could think to do was circle my cart until I was away from them. Since then, I had developed more effective strategies: flicking dirt backward with my foot, stomping in their direction. I could even cause strays to backpedal by standing in a dominant way. After that first encounter, I rarely needed to use my cart as a barrier. Now it seemed the only option.

As I stepped to the side of the cart, the kangal lunged and caught my heel. It thrashed and twisted its head, tearing a chunk of foam from my shoe. I spun, so I was facing the dog and walking backward again.

The kangal adjusted and snarled but seemed reluctant to attack in the narrow space between my cart and guardrail. When a car finally passed, the dog cowered, and Savannah and I were able to put some distance between ourselves and our attacker.

The kangal barked once more but halted its pursuit.

Down the road, once I was certain we were safe, I flung the stones into the forest.

Savannah was still pulling on my arm, so I yanked her back.

"Savannah!" I screamed.

She looked up at me with her ears pinned back.

"Sorry. I'm sorry, baby girl. I'm sorry."

I bent down and brought her over to me. She put her head against my chest.

"You did a good job. . . . You did a good job, Savannah."

I held her by the cheeks and kissed her forehead. My heart was still thumping.

We walked an hour more until we reached a restaurant at the end of town, where my exhaustion caught up with me.

A man in a suit greeted me at the door.

"Salaam."

"Salaam."

"Do you have food?" I put my fingers to my mouth.

"Of course. What would you like?"

"You speak English."

"More Russian and Turkish. And Arabic very nicely."

"Lots of languages."

"That yours?" He pointed to Savannah tied to the cart.

"That's my girl. From Texas."

"America?"

"Yes, sir."

"Come, come."

I followed him to the kitchen. He opened a freezer and pointed to my options.

"Chicken, kebab, lamb."

The chicken was resting in its own juices, so I pointed to the kebabs in a different compartment.

"How many?"

"Three. And some vegetables, and a coffee, please."

"Very good. Please, have a seat."

I went to the back corner, nodding to a group of men who looked at me as I passed. When I sat down, relief found me. There was no wind or fog or pursuing dogs. It was warm inside. My fingers stung as they came back from the cold. The owner placed a cup of Nescafé in front of me, and I wrapped my hands around it.

"Very cold, today," he said.

"It is. Too cold. Can I have three pieces of lamb as well? The ones with the bone."

"Three kebabs and three pieces of lamb."

"The lamb is for my dog."

"Very good. No problem. Three kebabs and three pieces of lamb."

The owner went off. I looked down at the chunk missing from the back of my shoe, then to Savannah gazing through the window at me.

I could keep our things well-maintained, my socks dry, our tent neatly folded, and I could choose quiet roads to walk and usually the right people to trust, but no matter how adept I became at navigating the world on foot, a certain level of randomness was unavoidable. It was a challenge inherent to the adventure but also the beauty of it. The world contained forces greater than our intention. Savannah and I were specks of dust with a trillion unknown actors spiraling around us. Sometimes that meant encountering a Turkish wedding, other times it meant fending off an aggressive dog. I couldn't control what we met, only how we met it.

THE CLOSING OF
THE WORLD

Pigs sank in the mud and men in wool coats negotiated terms in the rain. Beyond the open-air auction, a pack of dogs climbed over the road and surrounded me and Savannah. I threw stones at the road in front of them until I could manage a way through. Further up the road, I found a boulder to rest against. In the valley below, a man surveyed a vineyard with his Jack Russell. I pulled out my phone and scrolled until I saw a message from a follower that said the Kazakhstan border had closed. The embassy website confirmed he was right; the borders had been closed for three days.

Suddenly and forebodingly, the wind picked up and the rain turned cold. I shivered, rubbed my hands together, then warmed them with my breath. With the Kazakh borders closed until at least April 15th, every country bordering Azerbaijan was now shut and I had no way to leave, despite my visa expiring in two weeks.

"All right, Savannah," I said. "May as well get out of the rain."

We turned back and followed the same road we ascended, returning to the hotel at the last roundabout of Shamakhi. The front desk was empty, so I sprayed the dirt from my tires with a hose outside, then I dragged my cart upstairs and down the hall to the room I had occupied the night before.

After Savannah and I were cleaned up, I decided to get something to eat at the kebab shop below the hotel. The restaurant wasn't much larger than a walk-in closet. Against the far wall, a man slouched on a battered sofa and tapped out a message on his flip phone. Another man, who was missing his front tooth, smiled to me as he cleaned the counter. The kebab roasting on the spit behind him had clearly defined layers, so I knew it was authentic.

"Two, thank you," I said in Russian.

"Coronavirus," he said in English, looking back at me as he carved the kebab.

"Coronavirus," I agreed.

"Closed. Baki. Closed. Azerbaijan closed."

"Kazakhstan and Georgia, too."

"Tomorrow closed. Tomorrow everything closed."

"Coronavirus?"

"Nowruz."

He pointed out the window to the flame statue at the center of the roundabout.

"Clean. Everyone clean."

I nodded, unsure of what to make of what he was saying. I paid 150 *manat*, then left with the sandwiches. The owner followed me outside and pointed to the flame statue again.

"Nowruz," he said.

"What is that?"

The rain had slowed to a drizzle. A man in blue jeans and a denim jacket was leaning against the wall smoking a cigarette.

"Where are you from?" he asked in English with an American accent.

"America. What is that he's saying?"

"Nowruz. It's a Muslim holiday for spring. We place fires in the road and plants on the tables to say things are beginning again. For ten days, it goes on. Ten days it will be a party."

The man drew hard on his cigarette and his eyes shone from the ember.

"Your English is fantastic."

"YouTube."

For the remainder of the afternoon, I stayed in bed and attempted to plot out my next move. I scoured the American, Georgian, Azeri, and Kazakh embassy websites. I messaged Giga about returning to Georgia. He messaged his friends in the government, but they said the border closures would be in place until the infection rate dropped significantly. There were American consulate flights from Baku, but they weren't accepting dogs, and I wasn't prepared to leave the Caucasus anyway. Every country in the region claimed the border closures were temporary. Kazakhstan would reassess in two weeks. If they reopened even briefly, that would be enough to time to catch a ferry across the Caspian. From there I would have two weeks of walking to the Uzbek border. Then I'd just need to wait until Uzbekistan opened their borders and I'd have another two months of walking to Kyrgyzstan.

I was certain the closures would work, the infection rates would plummet, and the borders would reopen in two weeks. I had to be ready when they did. Alat, the port town where the ferry departed for Kazakhstan, was too small to stay in for any extended period, but I could walk to Baku, touch the Caspian, then taxi to Alat once the ferry was running.

Later in the evening, I heard someone in the hallway, so I stepped out of my room and spotted the owner of the hotel. He gave me a confused look as I handed him money for the night.

"I'm sorry," I said. "No one was here."

"No problem. Come, come."

"Where?"

"Come."

I looked back to my room. Savannah was standing in the doorway with her tail wagging.

"I'll be right back, baby girl."

I followed the owner down the hall to a room that was more spacious than my own. It had four twin beds, a faux-leather sofa, and a table of fruits, cheese, energy drinks, beer, and vodka. The room reeked of cigarettes. Two beer-bellied friends of the owner were picking at the fruit.

"Come, come," said the owner.

He gestured for me to sit on the sofa, and the men made room for me.

"Salaam. Salaam," I said.

"Here. Eat." One of them handed me an apricot.

"Vodka." The other poured me a shot.

The drink was somehow worse than Dusica's rakija.

"Wow. That was horrible."

The men laughed then refilled their glasses and drained another shot.

"Good!" The owner gave me a thumbs-up. "Eat, eat."

I pulled a few grapes off the vine and noticed a television playing in the corner. A newswoman was standing in front of a graphic demonstrating the airport and border closures. The graphic zoomed in on Baku, then showed the roads closed around it. Then the screen flashed a map of the world where every country was colored either red, yellow, or green. Every country bordering Azerbaijan was red.

The next morning, it was still raining, but Savannah and I departed earlier than the day before. At the auction, there were no animals and no auctioneers. Up the road, no wild dogs slunk over the hill to harass us and after two hours, we rested at the same boulder overlooking the valley. I decided that we would take the long way to Baku to burn some time. There was no point in hurrying. The world was closed, and we could only bide our time until it opened again.

The protest consisted mostly of men, but occasionally a group of women could be seen whirling scarves and shouting "down with the enemy!" Initially, the demonstrations annoyed me. The chanting woke me from a deep sleep at two in the morning. But once the weariness fell from my eyes, I was able to appreciate the magnitude of what I was watching—the outbreak of war amid a global pandemic.

Valerie, the brilliant Swiss woman I was living with in Baku, was annoyed by the demonstrations for less self-indulgent reasons than myself. She had been teaching in Azerbaijan for two years and she had seen first-hand how indoctrinated some Azeri students could be in their hatred of Armenians. Local newspapers read like a combination of the *Daily Mail* and Soviet propaganda. Anger was justified by reports on "The Enemy."

Valerie shook her head. "They're already calling for war, and who even knows what happened?"

Early into my time in Baku, Valerie and I had met while I was walking Savannah and Valerie was walking her dachshund mix, Mamba. We got on effortlessly and almost immediately began spending our days together. Valerie had a master's degree, played violin, and spoke four languages. After a few weeks, while telling her what a difficult time I was having trying to find a place to rent with the rental agencies closed, she suggested I stay with her.

Valerie's apartment was in the heart of the city. Below us was Nizami Park, to the east was the amber glow of Old City's limestone, and down the street was the promenade with a Starbucks and a Hard Rock Cafe. For all the dirt roads I walked in the Azeri countryside, Baku was a surprisingly developed metropolis. Government attempts to expand the city were happening so quickly that it was one of the few capitals with an excess of housing. Our apartment with its three balconies ran a mere $400 a month.

When calls for war began carrying through the night, we'd been in lockdown for weeks. Each morning, the pandemic quiet returned, and the only people on the street were government-employed babushkas, sweeping at nothing with their sorghum brooms. Thankfully, exceptions in the lockdown were made for people with dogs. Valerie, Savannah, Mamba, and I were allowed out twice a day, and we stretched those allowances as far as they would take us, which wasn't much. Baku was sweltering in the summer, reaching one hundred degrees by late morning. Usually, we only left our air-conditioning at dawn and after sunset. In the morning,

Valerie studied Russian, and I worked on writing a science-fiction novel for the fun of it. In the afternoon, we played ping-pong on the living room table.

When Azerbaijan's seven thousand hospital beds filled up, total lockdown went into effect and the arbitrary blessing of our birthplaces was made starkly apparent. While thousands of Azeris lost work, fell sick, and went hungry, our passports and currency proved unjustly powerful. We had food, shelter, and we isolated in luxury. We had done nothing to earn our privilege and yet, as two foreigners, we spent our evenings sitting on the balcony sipping wine, playing rummy, and watching the sun ricochet between the city windows.

Near the end of summer, the temperatures dipped from their suffocating highs and the results of a two-month lockdown could be seen by new lows in the infection rate. Lockdowns were loosened and we were free to go for walks whenever we felt. Usually, we strolled along the Caspian Sea, then wove through the sinuous streets of Old City. Sometimes we walked to the flame towers and into Bayıl yolkalıq, a park that was always empty and where we could sit on a concrete wall facing the city. We took our walks every day, imagining time stood still.

With Valerie, my growing desire to be in one place with one person was being satisfied, but also fed a gnawing disquiet in me. Lockdown was giving me something I couldn't have. The walk wasn't finished. As always, I would leave. I'd close my eyes and be under the sun, sore and tired, pushing through the elements once more.

My comfort was a mirage, and in August that bore out.

Valerie received word that her last-ditch application to teach at a private school in Rome had been accepted and that she would leave for orientation in three weeks. Once her departure was set, the soft walls of our fort buckled, and the sheets fell in.

Dreading my return to solitude, I became withdrawn.

Valerie left for Rome and a few weeks later, a flight opened to Turkey that would accept Savannah.

When I landed in Istanbul, I grew depressed. I left a fortress of pillows and sheets for the thin comfort of nylon snapping in the wind.

THE SUSPECT

With both hands on his staff, the shepherd leaned forward to watch his flock graze the rocky hillside. Like most Turkish shepherds, he wore a suit and a flat cap. His suit was brown and dirty, but loose-fitting enough to be comfortable in the heat of the sun. Before us stood the Aintab Plateau: dry, boundless, and feathered by fields of wheat. As I approached, the shepherd raised his hands as though already admitting he had no answer for what I was going to ask.

"Can I go up this way?" I said in English.

I pointed to the path climbing into the forest.

"On foot?" I said in Turkish.

The shepherd spoke, but I didn't understand him. He wavered a hand to say "Maybe." Then he stood proud and mimed a shotgun.

"But can I cross?" I gestured.

He shrugged and mimed a shotgun again.

"Okay. Thank you." I put a hand to my heart.

The shepherd returned the gesture, then turned back to his flock. The shadow of the mountains touched the highway, but beyond the asphalt the fields still shone in the sun. I had three miles to the top of the mountain and two hours of daylight remaining. It would have been easier to follow the highway—to the north it traced a river to Osmaniye—but I was tired of walking large roads. I wanted to sleep in a forest where it was cold and I could be free from the noise of passing cars.

After a few hundred yards, the dirt road became a path that rainwater had carved a gully through. I kept the cart tires on either side of the trench, but there were large stones sticking out, so no matter what I did the cart rolled unevenly and required a concentrated effort to push.

Savannah trotted patiently beside me. Her tongue was out. Her fur was short. We had covered twenty-one miles already, so she wasn't full of energy for racing up and down the mountain in pursuit of new scents. Since leaving Azerbaijan, we had walked from Istanbul to Gaziantep and planned to loop along the Mediterranean and back to Istanbul. Turkey was one of the few large countries I could enter to buy myself time until Uzbekistan or Kazakhstan reopened, and I could resume my primary route.

Thankfully, Turkey was perfect for walking. There was a variety of landscapes, hearty food, and because of ablutions in Islam, public fountains in every town. Still, I was as bored as I'd ever been. Turkey was too calm. I was never tense. I was never excited. In Gaziantep, one of the great, bustling food cities, I spent three days drifting the streets like a ghost. In the countryside, I camped wherever I wanted because I knew if someone discovered me, they would be warm and hospitable, and I would love meeting them. If it was a shepherd who came across our camp, they would have friendly kangals for Savannah to meet as well.

Maybe I had been walking too long. Maybe it was the five months with Valerie. Whatever it was, for the first time on my walk, I was ready to be finished with it.

Another hour passed, and Savannah and I had pushed a mile and a half up the craggy path. The western face of the mountain was dim, and the air was chilly. Trees blocked my view of the plateau. I walked in silence so I could listen to the branches creak, the birds whistle, and the mice rustle the floor.

From around a steep bend, two men appeared on a motorbike in neutral. They wore army fatigues and came to a stop beside me. The man driving was young and the man holding his waist was old. The older man spoke in Turkish, but I couldn't understand him and there was no internet to translate.

"On foot," I said in Turkish.

They looked over my cart, nodded, then continued silently downhill.

Savannah and I walked a little further before the puttering of their motorbike made its way back to us. The men pulled alongside me and asked for my passport.

"Why?"

"Military."

The old man tapped the badge on his shoulder.

I withdrew my passport and handed it over. Once the man found my visa, he shut the passport and handed it back.

"Thank you."

They turned the motorcycle around, shut off the engine, and descended again.

It was late enough that I considered pushing into the forest to look for a place to camp, but the ground was steep, and it seemed unlikely that I'd find anywhere open enough to camp, so we soldiered on. By looking at my map, I could see we were almost at the top and that the peak of the mountain was level. I imagined a grassy clearing fenced by pines where I could wake to the smell of earth then boil water for coffee with my sleeping bag over my shoulders to keep me warm.

A half hour later, the trees gave way to sky. Savannah and I were nearly at the top. Sweat caused my shirt to stick to my chest. Ahead of us, two men on a motorbike rolled into view. Before coming to a stop, the man on the back jumped off and jabbed a shotgun against my ribs.

At first, I saw a gaping hole in my chest and my organs strewn across the forest floor. Then I saw my torso in the forest and my legs on the path. After that, I wondered how long Savannah would stay with me and if my parents would find her. I knew she'd stay with me as long as she could, but eventually she would need water, so she'd have to descend to town. Once she had water, she'd return. And after a few days of not posting, and when someone noticed my GPS tracker hadn't moved, my parents would know something was wrong and they would fly to Turkey. It would take them a few days to reach my body, but they would find Savannah beside me. If I had been smart, I would have kept a small GPS on her collar, but she only needed to survive a week on her own and I was certain she was capable of that.

The man with the shotgun shoved my shoulder to turn me around.

I was trembling and surprised by my unbridled fear. I thought I had conquered my fear of death years before. When I was withering from the bacterial infection, I had been at peace with death, but now, face-to-face with it once more, I was terrified. I hadn't returned home. I hadn't met someone. I had skimmed across the world, but what use was that? What had I accomplished? What lasting good did I contribute?

I braved a glance over my shoulder. One of the men was going through my things and throwing whatever he didn't need onto the path. His clothes suggested he could have been any villager in Turkey.

"Take anything," I said.

The man with the shotgun took my backpack from me and tossed it to the man going through my cart. Then he pressed the barrel into my down jacket so I could feel the cold metal against my back.

My hands shook wildly.

Savannah was somewhere nearby, maybe right beside me. I wasn't sure.

"Identification! Where identification?"

"My backpack." I pointed to it.

The man going through my things pulled my journal and my toiletry bag from my backpack.

"Where identification?" he yelled.

Although I could still feel the gun to my back, my trembling subsided a fraction once I had something to focus on other than my impending death. I was realizing the men weren't common thieves. If they had been bandits waiting for a passerby, then the robbery would have already happened. Instead, my things were on the ground, my camera had been ignored, and I was being asked for my license.

"My backpack. The top," I said.

I looked behind me to the man with the shotgun. He was reassuringly relaxed.

"Backpack," he said, using the shotgun to gesture me over to it.

With my hands in the open, I went to my backpack, unzipped the top pocket, and stepped back. The man withdrew my wallet and found my license.

"New Jersey? American?"

"Yes."

"Where passport?"

"In my cart."

My passport was in a waterproof bag along with my laptop and Savannah's paperwork. After the attempted robbery in Panama, I kept my most important paperwork buried, so it couldn't be discovered if someone decided to go through my things. I looked to the man with the shotgun, and he nodded to tell me to get it.

I handed over my passport. The man aimed his flashlight on my photo and examined the text. Then he tapped the cover by his ear and listened to the sound.

"Bad."

"That's me. Thomas Turcich."

He wagged a finger.

I looked again to the man with the shotgun. He stood a few feet off and spoke with his partner. His partner tried to call someone, but there was no service. They spoke again, then the man with my passport began throwing things back into my cart.

"You," he said.

I repacked everything and put on my backpack.

"We go." He pointed uphill.

I began trembling again. I imagined they were walking me off the path to shoot me.

"Okay. Okay," said the man with the shotgun.

I pushed the cart uphill while he walked a step behind with the gun aimed at my back. We crested the mountain and came to a clearing that on any other night would have made an ideal campsite. The man with the shotgun patted his hand down in the air to tell me to relax. The other man held his phone in the air.

"Phone," I said, pointing to my backpack's hip pocket.

I withdrew my phone slowly and showed it to them, so they knew it wasn't anything else. Then I raised it in the air in hopes of finding reception so we could translate and I could figure out how to prove my identity.

For twenty minutes we both kept our arms raised in search of service. When their line finally got through, the man stood on his toes and spoke with someone. After he hung up, he let out a loud whistle. From within the forest another whistle sounded in response. A few minutes later, a pickup rolled onto the road and a man in a vest and şalvar pants stepped out. He looked at me disdainfully, took the shotgun, cocked it, then stood beside the truck with the gun pointed at me.

I nodded to him, but he offered nothing in return.

"Okay. Okay," said the kindest of them.

We loaded my cart into the pickup, then I climbed onto the bed with Savannah and was told to sit against the side. The man in the şalvar pants stood in front of me with the shotgun across his chest. The engine started and we rolled off under the black slate sky. The wind was biting as it swept over the car. I was in shorts and didn't have my hat. My legs and ears stung, but I was grateful to be against the cab. Savannah stood, balanced tenuously as we sped down the uneven road. The man in the şalvar pants squinted against the wind. When he looked at me, I smiled and shouted, "Feels good!"

He held his eyes on me for a moment, then looked down the road again.

We drove long enough that Savannah gave up standing and my back was bruised from hitting the side of the bed. Eventually, I spotted a white glow in the distance. As we neared the light, I noticed that we were approaching a substation and at the gate were men in military fatigues.

The guards waved us through, and the truck pulled to a stop once we were inside.

The man in the şalvar pants stepped down, handed off the shotgun, then stood by the gate and watched me with his hand on a pistol inside his vest. I was told to sit with Savannah and keep my legs hanging off the truck. A dozen men formed a semi-circle around me.

From a car parked to the right came the superior officer. He was round and smooth, and seemingly annoyed at being bothered after-hours. Another officer handed him my license and passport. He glanced at them, then handed them back to me.

"What is that?" he said, pointing to the cart.

"My things: clothes, water, food, tent, a sleeping bag. I push it. I walked from Istanbul. I've been walking for five years. I walked the Americas, down Europe, across Morocco, Algeria, Tunisia. From Italy, I walked to Azerbaijan. I walked across Turkey last year, along the Black Sea. I crossed the Bosphorus Bridge on foot. I was the first private citizen to cross it on foot. It was in the news. It was everywhere. I'm sorry I came up that path. I was trying to avoid the highway. I thought the forest would be peaceful. I thought I'd find a quiet place to sleep."

"Did you fly with that?"

"The cart? Yes. I've flown with it a dozen times. It's luggage basically."

"You flew to Istanbul? Where did you fly to?"

"From Baku to Istanbul, yes."

"There have been bombings, you know? The terrorists are bombing planes. There are bombings in these mountains. There was a bombing not long ago."

"I didn't know. I'm only walking. I was going to sleep in the forest and be gone the next day."

"You flew with that from America?"

"From Panama to Colombia, from Uruguay to Philadelphia, and from Philadelphia to Denmark."

"From America?"

"From America to Denmark, yes."

"And you're American?"

"I'm from New Jersey. I was born in Philadelphia. It's on my passport."

"Passports can be fake."

I didn't know what to say. I looked to the man who had been giving me reassurance, but he was indifferent now. If they didn't believe the authenticity of my passport, I wasn't sure what I else I could offer.

"It's not fake," I said. "It's stained because it got wet in a rainstorm in Argentina, but the Turkish visa is in there. You can see it."

"Kurdish terrorists fake passports every day. Why are you pushing that here? What's in it?"

I couldn't understand his fixation with my cart. I knew it was odd to be crossing an undeveloped mountain by the border of Syria with a dog and baby carriage, but they had dug through every bit of my cart and found nothing. They saw there was only camping gear, food, and a camera inside.

"It has my things in it," I said. "I've pushed it for years. It's my home. You can go through it again if you want."

Outside the light of the substation, the forest was dark. We were removed from everything. The officer continued his loop of questions, and I could find no way off. He asked why I was in Turkey, whether or not I knew any Kurds, and what I could tell him about the PKK. The man across from me watched me like an owl. His eyes were fixed. His hand was stayed to his pistol. I laughed and joked when I could in an attempt to relax the commanding officer, and for brief moments he seemed willing to let go of the questioning, but he always rediscovered his concern.

While the questions continued, I opened my phone and saw I had a bar of service. I opened Instagram and waited for my profile, its blue check, and a few photos to appear. Once a few images were loaded, I passed my phone to the commanding officer. He held it away from himself and squinted. Then he found his reading glasses in his pocket and put them on.

"Instagram," he said.

"That's my page. That's me. I'm The World Walk."

The younger soldiers came forward and huddled around the officer. They chattered in Turkish, buzzing like the substation. One of them found my profile on his phone and followed me.

"This is you?" the officer asked.

"That's me. I'm just walking. I'm just passing through. I didn't know about the mountains and the terrorists."

The men laughed at a photo of Savannah, then pointed from her to the photo. One of them rubbed her head. When I saw the man in the şalvar pants release his pistol and tap out a cigarette, I finally relaxed. For a while, the men went through my Instagram, and I shared some stories.

"Can you return me to where you picked me up?" I asked.

"No. It's not safe. There are terrorists in the forest. No more walking in the forest, okay, Thomas? We will drive you to where it's safe."

Three soldiers drove me and Savannah to the outskirts of Hasanbeyli. By the time we arrived it was midnight, so I used the light from their pickup to set my tent in a field set back from the road. The men stood with their hands on their hips and watched me make camp. Each time I unpacked something new, they asked me about it, and I would translate an answer.

They were pleasant to be with now, but I was tired. I shook their hands and thanked them before I even had my mattress inflated. When they left, I ate a few peanut butter jellies, edited and posted a video from my day, then fell asleep.

The next morning, it was raining. After walking for a bit, the rain stopped, and I found a cafeteria for breakfast. Savannah crawled under the cart while I went inside. I had a çay, some doughy white bread, and a bowl of *mercimek*—a yellow lentil soup that I had dreamed of every hour of every day since my first spoonful.

Beyond the restaurant, the sky was gray and fast, and the mountains were blue and rolling like a sea in a storm. Savannah was happy. The road was narrow and peaceful.

After being held up at knifepoint in Panama, I developed the need to keep my back against the wall of any room I entered. For years, I was paranoid about leaving my things unattended for even a moment. But now, the morning after being held up at gunpoint, it was as though it never happened. I had been on the road long enough to know that just about every person was kind and only trying to make some money and spend time with their family. Locals were friendly, my days were calm, and I would find more good food ahead.

I was living a fantastic life, yet boredom had settled over me and refused to leave. After years of walking, the thrill of the unknown had dulled to a monotonous hum, and adventure had become routine.

BUTTERFLY VALLEY

On New Year's Eve, I arrived in Kaş, a port town on the Mediterranean. I knew someone vacationing there—one of Valerie's coworkers in Azerbaijan. She said I should stay a few days, and because I had no good reason to decline, I didn't. I rented a room in a hotel beside a Greek amphitheater. In the morning, the hotel manager prepared every guest a full Turkish breakfast—*simit, menemen,* olives, jams, and cheese.

On my second day in Kaş, I met Mina, Merve, and Ceyda—two daughters and their mother who were lingering in Kaş while university was paused. Ceyda was a teacher from Ankara. Her ex-husband was a Brit. She and the girls held dual citizenship in the United Kingdom and Turkey. Merve was going to school in Australia. Mina in the UK. They were friendly, liberal, gregarious, and they snatched me up and carried me about in their satchel.

Each day, I met them at a different beach. We went for a walk around the peninsula and watched the sunset from the amphitheater. On Friday, we met at the farmer's market for *gözleme* and pomegranate juice. Initially, I thought I would leave Kaş after a week, but one week turned to two, two turned to three, and after a month, Ceyda was negotiating rent on an apartment for me.

By then, I had befriended other transplants waiting out COVID on the Mediterranean as well. Dave was an Aussie divorcé with short blonde hair who scooted around town on his moped picking up whatever beautiful woman caught his eye. Burju was a well-read Turk who recently gained German citizenship and offered Mina and Merve a fount of sisterly advice. Reeka was a Sri Lankan/British tarot reader who had been walking the Lycian Way and adopted the dog that had been following her. Egil and Tanya were Icelanders who'd been together a decade, and each ran their own business—warehousing for Egil and high-end hair extensions for Tanya.

When I moved into the apartment, Ceyda found and negotiated for me, we threw a housewarming party. Over a few hours, we ate mezes, fish, and a pot of borscht. As a thank you, I gave Ceyda a bottle of Baileys. After a few sips, she became flushed and giggly. The rest of us drank raki, our glasses turning cloudy when we added ice.

Even in winter, Kaş was warm. Each day, I went to the coffee shop around the corner, bought a cappuccino, and sipped it on my balcony in the sun. Between the houses ahead of me, I could make out a sliver of the Mediterranean. After breakfast, I took Savannah on a walk, for at least an hour. When I needed a jolt, I jumped into the sea. Later, I studied for two or three hours. With a highlighter and a pen, I pored over *The Great Convergence*, *Erdogan's Empire*, and *Silk Roads*.

> *"The call of Constantinople echoed loudly around all of Europe in the eleventh century. Documents record that in the eleventh century it was home to men from Britain, Italy, France, and Germany—as well as from Kiev, Scandinavia, and Iceland."*

For each of our birthdays—there happened to be many—we rented a boat and took it on the water for a day. The water was as clear as the air. At any point but the deepest, you could see the floor. We drank pink gin and tonics, I smoked cigars, and the captain cooked fresh fish for lunch. Once we were fat and content, we went around and shared a word that we believed summarized each person. One word inevitably became many, but it was a good way to focus on the best of everyone.

"Fatherly," Merve said about me. "I can't wait to see Dad-Tom."

I thought it a great compliment. Dad-Tom was a long way off, but the idea of being a father resided in my deepest imaginations. Since Spain, I had never stopped fantasizing about my future home and family. The fantasies made my solitude heavier, but the nearer I came to the end of the walk, the more frequently they ran freely.

After two months, I had friends in every corner of town.

On a hike to the bay opposite Kaş, I met Yari, a lanky, self-contained PhD student with round glasses and curly chestnut hair. She wore boots and technical pants that outclassed our thirty-minute walk. When we reached Limanagzi, a secluded bar on the bay, men were hauling two-by-fours off a dinghy to repair the deck. Yari and I sat over the sea.

"I was an engineer for Mercedes, but when I was protesting for gay rights in Istanbul, I was hiding behind a car being hit by a government water cannon and I noticed the truck was made by Mercedes. I realized that I couldn't continue working for them. I wouldn't contribute to an industry leading to the destruction of our planet and the oppression of human rights, so I quit, and I applied to PhD programs. Well, I applied to one program, where my ex was studying, but I got in, and that's where I am now."

A few days later, I asked Yari out and we went paddleboarding across the harbor. She marveled at the small wonders of the world in a way that momentarily helped me rediscover my appreciation of them.

"The glimmer! Look at the glimmer!" she said as we drifted over the water.

The ripples in the light were like diamonds.

When we reached the opposite shore, we carried our paddleboards across the street and set them in the sea. We paddled to a beach, rested in the sun, then found the tide too strong to go back, so we left our boards by the water and walked barefoot to her car.

"Don't you love the feeling of the stones on your feet?" Yari said.

I looked down at the pebbles packing the concrete walkway and wondered if it was possible to exist solely in the present as Yari so often seemed to do.

In a gradual way, Yari and I took up together. She worked long hours on her PhD and due to COVID she was reluctant to come out. We didn't see each other more than once or twice a week. The rest of the group filled in my days. Whether it was swimming, partying at my apartment, or sharing a three-hour breakfast, the group in Kaş provided me with as much warmth as any campfire. However, by the beginning of April, the ends of our group were fraying. Egil needed to get back to his warehouse, Dave set sail on the Mediterranean, and with a vaccine available, I flew home for three days to get the jab, then put together plans to walk Uzbekistan and Kyrgyzstan—the only two countries on my route that were open.

One thing Yari wanted to do before I left was hike part of the Lycian Way—a trail that followed the Mediterranean cliffs and passed villages of the extinct matrilineal society of the Lycians. Ruins of the ancient civilization dotted the coast. A towering Lycian tomb even marked the corner near my apartment.

Two weeks before my flight to Uzbekistan, Yari and I taxied to Ölüdeniz to join the start of the trail. Savannah was excited to be on the move, but it was hotter than we expected and there was less water than we anticipated. For a few days, the going was tough, but eventually we came to Butterfly Valley, a thirteen-hundred-foot gash in the plateau that promised an escape.

After a few lazy switchbacks, we reached a point in the path that dropped straight into the valley—an almost sheer descent. There were makeshift slides and steps and a thick rope bolted into the rock. For a careful hour, we passed our backpacks and Savannah to each other. When we finally reached the bottom, we followed an overgrown trail until it opened to a simple resort with showers, bathrooms, a wooden cafeteria, and a long, secluded beach.

Yari and I rented a campsite and set our tent. It was Worker's Day, so the owner of the resort gave the staff the day off and as much as they could drink. By nightfall, there was a ten-foot bonfire and a woman twirling fire poi. There were only twenty of us. Savannah was roaming about. I sat between Yari's legs, and she had her arms around my neck as I listened to Selda Bağcan's clear, bittersweet voice on the speakers.

After a few beers, I left the party to be on my own. Savannah found me in the tent and curled outside it. As I was dozing off, Yari came to the tent, too.

"Tom, you have to see the stars. I've never seen so many."

"I saw them. They're beautiful."

"But you have to see them now. You can't see this many stars in the city."

She was crouched outside with her eyes skyward.

"I'm happy to lay down right now."

Yari looked at me, then went off.

The woman I wanted to be with had asked me to join her on the beach to look at the stars, and the only thing I thought to say was "I'm happy to lay down."

Maybe that wasn't wrong. Certainly, after a thousand nights camped beneath the night sky, it was understandable, but it wasn't who I wanted to be. I left home to suck out all the marrow of life, to feel the stars dripping through me and the rivers running cold in my veins, but the more I saw and the more I felt, the less significant any one thing appeared to be.

The stars obliterated me long ago. What more could they offer? I was dust already. The warm wind, the trees clinging to the stone, and the dark red twilight had pressed me ever flatter. The vastness of the world humbled me a million times over. The shredding of my ego had been sweeping and pitiless. If my obliteration wasn't yet complete, I feared I'd unravel. I needed something sharp, something human to hold onto—and the stars could never offer that. I understood I was nothing, but I needed to *feel* that I was someone, and more specifically, I needed to feel that I was someone *to someone*.

THE FINAL ADVENTURE

Our horseman was a boy in camouflage. He knelt beside a boulder and fed twisted branches into a fire. His mares were tied off by the lake. Across the water, dawn washed Gora Babash-Ata in a soft orange light. Fresh landslides in the mountain face offered signs of time's unending chisel.

After finishing her horse meat, Savannah burped then came to sit beside me. I put an arm around her and sipped my instant coffee. The meadow bloomed with purple, blue, and yellow wildflowers.

Kyrgyzstan was likely the last foreign country we'd walk. The three foreign countries remaining on my route—Kazakhstan, Mongolia, and Australia—were closed due to COVID. With no end to their closures planned for the near future, I wasn't willing to wait around another year. If none were open before my Kyrgyz visa expired, Savannah and I would fly to Seattle and walk the final seven months of our journey to New Jersey. I wouldn't complete the route I planned, but seven years of walking was long enough.

From around the boulder, my guide Husnidin appeared. He was an old yak with the verve of a stallion. He raised a handful of mushrooms triumphantly.

"You found that many? I looked for an hour and only found two," I said.

"No, not that many, but something before our crossing. The pilgrims picked the mushrooms. Kids with their parents, so there aren't many left. There should be more wood, but there are too many people. You saw how far we had to go. There won't be wood for the pilgrims who come later. It's good you came now. It's a good season. We can still have our morning coffee and not need to burn horse cakes."

"You've done that?"

"Only a few times on hikes when we were gone for too long. They burn weak and low. Wood is better. Gas is the best."

Husnidin handed the mushrooms to our horseman who threw them in with our pasta. Once we finished eating, we packed our panniers and slung them onto the horses. Husnidin and I took a few snacks from our food pannier to keep in our backpacks. I had a Snickers from town that I'd been saving.

Our horseman rode the lead horse, while Husnidin and I walked. We followed a narrow path through the boulders until leaking out to a tin shelter by the lake. Savannah ran ahead to greet a shepherd dog outside the fence. Two men and a boy came to speak with Husnidin. After sharing some news, we returned to walking.

"They're sacrificing a lamb tonight."

"For what?"

"For the boy, for his health. He is having problems with shaking."

"Seizures."

"I don't know. It would be good to stay tonight. There will be plov, lots of plov. Savannah! You love plov!" Husnidin chased her until she barked, spun, and darted off. Husnidin laughed uproariously.

"Never enough plov for Savannah. She wants to stay in Kyrgyzstan forever so she can eat plov until she's fat."

At a green slope of Gora Babash-Ata, we said farewell to our horseman. While Husnidin, Savannah, and I crossed the mountain pass, our horseman would take the horses to town the long way and arrive in Arslanbob sometime in the evening. If our crossing went well, we would beat him to town by several hours.

Husnidin, Savannah, and I walked up a hill full of wild onions and rhubarb. I broke off an onion stalk to chew as we went. Atop the hill were boulders to sit on. The three of us sat together and took in the view.

At our height, the lake, Ozero Kolkulan, was a matte blue puddle caught in the jagged walls of towering stone. By the tip of a peninsula that jutted into the water, a small wooden mosque was visible, but only because I knew it was there. Across from the mosque, on a different lake-shore, was the tin shelter where the boy and his family were staying. We stayed there early on when it proved a timely place to escape a rainstorm. There was an abundance of blankets, pillows, carpets, pots, and wood left for pilgrims. Since we were the only people there, Savannah and I had our own room and luxurious beds of a dozen thick blankets. A rat or two might have slipped by in the night, but Savannah chased them off.

Behind the lake, the mountains were layered one after another until fading into the sky. We had walked the passes between them. Certain valleys had a single family in them; others had two. Some were empty. During the summer, the valleys were where the shepherds brought a town's livestock for fattening. In one valley, Husnidin despaired at a flock of grazing sheep that numbered in the thousands.

"This used to be wildflowers," he said. "Now there's nothing but grass."

Wildflowers or not, the valley was still the most beautiful place I had ever laid eyes on—though that laurel was continually overtaken in Kyrgyzstan.

Husnidin pointed to a long shadow on the lake's water.

"It will be busy tomorrow," he said. "Four or five families coming."

He shielded his eyes with a hand and squinted.

"You see?"

He traced the peaks of the shadow with a finger.

"Five families. Maybe there will be more lamb and more plov. Savannah wished we stayed."

He found her beside him and rubbed her head.

After we began again, we entered the shadow of the mountain where no green grew, and the stones were loose. We hugged a path on the mountainside that took us to a glacier that stretched from the top of the mountain to the valley below. A few days before, we had drunk from the stream at the glacier's end.

The top inch of the snow was soft from the sun, which made for easy walking. The soles of my shoes were smooth from having walked Uzbekistan in them and not replacing them in Bishkek for fear of blisters. Husnidin's backpack was heavier than mine, so he took more breaks on the glacier than I did. Sometimes when he stopped, I sat in the snow and watched him. He was a fleck of red on a bright white slide.

When we reached the top of Gora Babash-Ata, there was a tiny lake that was frozen except for its middle, where the water was a deep, unsettling black. I made a wide arc around it, but even at a hundred feet, the water threatened to pull me in. On the other side, up a small rise, the mountain opened and the view south unfurled.

"This is where we go down," Husnidin said. "Let me see if there is still snow."

Husnidin walked to a precipice and peered down. Beyond him was his home: Arslanbob—a shallow valley hemmed by cliffs to the west, the largest walnut forest in the world to the east, and air made dim above it from the smoke of a coal fire in every home. Across the green sea, a few dozen mountains ripped the sky. Furthest was the Pamir Mountain Range, peaks that from our distance seemed like clouds at the margin of the world.

After a minute, Husnidin came back from his inspection.

"I thought it would be gone now, but there's still snow."

"What does that mean?"

"In summer we can run down, now we can't go this way. There are two options: go down the rocks over there or cross the snow and go down the other rocks."

The rock face before the snow looked like a petrified waterfall protruding from the earth, its surface a series of uneven ridges and hollows. The rock face beyond the snow was only moderately better.

"I don't know. Can we sit for a minute?"

We huddled against a stack of stones, and I bent over my Snickers like it was a Bible. When I finished, Husnidin spoke.

"We can't wait long or there might be wind."

"Okay."

"Which way do you want to go?"

"The one farther away, I guess."

My stomach churned.

When Husnidin stood, Savannah spun to her feet. We walked together until reaching the hundred-foot stretch of snow that divided our two paths. Husnidin and Savannah crossed the snow with ease. I started after they made it to the stone on the other side.

The snow wasn't steep, but to my left it disappeared down the cliff. I stared at the edge, and there it was again—death. Just like when I was sitting on Shannon's lawn at seventeen, the understanding of death's finality overwhelmed me. I could feel its hand on my shoulder, spreading its chill, clouding my thoughts, hastening my breath, and forcing me to the ground until I was clutching the snow. I could think of nothing but the absolute darkness.

"Don't do that!" called Husnidin. "Stand straight. You have to stand straight."

The lower I cowered, the faster the snow gave way, but suddenly Husnidin was beside me, wedging his feet against my own and preventing me from sliding further.

"What you're doing is more dangerous. You have to stand straight. Don't lean."

"I can't. My shoes are too slippery."

"Then we'll switch."

For a moment, I was warm with gratitude, but then I imagined Husnidin slipping, and Savannah and me stranded on the mountain.

"No, you'll slip. They're too smooth."

"Take them off. I'm the mountain goat, remember?"

Carefully and awkwardly, I undid my shoes and handed them to Husnidin. He pulled on my shoes, and I tied on his boots. Once Husnidin had my shoes on, he jumped in the air and brought his knees to his chest.

"Oh, these are nice! So light! Like air."

Husnidin brought me to my feet and with his help I found my balance. My fear lessened as I felt the boots gripping the snow. Husnidin walked beside me. I stood more upright, but once I reached the stones, I collapsed onto the ground and held my hands over my face.

"That's good practice," said Husnidin. "Next week we'll come again, and you'll be jumping on the snow like me."

"Is that the most scared someone has been up here?"

"No, of course, no. There was a woman who wouldn't come down from the rocks. She was crying and yelling at her husband until she was too tired to yell. It took an hour to move her."

I spent a while gathering myself, but going down the rock face was easier than I imagined. I kept telling Savannah to slow down because I was afraid that she'd slip, but she made light work of the descent, scrambling far below before climbing back up to check on me.

Beneath the rock wall was a tremendous landslide of silt. We ran down, and because the land was so steep, there was no stopping. Only when we came to a wide flat stone that stuck out of the silt like a spearhead could we rest. On the stone, I took off Husnidin's shoes, dumped the silt that had gathered in them, and handed them back. Once I had my sneakers on, we started again.

We ran to where the silt gathered in a dell against the hill then we ran over the hill to where the earth was sparse and bouldery and Arslanbob was in view.

Our way continued and Husnidin kept running. Savannah and I ran after him. Sometimes there was a path; sometimes there wasn't. We dodged divots and avoided stones. We ran across the balds where wild horses scattered when they spotted us. We followed switchbacks through the wildflowers until the path wove beside a stream that gurgled white and gray. With each step, the mountains receded further behind. Walnut trees sprouted and multiplied, and we flew between them like wisps. My legs burned. Sometimes when I needed to jump, I feared my knees would buckle and I'd fall to my face. But we never slowed. We ran even when it hurt, and the air stung our lungs. Over another stream, across another field, down another hill, the path carried on. Despite our exhaustion, we ran faster because we knew somewhere just ahead was home.

THE SHADOWS OF A NEW MOON

The scent of lavender held me. I hadn't said it aloud, but I was in love with her. It came upon me slowly, sometime in Uzbekistan, when we were talking every day. For a while I resisted it, perhaps out of habit, but I was too tired for that anymore. When I landed stateside, I took the first opportunity to see her again.

"How was the walk?" I asked as Yari sat down to join me.

"Clarifying."

"That's good."

I passed her my beer. She took a sip then passed it back. After we finished, we walked down the street. Chatter from the few open restaurants filled the night like a chorus of cicadas.

While we waited for a table, we talked about nothing.

"Thank you for the Dr. Seuss books. I love them."

"Of course," I said. "You need to have at least a few of them in your library."

"The colors. They're like the Mediterranean. They're like Kaş."

"*The Lorax* is such a dark story, I forgot how dark it is. Maybe it was the colors, but I didn't remember it that way."

"It's hopeful at the end."

"The earth is destroyed."

"But he's given a seed." She held up her finger to accentuate her point. "And there's hope."

"That's a lot riding on a single seed."

Yari tilted her head and seemed to consider me for a moment.

"So we're good like this, right?"

"Yeah," I said without thinking.

"Okay. Good."

Quiet spread over us. I brought up some mundane topics to keep the conversation going, but I was thinking about what I had said earlier when we were in bed.

"Take a chance. Maybe it won't work."

Yari didn't say anything after I said that, but she kissed me, and we made love. I thought that meant she was taking the chance, and that my last-ditch effort had won her over, but now I wasn't sure.

After we paid and left the restaurant, we held hands at the corner, waiting for the light to change.

"What did you mean back there? By good like this?"

"I mean we're just going to enjoy these next few days, right?"

"And that's it?"

The light changed and we crossed the street. She was thinking.

"You see how I am here, Tom. I have to teach soon. I have the PhD to work on. You know how seriously I take my meditation, how I'm trying to stay in the moment. I don't want to look at my phone. I don't even respond to my family sometimes."

She continued, but I didn't hear her until something struck a nerve.

"After seven months, when you're finished walking, you can contact me."

"No," I said quickly. "No, no, no. I'm the one who came here to tell you I want to be with you."

"Okay. I misunderstood."

"I'm the one with stronger feelings. It's up to you whether you want to be with me."

"I misunderstood."

We were silent after that. After a few blocks, I became fixated on the image of the half-used box of condoms in her nightstand.

"You slept with someone, right?"

"Yes. Three times."

"Okay."

"It was only sexual. And it was after we talked about it. We agreed to tell each other if we had feelings for someone else. That's what we agreed upon."

"I know. It's fine. It doesn't matter."

We continued holding hands and I didn't care that she had been with someone else. We were never dating.

"I guess we're just in different places," I said.

When we got back to her apartment, we made love again, but this time I felt sick afterward. I got up straight away, went to the bathroom, and came back to her reluctantly. She lay her head on my shoulder and put her arm over me. The warmth I felt for her was like a fever.

"I have to go one way or the other," I said. "I can't keep doing this in-between. We're either together or we have to stop talking. The in-between is too painful for me when I'm out there on my own. I want someone to rely on and I want that someone to be you."

She was so happy when I confessed this. She drew me in to kiss her. We kissed for a while, but then I pulled back.

"So what do you think?"

She withdrew, and I fell to my back.

"Can we talk in seven months when you've finished the walk?" she said, leaning over me.

"We have to go one way or the other. It's too painful for me."

"Well, I have until Friday morning to think about it, right?"

"Sure," I said meekly.

But not much later, she said she couldn't do it. She couldn't give me what I wanted. She didn't want to be relied on.

I didn't hear her though, not really. I wanted to be with her, so I pulled her to me, and we put our arms around each other. Then we talked for an hour about how we felt about each other, and I realized over and over that she would make no concessions. The best she could do was put her hands on my cheeks and say, "I care for you a lot and I'm really happy you're here right now."

There was no future for her, or maybe there was and I wasn't in it.

Either way, I felt sick lying in bed with her that night. I couldn't sleep and at 1:00 a.m., in a wave of jealousy, I questioned her about the condoms and why she suddenly started birth control. She went over the details patiently and I felt like a fool for getting upset.

"One thing you can count on me for," she said, "is brutal honesty."

That was true. I believed every word she said, only sometimes it took a while for the truth to sink in.

"Why don't you go for a walk?" she said.

I went out under the shadows of a new moon and felt liberated in the crisp air. While I walked, I thought about what she said to me earlier:

"There's a Buddhist saying, something like 'I love the apple even though the apple doesn't love me back.'"

I understood what she meant, but for all my years of walking, I wasn't a monk. I hadn't transcended my emotions, and I did care if the apple loved me back. I couldn't go two more days pretending I didn't.

I fell asleep on the sofa downstairs. At 3:00 a.m. she called me, worried. I went upstairs and fell asleep. When I woke the next morning, I packed my things.

Two days later I was in Seattle again. When I was reunited with Savannah, I cried.

THE DULL PAIN OF IT ALL

As the morning sun broke through the pines of the Pacific Northwest, a fog rose from the damp asphalt and the small town of Marblemount stirred to life. From the general store, I bought a coffee and an apple Danish and sat with them on a bench outside with Savannah at my feet. This was the last place to buy food before a ninety-mile stretch of forest that made up the Northern Cascades National Park.

My body felt better than I anticipated. Over the past two days, Savannah and I had walked twenty-four miles and each morning, I woke to feel remarkably fresh. My new habit of meditating and doing yoga each morning was making a difference, yet despite my body feeling strong and my spirit riding the high of walking again, I felt on a deeper level a profound exhaustion from defending myself against my self-imposed solitude over the past ten years.

During all those years of walking, I knew in the back of my mind that I was protecting myself and the walk from romantic love, but it wasn't until the week prior that I could see the armor I'd worn. I donned it at twenty-two, in order to end things with Layla; I knew if I left walking around the world an unfulfilled dream, a seed of bitterness would take root in me. I was still in love with Layla when I acted against my emotions and broke it off. I remember thinking afterward that I would see the walk through even if it killed me because I could imagine no greater sacrifice than giving up a life with her.

After our breakup, I wore the armor willingly. If I was going to walk around the world, I needed to. Romantic love and The World Walk were incompatible. It wasn't like being in medical school or doing a PhD. Though arduous journeys in their own right, neither necessitated removing oneself from every creature comfort as walking around the world did. PhD students lived in one place for years. They had rooms, beds, a roof, friends to get drinks with, and a community with which to commiserate.

While walking, I had none of that—at least not with any consistency.

Looking back, I could see how the armor protected me as I went. I straightened it, tightened it, and it kept me safe from loneliness. It held together as I navigated new cultures, as I raised Savannah, as I pushed my body, as I walked for months in the desert, as I climbed mountain after mountain, and most importantly, as I fell asleep each night.

But after ten years, sometime in Azerbaijan or Turkey, it began to crack.

Egil and Tanya noticed immediately.

"After we met you, Tanya said how interesting you were, but we both knew you were done with the walk."

It was true, but the walk wasn't done with me. I made a pact with myself to finish it.

For a few months more, I did my best to keep the armor patched together, dismissing my feelings for Yari and bounding my desire to share myself with someone. But that was no use anymore. The weight of the armor was no longer worth the protection it offered. So rather than allowing it fall off piece by piece during my walk across America, I cast it off all at once by going to see Yari.

The relief was total. No longer did I carry that weight. No longer did it bite my neck or constrict my movements. I returned battered, bruised, and weary, but allowing myself to be exposed and unprotected for the first time since twenty-two.

And now I sat outside the Marblemount General Store, tired and aching, but with the strangest sense of lightness. While I considered this, a burly man with a generous smile leaned against a post to say hello.

"I can see it in your eyes," he said not far into our conversation.

"Yeah?"

"I had the same thing after a year in 'Nam."

"That's so much worse, though. I haven't been to war, just on my own."

"But it's there. I see it in your eyes. You're older. It wears on you, ages you."

I nodded. I couldn't remember having such a personal conversation with a stranger so quickly while I was abroad. Now they were happening every day. The day before I found myself consoling a barista about her ailing mother and the inevitability of death.

The bearded vet continued.

"After these seven months, you'll be finished. I mean really finished. For me, all it took was that one year in 'Nam. I got here and I've been content ever since. At a certain point, you understand there isn't anything more you need than a good woman by your side and a little peace and quiet."

"I can't wait."

I left Marblemount at noon. My cart was weighed down with protein bars, cans of beans, and soup. For miles, the road was flat, the sky was cloudy, and a breeze cooled the air. We passed a few farmhouses drifting in high seas of grass. To our right, the Skagit River roared.

Eventually, the road began upward, as it had so many times before, and I was surprised at how well my legs handled the climb. It had been months since I pushed the cart uphill. Uzbekistan was flat, and horses carried my things in Kyrgyzstan.

By five, Savannah and I had covered twenty-one miles. That was more than enough to be considered a fine day's work, so I turned down a service road looking for a place to sleep. Not finding anywhere ideal, I parked the cart, sat on the road, and set out Savannah's food.

Savannah started eating immediately. I rested beside her and gazed into space. In all likelihood, I could set my tent toward the edge of the service road and no one would bother us. I was tired enough for that to be appealing, but the road was steep, the gorge was loud, and I knew I'd wake in the middle of the night regretting not finding a better place.

I looked over my map and considered where else we might sleep. In eight miles there was a campground. It was five thirty already so even if Savannah and I walked nonstop, we wouldn't arrive until after sundown. But that was good enough. I let Savannah finish her food, then I covered the bowl and put it back in the cart.

"We're not done," I said aloud.

For two hours, Savannah and I walked without rest. After we crossed Gorge Lake, the road turned suddenly steep, and the day caught up with me. I pushed the cart uphill for a few minutes, then stopped to catch my breath. Five minutes on, I started again. A few minutes after that, I took another break. We had walked twenty-seven miles. My calves were throbbing.

With my phone I inspected the elevation gain ahead of me. The road was steep for a little over a mile until it leveled out.

We began walking again. The cart pressed against me, and I pushed back against it, fighting gravity with my weary body. I was wrecked—physically, emotionally, and spiritually, but I knew each step uphill was a step closer to relief.

"Finish it," I said to myself.

"Finish it."

My legs moved steadily beneath me.

"Finish it."

I found a rhythm between the words and my breath.

"Finish it."

Inhale.

"Finish it."

Inhale.

In six years of walking, I never spoke to myself in mantras, but a mile of road had never represented so much. It was the entire walk. It was my life after the walk. It was the past six years, and the seven months remaining. It was my exhaustion. It was me dragging myself to the finish line. The road grew steeper, but my legs kept moving.

"Finish it!" I shouted. "Finish it!"

Savannah raced ahead of the cart, pulling the leash. The road was unforgiving.

My chanting went on, becoming nonsensical.

"Fina shit. Fina shit. Fina shit."

Then meaning returned.

"Finish it."

My back was knotted.

"Finish it."

The road curved and I thought I could see where it leveled out, but minutes later I realized it still carried upward. My legs screamed. My heart was in my head. I started to lose focus.

"Finish it."

The words were empty.

"Finish it." I pleaded.

Tears fell from my eyes.

"Finish it."

"Finish it."

When the road finally leveled out, I didn't celebrate.

I didn't throw my fist in the air.

A half hour later, I staggered into the campground and found a clearing where I could set my tent. Across from me families played games, drank, and laughed. One had fairy lights strung between the trees. At another, someone was playing guitar. I laid out my tarp and sat down.

I hung my head and marveled at the totality of my exhaustion. It wasn't the thirty miles I walked that day, it was the twenty-five thousand before it. With my armor cast off, it felt as though I was seeing myself for the first time in a decade. My skin was shriveled and pale, and my body was bruised beyond recognition.

How many hits had I taken? No close bonds. No love. No Sunday dinners. The careful separation. The practiced Stoicism. The ports I had to leave again and again. The dull pain of it all was unbelievable—how pervasive, how deep it ran. How many wounds did I suddenly find? And at my stomach, the cut of indifference. It would heal quicker than the other wounds, but it was a sharp pain.

I closed my eyes and swam down, down into my mind in search of shelter, far from the aches covering me, where the water was cold and the sunlight was far away, where pressure gripped my chest and threatened to crush me, where in the icy darkness there lay something shimmering.

A memory.

The warm wind on my face. The smell of lavender and the sea. The weight of her body on my legs and my hand on her thigh. Her arms around me and my face in the nape of her neck. The memory wasn't tainted by knowing her indifference because it wasn't about her. It was how I felt. It was wandering the wilderness for a decade, and finally, finally, allowing myself to rest.

THE WILDFIRE

"I don't believe it."

"I know."

"I walked across Mexico and I never had tacos this good. Let me have another bite."

Bonnie held out the taco. A corn tortilla rippling with fragile bubbles shone under a brush of oil. Carnitas and cheese dangled and dripped. When I bit into the taco, the spark of lime rose above a burst of fat to send a rush of satisfaction into my most ancient wiring.

The owner leaned on his forearms and peered out the window of his chrome food truck. Behind him, his daughter moved spices to make room for the groceries she'd bought from the store across the parking lot.

"Isn't it good?" Bonnie said.

"The lengua is good, but these are amazing. How have you never been here before?"

"Two weeks left and I'm just discovering the place."

"All the meals you could have eaten . . ."

"Heartbreaking."

Five nights before, while I recovered in a hotel room after crossing the Cascades, Bonnie and I met on Tinder. Her profile said she was from Alaska, had been a paramedic there, and was now in medical school. My profile said I was walking around the world with my dog.

On our first date, Bonnie said, "I've finally met someone more interesting than me."

"Yes, you have," I said in jest.

Bonnie was doing a family medicine rotation in the valley over from me, Omak. After two dates, she offered to have Savannah and me stay at her apartment when we passed by. So, after leaving the hotel, I walked a day, camped at the top of the pass, then hurried downhill. A mile from her apartment, she appeared in the distance, jogging toward me with an excitement mirroring my own.

While we lay in bed that evening I said, "I thought I'd stay another day if that sounds good to you."

"Two days of walking and you already need a day off?"

"I must be getting old."

In my earlier years of walking, stopping for three days at a hotel, walking two days, then stopping another day would have been unthinkable. But I was in the United States now; I had citizenship, not a visa. Winter loomed and I needed to reach Lexi's home in Denver before the worst of it set in, but more than anything, I needed to do absolutely nothing with someone.

The next day, we drove to a lake in a valley of uneven hills and placed our blanket on a beach just wide enough for the two of us. Savannah trotted into the shallows, drank, then dug herself a bed at the base of a bush. Across the water, a hill was dark with green pines but behind us the hills were bare and only the charred spindles of trees remained. Farther on, across a stretch of amber grass, the peaks of the mountains were shrouded by the orange smoke of a wildfire.

"I thought I'd be working at the tire shop the rest of my life," Bonnie said, opening the cooler for a beer. "It was difficult to imagine anything else up there. It's only because of my boss, Dane, that I applied to medical school. I never gave it a thought until he told me I should. I didn't think I'd be accepted."

"Do you miss it? Alaska?"

"Parts of it. It's a great place to be a kid. When I was young, and my parents were trying to establish their shop, they expected me and my brother to spend every minute outside. We would build these insane structures out of tires in the back: towers, forts, we even built a zip line."

"You built a zip line?"

She laughed. "It's sort of the natural progression when there's nothing else to do."

I stayed with Bonnie another night and the following morning I asked to stay a third. Since it was Labor Day, we drove an hour to Chelan. At the end of the main street was a meandering lake lined with houses, parks, and a running path. Bonnie and I set our things on a shaded bank then we jumped in, and she swam over and wrapped her legs around me.

After that, we were cold, so we lay on our towels in the sun. Savannah stayed close unless she wanted to say hello to someone sitting on a bench. There were paddleboarders and families blasting music from their boats. Behind us, bachata played from the speakers of an amphitheater where girls were learning to dance. On a distant mountain, another wildfire swirled.

"I have to ask," I said. "You've read some of my blog posts, right? I assume you looked me up?"

"Your Tinder profile said you were walking around the world. I had to make sure you weren't a liar."

"That would be a bold thing to lie about."

"Very."

"But so you've read some of them?"

"The past three, I think."

"What do you think? Meeting me at my most vulnerable?"

"It sucks to be rejected, but at least you were decisive. I was on and off with a guy for three years. It was terrible."

"When was that?"

"It ended in January."

"You ended it?"

"More or less. I realized where I stood and that nothing was going to change. When you're young, you think you can become someone that will make them realize they want to be with you, but it doesn't work that way. You are who you are, and they are who they are. Better to be with someone who wants to be with you."

"How terrible would it be if you had to change your whole personality to be with someone? What's the point? This is supposed to be someone you're going to spend your life with. If you can't be yourself with that person, then you'll never be yourself with anybody."

"We think loving someone can overcome anything, but love isn't enough."

"When my first love and I broke up, I remember my friend saying, 'I thought you would be together forever' and I told him, 'Life is more complicated than that.' I didn't realize I knew that until I said it."

For the rest of the day, Bonnie and I were in and out of the water. Occasionally, she called her friends. I read *Agent Sonya* and focused without trying. We had a few beers, and I lit a cigar and soon it was like we were floating in the water even when we weren't.

"You've been very healing for me," I said.

"Nothing heals like a rebound."

"No, it's not that. I mean, that's part of it. I just needed this a lot. I needed to feel affection without having my guard up. I've been on the road for too long. There were moments here and there, of course. I've always had Savannah for companionship, but I haven't been able to relax with someone in years. Right now, I don't think I could possibly feel any better. It's a perfect day."

"It really is."

Gradually, the westering light washed the ground and emptied the park. People rode home in their boats. Even Savannah was ready to leave; she barked to tell me it was time.

I drove and Bonnie fell asleep in the passenger seat. I kept my hand on her thigh, and she kept her hand on my hand. When we pulled up to her apartment, I woke her. Then we showered, went to bed, and she dozed off again. For a while, I drifted in the space between awake and asleep. I clung to the deep sense of peace I was feeling, saying to myself, "Remember this. This is important. This is how you're supposed to feel."

The next morning, Savannah and I started walking again. I didn't bring my cart, though. After Bonnie finished work, she picked us up twenty miles from her apartment. We spent another night together and the following morning, she drove us to where we left off. I wanted to stay the remaining two weeks Bonnie had in Omak, but I feared the weather I might be pushing through in Idaho and Wyoming if I did.

On a dirt road, I dragged my cart from the back seat, put the tires on, then turned to Bonnie. We kissed, then held each other for a long time. I watched the hem of her dress dance in the hot wind. There was something uncommon between us. Perhaps it was only that I was ready for Bonnie and that Bonnie was ready for me. Maybe that's all it was, but I had camped everywhere between the coast and the mountains, and save for a few nights in air-conditioning after weeks in the summer sun, I couldn't recall ever sleeping better than when I was beside her.

"It was perfect," I said.

"It really was."

We let go. Savannah had jumped in the car and was watching me from the back seat.

"Come on, Sav. Time to go."

She didn't move.

"I don't want to go either, but it's time. Come on, baby. Time to go."

When I reached for her collar, she jumped outside. I clicked on her leash, kissed Bonnie goodbye, and continued my way home.

After forty minutes, I reached a dead end on the back road I'd been following. To return to the main road, I cut uphill. Seeds from the dry grass clung to the hair on my legs. Three deer burst over the hill and bounded by me and Savannah. The nearest of them, passing six feet from us, had twelve points. I turned to watch how it disappeared down the river gorge, then paused to consider Washington's monumental beauty. The state changed its dress in every valley. Only a mountain pass before, we had been in the Cascades, where the land was verdant and brimming with pines. Now the mountains were an iron red and the ridges were dark and dramatic.

The main road was loud and busy, but the sun was behind us and to the east, so Savannah had shade to walk in. It took a few hours to find another back road, but once we did, Bonnie called.

"Maybe this is crazy," she said. "There's a town twenty miles from where I dropped you. Do you want to get dinner there tonight?"

"The Red Apple Inn takes dogs. It doesn't look like a great spot, cinderblock walls and who knows how the beds are, but the reviews say it's clean."

"You looked up a hotel?"

"I was just about to call."

After a night at the Red Apple Inn, Bonnie and I had a few days apart. We spent the following weekend in Republic—a town twenty-five hundred feet in the mountains with a population of one thousand that somehow churned out two homegrown, far-right pamphlets that could be found at the entry of every store. Bonnie drove two hours to meet me. We bought each other gifts without knowing the other was doing the same. I gave Bonnie an orchid. She gave me two disposable cameras. After our weekend in Republic, we were reluctant to separate, so while I walked a day, Bonnie studied at a cafe, then drove to camp with me at night. The next day, she left before dawn to arrive at work on time.

Soon after that, Bonnie's rotation in Omak ended and she returned to Seattle. We spoke on the phone every day. When my reception was strong enough, I pushed out any worry of my external batteries dying so we could video chat for hours. When I was out of service, I checked my phone incessantly to see if I had regained enough service to allow a message from Bonnie to come through.

Over the few weeks that followed, I crossed Washington, cut through the lush Idaho handle, passed the Continental Divide at the same point as Lewis and Clark, entered Montana, then turned south for Denver.

Bonnie's next rotation was in Cheyenne, Wyoming. On her drive out, she met me in Thompson Falls, Montana.

We booked a log cabin at a roadside hotel that had a path to the river. By the water, Bonnie picked flowers and put them in my hair. At night we sat on our porch and shared a bottle of wine and listened to music. Even though we were close to town, the lights were weak, and we could see the stars. When it was too cold, we went inside and everything was the same as it was outside, but we were warmer and closer together.

"I love you, Tom."

"I love you, too."

That was it—no idiosyncrasies, no dilemma, no questions, and no fractures—love. We'd known each other for a month, but that night an hour was a minute, a day was a week, and we were both forever and rare. We wanted it that way: to exist in no other place and to be nowhere else ever again.

WINTER IN THE WEST

Though I huddled against it, the sagebrush did little to slow the unrelenting wind that had been going since Savannah and I departed Jackson and entered Wyoming's high desert. I thought my walk across America would be an easy one, but Wyoming could have been Peru or Chile for its barrenness. Between Rock Springs and Rawlins, there was a Love's truck stop then nothing apart from sage for a hundred and twenty miles.

Currently, Savannah and I were halfway through that stretch. We had been following a dirt road along train tracks and a few modest oil wells dutifully turning over. A train passed in the morning and the conductor waved, but other than that, we'd seen no one. Ahead, the road took the long way around a table of land. The sky was near, and the clouds were layered like the mountains in Kyrgyzstan.

My water wasn't boiling, but I needed coffee, so I set my food crate beside the stove and used the lid to block the wind. The water warmed a few degrees, but the wind was too strong. I turned off the stove then opened the bottle of instant coffee and tapped some crystals onto my palm. I threw back the crystals, washed them down with the water in the pot, then packed my stove and returned to walking.

On the road, the wind was in my ears and the cold assaulted my joints.

Still, I felt free.

The expansive landscapes of the American West seemed to shoot my worries to some unreachable horizon. I released myself from the responsibility of sharing my journey—I stopped posting to Instagram, I stopped writing blogs, and I stopped making videos. I wanted to experience the final section of my walk in as pure a form as possible, and when I wasn't looking for beauty or conflict to extract from my days, every moment became pristine and singular. I saw fragments of my new self reflected against the old—a boy and a man, a tourist and a traveler, a wanderer and a seeker.

Savannah walked in front of me. The wind brushed her coat, so she appeared bald on one side. We crossed the train tracks, passed the oil wells, then followed the road until I noticed power lines cutting over the sage. I looked at the map to find where they led, and saw that if I followed them, they would intersect with the road on the other side of the table and save me an hour of walking. A little farther on, I discovered a trail below the lines.

As I turned east, the wind was at my back. The trail was less traveled and my cart jostled wildly. One of the bars holding my back basket snapped. I sat on the ground and sawed off the other bar with my Leatherman, then stuffed the basket into the main compartment of my cart. It ruined the weight distribution and made pushing the cart more difficult, but there was nothing else to be done. When we reached a dale splitting the rise of land, our way improved. The path became flatter and wider. In the distance, I spotted a man standing in the sage.

"Savannah," I hissed. "Savannah."

She paused and looked back. I held up a hand so she would stay.

The man must have been seven feet tall. He was looking into the valley where a herd of pronghorns grazed. That's all I could make of him. I saw no pickup or four-by-four. I might have been on his land, but there were no fences or signs to warn of trespassing. I couldn't tell if he carried a rifle.

Slowly, I started forward.

"Stay," I whispered to Savannah.

Once I was near her, she walked just ahead of the cart.

The man didn't move. I was waiting for him to notice me so I could wave—there was no way to go unseen—but when the man turned, I saw it was no man at all. It was an elk that spotted me, then bolted into the valley.

I glanced behind me, then forward again. My fear swept away as I was assured once more that we were alone.

At a pinch in the dale, the table sheltered us from the wind. It was peaceful there, so I sat to watch the pronghorns. Savannah walked ahead and I wasn't sure where she had gone, but she never went far, so I didn't worry. I lay on my back and watched the clouds collide and break apart. I couldn't wait to be in my tent. The short days meant I was spending fourteen hours of each day in it. Savannah had her down jacket and a sleeping bag; it was the only way to get her through the nights. I sat up to look for her and when I couldn't find her, I whistled and waited, but she didn't appear. I stood and searched until I saw her in the valley, chasing the herd of pronghorns.

She stood no chance of catching them. Pronghorns were the second-fastest land animal in the world. They managed the uneven land like an arrow through the still air. At full speed, they were difficult to comprehend—fast enough that they seemed to float.

With both hands, I whistled. I worried the elk was down there, and I worried Savannah might be trampled by it. But she kept running and vanished around a knoll.

After ten minutes, I spotted her clambering up the hill, panting and bright-eyed.

"You almost have them?"

I set out a bowl of water, and she lapped it up.

We stayed another ten minutes, then walked until we found a clearing to make camp.

It was only four, but Wyoming was already mean. As the sun neared the horizon, the cold turned the wind into a whip. While I tried to set my tent, the wind struck me and made a routine affair a battle. I was practiced, though—stake the corners upwind, downwind, lock in the poles, pull the ropes taut, throw my things inside to weigh it down.

By the time I crawled into my shelter, my heart was racing and I was lightheaded from being too hot and too cold at the same time. Inflating my air mattress slowed my breathing, but it wasn't until Savannah and I were in our sleeping bags that I relaxed. Soon it was dark. I turned on my headlamp. For a while, I listened for any weakness in the tent. The wind wouldn't let up, but I had staked it out well.

I pulled loose branches of sagebrush from outside the campsite, piled them in my arms, then carried them to the fire pit and dumped them there. After twenty minutes, I had a large enough stack, but I decided to wait before starting a fire. The sun was still up and there was no wind. Savannah and I were the only ones at the campground.

To keep warm, I walked to the shores of the reservoir. The snow-capped peaks of the Wind River Range were far to the east but close in the reflection. The water was blue and orange from the sun. I was reading *Bury My Heart at Wounded Knee* after swapping it at the Horse Prairie Stage Stop for my copy of *Mountain Man*. The book was perpetually breaking my heart and giving me a greater appreciation for public land. How we paved over such majesty for suburbs and strip malls, I didn't know.

> *"They made us many promises, more than I can remember, but they never kept but one; they promised to take our land, and they took it."*

From up the road, I heard a car approaching. The car sped around the campsite, disrupting the quiet, then stopped near my cart beside the wooden fence. Savannah looked to me.

"Go ahead."

She raced off, and I walked up the beach after her.

Once Savannah reached the car, Bonnie stepped out. Savannah jumped on her then whined and wriggled between her legs. Bonnie tried to keep Savannah from pawing, but Savannah unleashed a fury of excited mitts to her calves. When Savannah finally slowed, Bonnie and I kissed.

"What do you think?" I said, gesturing to the view of the mountains and the reservoir.

"I didn't know Wyoming was so beautiful. Cheyenne is a truck stop."

"No wind tonight either."

From the passenger seat, Bonnie passed me two bottles of wine and a bag of Thai food. We took everything to a picnic table overlooking the lake and I folded my tarp on the bench to keep our bottoms warm.

Savannah rested her head on my knee and sniffed at the food. The wine was a tonic and the hot meal pushed out the sparse days behind me. I pulled Bonnie by the waist so she was nearer. I had sent her a postcard every week we'd been apart.

When we finished eating, we went to the shore and chased Savannah on the beach. As night encroached, we built a fire and the cold moved us closer and while I stared into the flames, I came to the realization that I had never taken a wrong turn, never been delayed, and everything I thought was a mistake was simply growing up and finding out. The six-and-a-half-year path that seemed so jagged was in fact a straight line to exactly where I needed to be.

"You can't be outside tonight."

The mother looked to me from over the center console of her minivan.

"With the wind chill, it'll be negative thirty."

"I was hoping to sleep at the church," I said. "I tried the number, but no one answered. Do you know if it's open?"

"I have to imagine it is, but if it isn't, the people who manage it live in the house next door. The pastor lives a ways away. I have his number. I'll try calling him."

While the woman dialed, I looked to the grain silo and the town of a few dozen houses. There was no restaurant, no school, and no post office. The Coloradan plains were snowy and unbroken.

"No answer," the woman said. "I wouldn't worry about it, though. Head over there and try the doors. It's too dangerous to be out tonight. I'll keep calling to let them know you're there. Anyway, they're a church. They'll understand."

"Thank you. Thanks for calling."

We shook hands, then I touched a hand to my heart.

"Be safe," she said.

After she drove off, I walked into town and followed the gravel path to the church.

Savannah put her nose to the double doors. They were locked, so I followed the ramp to the side of the building and sat against a secondary door that was out of the wind. Across the street was a farmhouse bordered by high trees. A black cat sat on the stoop.

"Come on," I said.

Savannah and I walked to the farmhouse and the cat darted around the side. I rang the doorbell while the wind whistled in the trees and slapped the loose siding of a nearby home. I rang again and knocked, but no one answered, so I returned to the church and huddled in the corner. I still had two hours of daylight, but I couldn't stay outside without shelter for long—even in Wyoming, I had never slept through a minus-five-degree night.

I reached behind me, tugged on the door handle, and discovered the door was open.

Savannah ran inside and I backed in with the cart. The church was more spacious than it appeared from the outside. Out of the wind, my face warmed, but the desire to make myself small and dense remained. I sat against the wall with my sleeping bag over me and drank the liter of chocolate milk I had carried from the town back.

An hour later, the front door creaked open.

Savannah greeted a well-worn man stomping snow from his boots. He held a plastic bag above her attempts to reach it.

"Savannah. Savannah. Let him be. Sorry, she's very friendly."

"Heard you might be in here." The man glanced at me, then looked at the kitchen to his right.

"I hope that's okay. I've been camping from Seattle, but it's too cold tonight. Thought we might freeze."

"Too cold for that. Not with the wind going the way it is."

The man moved to the kitchen, and I followed. He set the plastic bag on the counter and withdrew a Tupperware from it.

"In case you're hungry," he said.

He opened the Tupperware to reveal a mound of macaroni and chili sufficient for three nights.

"There are oranges and whatnot, too. Not a store around and we didn't know your situation, so we thought we'd bring something."

"It looks like heaven. Thank you. I'm burning five thousand calories a day, so I can always use more food. I'll get through that in no time."

He nodded to the counter, glanced at me, then pointed across the church.

"Thermostat is there."

We walked over to it. The man appeared reassured of my intentions once he saw my things tumbling out of my cart.

"It's just a few buttons," he said about the thermostat. "I'm sure you know how to work it. You can use the pew cushions if you want. There are some extra ones under the table there. Could make a nice bed."

"That's a good idea. Are you the pastor?"

The man smiled and looked me straight on for the first time.

"No. Not me. I'm retired. Still some ranching here and there, but I'm not the pastor. My wife and I manage the church. We leave the door open in case."

"I'm glad you did."

"There's nothing around, so you never know. We get cyclists every once in a while, but anyway, you look like you're situated, so I'll let you be. If you need anything, just come by. We're in the house next door."

"I really appreciate it. You're saving us. I'm Tom, that's Savannah."

"I'm Dale, and my wife is Linda. Sure she'll be over to check on you. Stay warm."

Dale left, and once I knew we had permission to be in the church, I settled in. I turned on the heat, then moved a table and a chair so I could sit facing the bay doors looking out to the plains. As I watched the wind shred the hard-packed snow, I wondered how I would adjust to life after the walk. The perpetual cycle of exertion and recovery had engrained in me a profound appreciation for the smallest comforts and brought me the greatest joys, but now the depth of contrast that I enjoyed for so long was what worried me. Where would I derive satisfaction when I wasn't finding a place to sleep each night, sheltering from the elements, or working relentlessly for each meal?

The Kansas farm roads were essentially wide trails aiming perfectly east to Missouri. I kept Savannah off-leash, and for the most part I could stare at the horizon without interruption. It was only the occasional streams, bordered by forest, that broke my view. When possible, we camped in those narrow forests to escape the wind, but more often we slept on the plains and prayed the ground would cool fast enough to calm the air. On one of those stretches, a cop pulled beside Savannah and me while we were resting. The cop lowered her window and didn't remove her sunglasses.

"You okay?" she asked.

"Oh yeah, just walking. Taking a break."

"Not hurt?"

"No, no. Doing well."

"There's no baby in there, right?"

"No, just my things, been walking from Seattle. Walking home to New Jersey."

"Okay. We had a few calls of someone pushing a baby carriage in the middle of nowhere, had to check it out. Sorry to bother you."

"No worries. Appreciate it."

Two days later, on another back road, a cop slowed behind me and flashed his lights. I put Savannah on leash, then sat on an embankment beside the road until the cop stepped out. The cop adjusted his body armor and raised a hand as he approached.

"How y'all doing?"

"Good, good, just walking." Savannah was pulling to say hello.

"You have some identification on you?"

"Of course."

I handed over my license.

"What's a guy from New Jersey doing out in Kansas?"

"Walking across the country. Been going for about four months now."

"Cold going."

"Especially in the wind."

"Let me run this and I'll be right back."

The cop went to his car then returned a few minutes later and handed my license back.

"Here you are, Thomas. Nothing in that, right?"

"Just my things: camping gear, water, food, clothing. Happy to open it if you want."

"No need. How'd you end up all the way out here?"

"Quickest way east from Denver."

"Got a long way to New Jersey."

"Another few months at least."

"Be smart as you go. A lot of cops would have pulled their gun on you out here."

"They would have pulled their gun on me?"

"Well, it's a small town and when there's someone we don't know, people start calling. A new guy walking the back roads in winter can be suspicious."

"With a dog and a baby stroller?"

He tapped his left shoulder. "Right here. That's where I was shot. Routine traffic stop, ten years back. Right in town. Pulled a guy over, met with a gun. Happened in a second. Happens all the time. We have to be paranoid. Just the way it is."

"Surely most people are just going about their day."

"Of course, but there are always a few that have warrants or just plain hate cops, so we have to be careful."

"Too many guns out there. Sure it's only become more difficult for you."

"Good guys and bad guys, but it's what we signed up for. I'm retiring next year after working twenty-five. Want to make it—plan on making it. Anyway, thanks for stopping. You need anything?"

"Got it all in the cart. I'm a professional at this point."

"Well, thanks again, Thomas. I hope you enjoy the state. Appreciate you understanding. Stay warm."

Another two days on, I turned off a dusty road and made for a strip of woods to make camp. Beside a frozen stream was a clearing tucked between two steep banks and protected from the wind by a few layers of leafless trees. My walking had been isolated and peaceful all day. I was relaxed. I sat on my tarp, smoked a pipe, and basked in our good fortune. Savannah ate dinner, then gnawed at a Dentastix. When I heard some-one's voice behind me, I stood and looked over the bank. Across the road, three cops traced the spine of a hill. I watched them for a minute, then sat on my tarp because I didn't want to be bothered.

A few more minutes passed and I heard someone approaching.

I stood again to see a cop in the field following my tire tracks. When he saw me, he yelled.

"Stay there! Don't move!"

The cop withdrew his pistol and aimed it at me. A rifle hung across his chest.

I raised my hands.

"Stay, Savannah."

"Here!" The cop shouted over his shoulder.

Four cops came racing down the hill, across the road, and into the field. The officer with his gun drawn walked toward me. When he was a few feet away, he looked beyond me to my camp.

"Anyone else with you?"

"Just me and my dog. We're walking across the country. Just staying the night. I didn't think we were on anyone's land."

"You have any weapons on you?"

"There's a Leatherman on my tarp and mace in my backpack."

"No guns?"

"No."

"Can you lift your shirt for me and turn around."

I did. He patted my pockets.

"You have identification?"

"My license is in my backpack, in the top pocket, sitting by my tent. You want me to get it?"

"No. Stay here."

The other officers stood a bit removed while the officer with his gun drawn looked through my camp then returned with my license. He handed it to another officer then came back to me with his pistol holstered.

"We had a call about a strange man walking with a baby carriage and a dog. It took a bit of searching but we found your tire tracks. I spotted them cutting into the field. That's how we found you."

"Wasn't trying to hide."

"What are you doing back here?"

"Walking across the country. We walked from Seattle."

"But why these back roads?"

"They're quiet, more peaceful than walking the highway. I can keep her off-leash, listen to my speaker. It's much nicer."

"You know we get a lot of thieves and migrants coming through."

"Here?"

"Last year we nabbed a felon on the same road."

The cop returned with my license and handed it to me.

"Was I doing anything wrong? I looked online and it said the area around the stream was public."

"This is someone's land, but you're fine. He won't mind. Just be gone by morning."

We shook hands, and a few minutes later, the convoy left in a storm of dust. I went to my camp and moved my tarp, so I could sit in the last beam of sunlight breaking through the trees. I packed a second pipe, and while I smoked, I recalled the days in Scotland when cops gave me sausage sandwiches and referred to Savannah as "my little friend."

In western Kansas, I connected with the Flint Hills Nature Trail, then the Rock Island Spur. In Sedalia, Missouri, I joined the Katy Trail—a 240-mile rails-to-trails. The trail was old and well-established. Bike shops, restaurants, and hotels offered a bounty of excuses to slow down. Through March, it remained cold and snowy, but the trails made for pleasant walking regardless of the weather. We were averaging twenty miles a day without much exertion. I jumped in the Missouri River every day.

We were ahead of schedule. Our homecoming was set for May 21st. My mom, my sister, and Philadelphia Sign were planning the festivities, but they wouldn't give me any details.

From St. Louis, I followed the Nickel Plate Trail out of the city. In Illinois, we were welcomed by the National Road Heritage Trail and the Pennsy Trail. The land was still flat but there were more trees than on the Great Plains. The trees made camping easier and the walking more diverse—I had something to look at other than the horizon. In Ohio, we came to our first hills since leaving the Rockies and as the weather warmed, the snow turned to rain. Finally, I was able to sit outside my tent at night and leave my sleeping bag at dawn.

When the land turned green, and the morning sun was strong enough to wake me, I passed my days like a child returning from school. My heart played with the memories of my previous seven years—I remembered my first birthday on the road when I was brimming with excitement and reckoning with my decision to end things with Layla. I remembered my second birthday in Bogotá with Fitz, drinking aguardiente and bouncing between clubs. I remembered my third with cousins in Montevideo; my fourth trudging in the rains of Germany; my fifth finding renewal in Tuscany; my sixth with friends in Kaş. And now I was spending my seventh birthday on the road. I was thirty-three, camped in a field—my kingdom the open air, the tilled earth, and everywhere beside Savannah.

By the time we reached Pennsylvania, I needed to slow down. I crossed the state eighteen miles at a time, taking long breakfasts and lying out midday to do nothing for hours. There were only a few bike paths, and the narrow roads were as stressful as they had been seven years before, but the camping was pleasant. We tucked in the forest where flowers bloomed, and the wind shook in the sky.

A hundred and thirty miles from home, and just ten miles north of Gettysburg, I descended from the Michaux State Forest and reached the Conewago Campground in the early afternoon. In the spring, Pennsylvania was humid, and it had rained the night before, so it was more humid still. The camp office was a white and green farmhouse with an ice machine on a wraparound porch. I knocked on the door, but no one answered, so Savannah and I walked down the gravel road to the first RV and found a man organizing logs beneath a blue tent.

"Do you know if there are any spots available?" I asked. "I tried the office and I tried calling, but I can't get a hold of anyone."

The man set down a log then came over and introduced himself as Mike.

"You should be able to find a place across that bridge. When I see the owner, I'll let him know you're here. Sure it won't be a problem."

Savannah and I found the clearing Mike directed us toward. There were no other tent campers, but the clearing was encircled by long-stay RVs. Each RV had an awning, and a few had foot-high fences around their modest yards. I parked the cart at a picnic table on the most level piece of land, made camp, then cooked pasta. There were no speakers blaring or engines running to spoil the sound of the stream and the birds.

Around dusk, Mike walked across the clearing to me.

"You want some firewood?" he asked.

At Mike's camp, I held out my arms and he piled logs to my chin.

"Come by if you want some more. If you're free tomorrow, you should join my wife and I for breakfast."

When I returned to camp, Savannah ran at me, jumped against my legs, then sprinted back to the tent growling and with her hackles up. I dumped the wood beside the fire pit then used pages of *The Economist* as fire starter. I dropped in a few logs and soon had a fire going. As the warmth from the flames grew, I picked a stick from the fire and used the end to light a cigar.

THE HOMECOMING

On our 1,861st day of walking, it was ninety-seven degrees, but we only had nine miles to home.

At two thirty, we started from my cousin's house on American. My cousin Brian and his wife Carly walked with us. Carly pushed my nieces Remi and Everly in their stroller. Bonnie had flown in from Seattle and was there, too. Ahead of us, the cameraman for a documentary was walking backward, occasionally wiping sweat from his forehead as he went. We took Second Street, crossed Spring Garden, and continued to Franklin Square at the base of the Ben Franklin Bridge.

Days before, I had put out word that anyone who wanted to walk the last nine miles with me and Savannah could meet us in the square. When we arrived, twenty people were waiting. They all knew my story, but I knew none of theirs. I shook hands, spoke with everyone, and took photos with the people who wanted them. At three, we left the park and Fitz came running down the street. We hugged as he joined the group.

"I was thinking I'd meet you at the homecoming, but then I remembered I moved back to Philadelphia for a reason. What good is being home if I don't join my best bud and Savannah for a few miles on their last day of walking?"

"Texas, Colombia, Italy, and Philadelphia. Glad to have you here, brother."

On the Ben Franklin, there was little shade. Savannah walked beside the railing for the meager shadow it provided. She was in her sun coat and doused with water, but she was still panting.

Partway up, I looked at the apartments beside the bridge and saw a GO TOM sign in a window and someone giving me a thumbs-up. In the next apartment building, people whistled and cheered from their patio. At the top of the walkway, we gathered for a group photo. Fitz and Bonnie were behind me. Savannah sat beside me.

When we were walking again, a clean-shaven kid named Anthony hurried so he was next to me.

"I've been thinking of doing something similar to you," he said. "But I got into air-traffic control school in Arizona, so now I'm not sure what to do. I have money saved, but if I go to school and work for a few years, I could leave when I have even more. I could leave with a hundred thousand dollars then not need to worry about finding a sponsor. I don't know. I want to leave immediately, but maybe it's best I go to school. I'm only young once, though, and when I'm older I'll have more responsibility. I might have a girlfriend and a house. I might not have the energy."

"That's true. Why do you want to walk around the world versus doing something else?"

"It seems like a great way to see the world, to really know it, and I think I'll feel like I wasted my life if I work all the time. Am I supposed to work until I'm sixty and then travel? I know I'll have to work no matter what I do, but it feels like I should prioritize other things while I'm young."

"I agree entirely, but there are a lot of ways to see the world. You don't have to go on a seven-year walk. If you're earning a hundred thousand a year, you can travel a lot and a lot more comfortably than I did. Walking around the world was incredible, I don't mean to say that it wasn't, but it was brutal, too. It's not for everyone. The only reason I made it was because I could never imagine doing anything else. I'd been dreaming about the walk for nine years before I began. It was like I was on fire. I think you need that. You'll walk through rain, over mountains, you'll camp in strange places, and you'll have to leave everyone you know. That weighs on you after a while. Maybe try a few walks around New Jersey first. Book a campsite, walk for a day, book another campsite. See if you like it."

On the Jersey side of the bridge, we walked down the steps and into Camden. News teams were waiting for us. So were two police cars and Lexi in her truck. Bonnie joined Lexi, so they could get ready for the homecoming. Fitz patted me on the back.

"I'm heading home," he said. "I'll see you at the finish line. The whole family will be there. My mom can't wait to see you."

Through Camden, we were escorted by the police along the trolley tracks and past City Hall Station, but I never asked for that. Occasionally, a cameraman jumped out of their car to film. We turned onto Haddon Avenue, walked by Cooper Hospital, under 676, then beside the brick row homes that should have had trees planted on their curbs, but only had electric poles and wires instead. Kids on their bikes asked where we were going. At El Rincon, a corner store, an old man whistled.

Another young man in our group came up beside me.

"Did you like Algeria?" he asked.

"Loved it," I said. "Incredibly kind people. Have you been?"

"Not yet, but I'm hoping to go with my dad soon."

"Wait." The boy's face was suddenly familiar. "You're Amar's son!"

Zach grinned. It had been ten years since I'd seen him.

"Your dad saved me. I wouldn't have even been able to enter Algeria if it wasn't for him and your grandmother. Rachid had one of his friends drive two hours to give me cash when I ran out. They gave me a cake on my thousandth day of walking, too."

He smiled again but didn't say anything.

"I'm glad you joined," I said. "Is your dad coming to the party?"

"He said he'd pick me up later, so he'll be there for a little while at least."

"Tell him he better make it."

Across the street from Harleigh Cemetery, the Gearharts, one of my second families growing up, pulled alongside us.

"Move it or lose it, you bum!" shouted Mr. Gearhart.

They reached out with water and gave bottles to everyone.

In Collingswood, people on their porches cheered us on. Children had WELCOME HOME written in chalk on the sidewalk. My fraternity brother Dave joined the group. So did Theresa and Shawn, a couple who bought Savannah and me a hotel room in Columbus, Ohio. People honked as they passed. A minivan drove by with high schoolers hollering as they hung out the side door. I walked by The Factory and searched for Tom, but he wasn't there. When I turned onto Strawbridge Avenue, he ripped down the street in a golf cart.

"What took you so long?" he said.

Everyone was walking in the middle of the street. Tom chugged a beer even though the police were in a car behind him.

"You're not walking with us?" I said.

"You'll have to try a golf cart around the world next time. Much easier than walking."

Tom whirled around and sped back to his house for another beer.

On the fence of my elementary school was a red sign.

CONGRATULATIONS AND WELCOME HOME
TOM & SAVANNAH!

The unofficial end of the walk was two miles ahead at The Taproom. That's where the homecoming party was being held and where everyone awaited us, but for closure, I felt the need to pass the place where the walk started. I turned onto Hampton Avenue where down the hill was the home I left seven years before.

At my parents' old house, rocking chairs still on the porch and the maple tree still blanketing my window, there was a group to cheer us on. I took a beer from a cooler in the driveway. Barb, my neighbor Bob's daughter, turned me by the shoulder to say hello, and I showed her Bob's

1933 track medal around my neck. For a moment, we cried. He passed while I was in Mexico.

Down the street, we turned at Cooper and followed it to Haddon Avenue. I'd done the same walk a thousand times. It was the way to Julian's, to the high school, to the soccer fields, and to the pool. More people joined at every block. We were thirty strong, then forty. We turned onto Crystal Lake and when we reached Park Avenue, I could see the end a few blocks ahead.

I stopped on the corner to face everyone.

"Before we reach the finish line, I just want to thank you for walking with me. A few of you even did the whole nine miles. That's crazy. It was hot today, even Savannah was struggling. It means a lot to finish like this. For twenty-five thousand miles, it was just me and Savannah. I shared the journey on Instagram, but I never really understood the connections I made on it. Until today, they always felt one-sided. It's nice to know that you were out there supporting us as we went. I can't thank you enough for being here."

"We're proud of you, Tommy!" Theresa shouted from the back.

"Now let's finish this damn thing."

The Taproom was obscured by a line of trees, but the size of the crowd became clearer as we approached. People were lining the sidewalk. They poured into the street. My fraternity brother Doug and his daughter Ruby joined us. I shook hands with my dad's childhood friend, Michael. I spotted Bob from Philadelphia Sign and reached for him, too.

When I turned into the parking lot, the size of our homecoming revealed itself. There was a balloon archway, camera crews, and hundreds upon hundreds of people cheering. I couldn't believe how many people were there—people I didn't know; people I did.

I unhooked Savannah's leash, and we crossed the finish line side-by-side.

On the other side, I wasn't overcome with excitement or joy, I was relieved. I hugged my parents and when my dad took my backpack, it felt as though an impossible weight had been lifted.

It was done.

Sixteen years later and I was finally free from the idea to which I had chained myself. I thought of dropping into my bed and sleeping forever, but instead I was met by the people who cared for me most. I hugged Lexi. I kissed Bonnie. I embraced Julian and Fitz.

Savannah was greeted by a bowl of ice cream—she had never had it before. Her eyes were wild as she lapped at it and while she ate, she received a thousand well-earned pets from the crowd.

"We'll watch her," my dad said to me.

I did some interviews, then I was set loose to meet everyone. Most of my extended family was there—cousins, aunts, and uncles. More fraternity brothers were there, too. They had signs printed. I shook hands with strangers and neighbors and old friends, and all of them congratulated me and I thanked them for being there.

An hour passed in a second and in the back lawn where there were picnic tables and grills, the crowd made a semicircle to watch the town commissioners name May 21st "Tom and Savannah Day." After that, Bob presented two giant checks for Ann Marie and Shannon's scholarship funds. Jack, Ann Marie's father, and Susan, Shannon's mother, were there to accept them.

After Ann Marie died, Jack moved out of town and into a farmhouse in South Jersey. My dad said he was happy. After Shannon died, Susan left Shannon's room untouched for years. It might still be untouched.

When it was my turn to speak, I held the microphone and paused to consider my life. I hadn't planned a speech; somehow it never occurred to me that I might need to give one. What came into my head were the words I said to Shannon's father at her funeral: "It's beautiful." I meant it in reference to the entire town being packed into the church for her, but I always regretted saying it. There was nothing beautiful about a parent burying their child.

"This is a terrible thing to say," I finally said. "But I'm lucky that Ann Marie and Shannon passed. Their deaths were what woke me to life. Without them, I would have never decided on a direction to set myself. I would have never walked around the world. I always thought part of them were caught in me like bits of shrapnel. I wish that wasn't the case.

I wish they were here. But it feels like a loop closed for me today and I hope my walk did the same for their families. It only happened because of them."

The temperature wasn't bearable until the sun was below the trees. Two grills were going to churn out enough hamburgers and hot dogs to feed everyone. Every once in a while, I noticed someone slipping Savannah a patty by the grill. Quite often, I was handed a burger and a beer, but I could never take more than a bite and a sip before setting them down to give my attention to someone who wanted to speak.

When I reached Fitz's mom, another one of my mothers, she clutched to me and cried.

"I prayed for you every night, Tommy. Every night. I don't know how your mother got through it. I'm so relieved you made it. I'm just so relieved."

For four hours, I was shuffled from person to person. Then suddenly, I looked around and noticed that most of the crowd had departed and only the close few were remaining. I sat at a picnic table with my parents, Lexi, Bonnie, Brian and Carly, Fitz, his fiancée Melissa, Julian, his fiancée Robin, Shawn, Theresa, and our family friends, the Moores. Savannah was snoring in the grass and even from afar I could see her belly bulging with food.

While everyone spoke and laughed and I was able to eat for the first time, I thought about how even though I was a different person than when I began, I returned as the same person to the people who loved me. Among them once more, I spotted the thread that stitched together my life. It was only because I was loved and loved deeply that I was strong enough to live with myself and withstand the ever-battering winds of change. Without a lifetime of love, I could have never set out on my own.

Love was the final arbiter.

Vedat and his son staring out to the Turkish plains.

Isabella saving for her business in San Sebastián.

Even Rob and his darkness in Georgia.

We were little things, none standing on their own, each determined by the great forces around them—government, geography, culture, and the love we were shown. Although we like to believe we're masters of our fate, our lives were decided long ago. We exist forever, like marks against the stone, but you are alive now.

Pay attention.

That's enough.

EPILOGUE

Pretending I was in Copenhagen, I carried my bike from my parents' apartment building, strapped on my helmet, then pedaled down the sidewalks. Across Haddon Avenue, the shops began. There was a Starbucks where the high schoolers gathered, a card shop at the next corner, and a Saxby's where most days I attempted to distill seven years into as few words as possible.

At Saxby's, I cut across the crosswalk with abandon. My view was that the cars were imposing on what would have been a pedestrian zone in every other developed country. A pickup stopped, I rolled up the curb cutout, then turned onto Washington and sped beside the Patco train line that I'd taken into Philly most of my life. I made a left on Euclid, then a right on West End. The houses of Haddonfield were old and gigantic. The trees were the same: towering over the street and showering me in mottled light.

For the most part, the drivers were careful, so I biked in the street as I rode by the soccer fields I played on as a kid and the pool where I swam. I pedaled uphill to The Taproom, then turned around the side and walked my bike through the entrance of Green Valley Tennis Club. On the far courts, I could see Julian, Fitz, and Ant warming up.

"What's up, Tommy?" Ant said as I came through the gate and onto the court.

"How these fools looking?"

"Lazy as always."

I set my backpack in a chair then withdrew my racket and took the backhand side of the court with Ant.

After a set, we were sweating and the clay had worked its way into our socks, so we rested in the shade. The women that were always there were there again, playing on the last court. Most of the old men were there, too—doctors and such. Julian knew them all.

"Your wedding is at a tennis club, right Fitz?" Julian asked. "Didn't you say they have clay courts?"

"Four of them, right on the water. Hoping to do a little tourney on the day of the wedding like you did. I don't think anyone really plays, but it'll be fun anyway."

"Excited for it, man."

"Melissa and I have a countdown on our bedside. I feel like I didn't notice it approaching until it went under a hundred days. Now every day it feels like the wedding is happening tomorrow."

"You came back at the right time, Tommy," Julian said.

"Appreciate you delaying your marriages for me."

"You moving out to Seattle after Fitz's wedding?"

"That's the plan. Hoping we end up in Philly for residency, but who knows, that's her walk. I'm not going to put my hands in it. I'm just along for the ride."

"Home for four months then gone again," Ant said. "We have to get in as much tennis as possible."

Fitz and Julian went back onto the court to hit some balls. Ant and I stayed in the shade.

"So tell me about it," Ant said, spinning his racket idly. "It's been weeks, and you don't talk about it at all."

"Yeah, no. I mean, it was just life by the end, you know? But it was incredible. Each morning, I would wake with a purpose—walk a little further down the road—and by simply fulfilling that purpose I was exercising, getting sunshine, trying new foods, seeing new places, meeting new people. Each day was packed. Those seven years felt like twenty."

"You miss it?"

"Right now? No. God, no. By the end, I was ready to hurl my cart off the Ben Franklin. It was a great life, but I've been waiting seven years to play tennis with you guys again."

"What about a story? You have to have a million."

"What type do you want?"

"How was ayahuasca? That was Peru, right? In the jungle? Before Julian visited?"

"In Iquitos, yeah."

"Were you nervous?"

"Before the first ceremony, definitely. I thought it would alter me in some permanent way, but it doesn't really. You just watch your thoughts from a step back like you're watching a movie. But the most amazing part was the morning after. Your field of view expands. It's like you're a kid again. That filter that narrows our perception of the world as we age gets lifted and suddenly there are possibilities everywhere. For a few hours you have this incredible, forgotten openness."

"But it doesn't stay with you?"

"The memory of it does. You remember how you experienced the world but can't anymore."

The four of us played another set, then we went to the clubhouse to share a few beers, prosciutto, cheese, and a baguette with the older guys. After that, I rode back to my parents, dropped my things, and took Savannah for a walk.

I kept her off-leash as we rambled away from the shops, passing houses from the 1800s, the historic high school, and the cemetery across from it. Downhill, we turned at Wallworth Pond and Savannah sprinted in the field beside the water. We crossed the pedestrian bridge then turned onto the Croft Farm Trail. Savannah was far ahead. Her tail was wagging.

After an hour, we rested on the wooden steps that looked through the trees to the lake. I lay back and shut my eyes, pressed my thumbs to my ears, and stayed perfectly still. For a moment, I almost lost the sensation of having a body.

But Savannah pawed me—time to get moving.

ACKNOWLEDGMENTS

The World Walk would have been wholly impossible were it not for the community that stood behind it. From the very outset, I've been blessed to grow amid a wonderful garden of humanity. I was raised with love and instilled with a quiet assurance that can only be matured under decades of unmarred shelter. Thank you, mom and dad, for that near-pristine foundation. And thank you, Lexi, for always being my first supporter. You showed me that everyone has their own path to walk, and they will walk it all the stronger when given love and warmth.

Thank you to my aunts, uncles, and cousins. When I was a boy, I was terrified of our raucous, frenetic family parties, but in them I learned how to defend myself and my thoughts, and to release the ideas that don't withstand the crush of a snarky remark or the incisive questioning of a cousin with a few drinks in them. You helped me refine myself.

Thank you, Fitz, for a friendship that has grown from soccer and *Need for Speed* to Colombia and Italy to your wedding and your own baby girl. You wrote in the journal you gifted me before I began that our friendship was the same heroic friendship that Aristotle imagined as the ideal—"made up of men who are good and alike in virtue; for each alike wishes well to each other . . . they are good in themselves." In many ways, we think differently, but in the thoughts that matter we tread alike.

Thank you, Julian, for a friendship that reaches from the tennis courts in Haddon Township to the Andes in Peru and the cities in Spain. You contain the rare tranquility that calms the earth and those among you. Your friendship has kept peace and laughter in my life, and your visits were founts of rejuvenation.

Thank you, Bonnie, my lovely, for your impeccable timing. How tragic it would have been to meet you years before only to lose each other amid the complexities of two young lives. As I write this, it's been nearly three years together and with each passing day, I find we fit together even better than the day before.

Thank you, Tom Marchetty, for being the first outside my immediate circle to believe in a madman. Why you did, I'll never know, but without your unflinching generosity, I would have never made it around the world. There's a direct link from you to Philadelphia Sign.

Thank you, Bob, and Philadelphia Sign. I would have been bleeding out my savings on rice and beans for two years were it not for your support. Often, while I was out on the road, I imagined myself as some old-world explorer with a generous benefactor back home—how fortunate a life!

Thank you, Mark Gottlieb, my agent, for seeing the potential of my story and guiding me through a world I know nothing of.

Thank you to my editor, Jesse McHugh, for your belief in my writing and your keen eye. You forced me to see my story with fresh eyes, to refine my language, and excise the unnecessary with even more ruthlessness than I already possessed. Your advice, and the sheer amount of time you committed, has contributed to my best writing.

Thank you, Zeki, at Timeks Hotel in Istanbul, for navigating the maze of Turkish bureaucracy to get me across the Bosphorus Bridge.

Thank you to all the farmers, ranchers, and shepherds who allowed me to sleep on their land. You afforded me many peaceful nights and